Psychoanalysis

Psychoanalysis

An Interdisciplinary Retrospective

JEFFREY BERMAN

SUNY PRESS

Cover illustration is from the Forces of Nature series. Arrangement of colorful paint and abstract shapes on the subject of modern art, abstract art, expressionism, and spirituality. Shutterstock

Published by the State University of New York Press, Albany

For information, contact State University of New York Press, Albany, NY
www.sunypress.edu

Library of Congress Cataloging-in-Publication Data

Name: Berman, Jeffrey, 1945– author.
Title: Psychoanalysis : an interdisciplinary retrospective / Jeffrey Berman.
Description: Albany, NY : State University of New York Press, [2023] |
    Includes bibliographical references and index.
Identifiers: LCCN 2023009064 | ISBN 9781438495682 (hardcover : alk. paper) |
    ISBN 9781438495705 (ebook) | ISBN 9781438495699 (pbk. : alk. paper)
Subjects: LCSH: Psychoanalysis. | Psychoanalysts.
Classification: LCC BF173 .B476 2023 | DDC 150.195—dc23/eng/20230707
LC record available at https://lccn.loc.gov/2023009064

10 9 8 7 6 5 4 3 2 1

To the memory of Paul W. Mosher,
trusted friend, mentor, and coauthor

Contents

Acknowledgments

I am indebted to the distinguished psychoanalytic clinicians, scholars, and theorists who made this book possible, first by reading my chapters about their work and then by responding thoughtfully to my questions: Sander L. Gilman, Joan Wheelis (and her late father, Allen Wheelis), Nancy J. Chodorow, Christopher Bollas, and Adam Phillips. I have been reading their books for decades, and their writings continue to inspire me. When I reflect on my gratitude toward these authors, I think of Sebastian's words in Shakespeare's *Twelfth Night*: "I can no other answer make but thanks, and thanks; and ever thanks."

As with my other books, I would not have been able to conduct my research without the invaluable help of the entire Interlibrary Loan staff at the University at Albany. Thanks to Timothy Jackson, Angela Persico, and Glen Benedict for fulfilling scores of Interlibrary Loan requests.

Part of my discussion of Sander Gilman's *The Case of Sigmund Freud* and *Freud, Race, and Gender* appeared in *The Psychoanalytic Review*, vol. 82, 1995, pp. 778–783. A shorter version of chapter 2, "Allen Wheelis's Depiction of Remediable and Irremediable Suffering," appeared in *Allen Wheelis: An Appreciation of His Work*, published in *Explorations: The Twentieth Century*, vol. 9, 1999, pp. 29–57. The discussion of Allen Wheelis's *The Listener* appeared in a shorter and slightly different form in *Psychoanalytic Books*, vol. 10, 1999, pp. 394–398. My review of Nancy Chodorow's *The Psychoanalytic Ear and Sociological Eye* appeared in the *Journal of the American Psychoanalytic Association*, vol. 68, 2021, pp. 1173–1181. My discussion of Adam Phillips's *On Flirtation* first appeared in *Psychoanalytic Books*, vol. 6, 1995, pp. 576–580. A brief section of my discussion of Christopher Bollas's fictional psychoanalyst "Mish Mash," based on the infamous Pakistani psychoanalyst Masud Khan, appears in my book *Psychoanalytic Memoirs*.

Having had the pleasure of serving for six years on the SUNY Press Editorial Board in the late 1990s, I know that the review process is thorough. I have certainly been the beneficiary of that editorial process in the present book. I am grateful to the anonymous reviewers who offered thoughtful suggestions for revising the manuscript before publication. I alone am responsible for whatever remaining weaknesses exist in the book. This is my fifth book published by SUNY Press, and, as always, I am beholden to James Peltz, associate director and editor-in-chief, for his unwavering faith in this project. Special thanks to my superb copyeditor, James Harbeck, for his help in improving my style and correcting factual errors. I am also grateful to my wife, Julie, for her love and support.

Finally, I dedicate this book to the memory of Paul W. Mosher, one of the towering figures in psychoanalysis, the recipient of the Sigourney Award, its most prestigious prize. Paul coordinated for the American Psychoanalytic Association the funding and production of an amicus brief presented before the US Supreme Court (Jaffee v. Redmond) that contributed to the establishment of the psychotherapist–patient confidentiality privilege. A founding board member of Psychoanalytic Electronic Publishing, he created a full text archive of the English language psychoanalytic research literature. Paul was a trusted friend, mentor, and coauthor. We cowrote *Confidentiality and Its Discontents: Dilemmas of Privacy in Psychotherapy*, which received the 2017 Book Prize from the American Psychoanalytic Association. We later coauthored the two-volume *Off the Tracks: Cautionary Tales about the Derailing of Mental Health Care* (2019). Working with Paul was one of the highlights of my life, and I feel privileged to have known him.

Introduction

Learning from Superiors

If one were to found a college of psychoanalysis, Freud states wistfully in *The Question of Lay Analysis* (1926), one would want to include branches of knowledge far remote from medicine: "the history of civilization, mythology, the psychology of religion, and the science of literature" (*SE* 20: 246; all quotations from Freud are cited to volume and page from the *Standard Edition*, translated and edited by James Strachey). Freud's insistence that psychoanalysis is a science led him to the conclusion that the study of literature is also a science, an assumption that no literary scholar would make today. Nor would most contemporary mental health professionals maintain that psychoanalysis is scientific. But apart from these claims, Freud makes a compelling case that future psychoanalysts do not require medical training. Psychoanalysts, Freud argues, do not use medical instruments, like physicians; rather, analysts work only with words, which can do "unspeakable good, and cause terrible wounds" (*SE* 20: 188). Words are always magical for Freud, and he was himself one of the greatest wordsmiths of the twentieth century. Freud structures *The Question of Lay Analysis* as a conversation or debate between himself and an "Impartial Person," and anticipating the latter's contempt of verbal dialogue, which occurs in the talking cure, Freud adds, "It is as though he were thinking: 'Nothing more than that? Words, words, words, as Prince Hamlet says.'" It's appropriate that Freud should invoke Hamlet here in recommending the widest possible education for analysts. Psychoanalysis and psychoanalytic literary criticism were born simultaneously, as can be seen in Freud's famous October 15, 1897, letter to his confidant Wilhelm Fliess, in which, after discovering the existence of Oedipal feelings within himself, he refers to the gripping power of *Oedipus Rex* and *Hamlet*.

1

Freud wrote *The Question of Lay Analysis* on behalf of Theodor Reik, a non-physician member of the Vienna Psycho-Analytical Society who had been charged with violating an old Austrian law against quackery. The charge was later dropped. Freud did everything he could to support non-medical training for analysts. He could not persuade American psychoanalytic organizations to drop the requirement for medical training—that decision came a half century later—but he succeeded in enlisting psychoanalysts from a wide variety of academic disciplines. Near the end of *The Question of Lay Analysis* Freud makes a surprising admission. "After forty-one years of medical activity, my self-knowledge tells me that I have never really been a doctor in the proper sense, I became a doctor through being compelled to deviate from my original purpose; and the triumph of my life lies in my having, after a long and roundabout journey, found my way back to my earliest path." Becoming a physician deterred Freud from his early goal of an "overpowering need to understand something of the riddles of the world in which we live and perhaps even to contribute something to their solution" (*SE* 20: 253), a goal he believed he fulfilled in the creation of psychoanalysis.

Elsewhere, Freud stressed the interdisciplinary nature of his creation—and his indebtedness to the arts. Upon being honored on his seventieth birthday as the discoverer of the unconscious, Freud disclaimed the title, admitting that the "Poets and Philosophers before me have discovered the unconscious; I have discovered the scientific method with which the unconscious can be studied" (Lehrman 164). And in "Delusions and Dreams in Jensen's *Gradiva*" (1907), his first extended essay on literature and psychoanalysis, Freud referred to creative writers as valuable allies: "they are apt to know a whole host of things between heaven and earth, of which our philosophy has not yet let us dream. In their knowledge of the mind they are far in advance of us everyday people, for they draw upon sources which we have not yet opened up for science" (*SE* 9: 8). Freud expected his readers to know that he was referring to Hamlet's words to Horatio—"there are more things in heaven and earth . . . than are dreamt of in your philosophy"—once again expressing his love for literature.

Few people realize that Freud wanted to become a novelist, as Wilhelm Stekel reported in his *Autobiography* (1950). "In my mind," Freud confided to him as they hiked through the forests of Berchtesgaden, "I always construct novels, using my experiences as a psychoanalyst; my wish is to become a novelist—but not yet; perhaps in the later years of my life" (Stekel 66). Freud never became a novelist—except to Freud-bashers, who accused him of fabricating fictions.

From the beginning, then, psychoanalysis has depended upon interdisciplinary knowledge, and its future development and survival will depend upon embracing its roots in multiple disciplines. Psychoanalytic interdisciplinarity is not a new idea, but in the following pages I discuss in detail six noteworthy contemporary clinicians and scholars, from a range of academic disciplines, who are shaping psychoanalysis. Offering a retrospective view of the writers' work enables us to see recurrent patterns that might not have been visible at the beginning of their careers. Following each discussion, I interview the author, who casts additional light on his or her work.

I began this book in late 2019, believing there was a timely double entendre in the approaching new year: 2020 would give me the hindsight, I hoped, to discuss my favorite contemporary psychoanalytic thinkers in a year that had a sonorous sound to it. Who knew that 2020 would be an *annus horribilis*, the year of the calamitous coronavirus pandemic, not to mention a frightening US presidential election unlike any other? Teaching through Zoom for an entire year, feeling isolated and anxious like everyone else, dependent on a virtual technology I did not fully understand nor know how to use, I was grateful for the return of in-person teaching in the fall of 2021. I could not see my students' masked faces, but I began to feel human again. I completed this book in early 2022, but just as the world seemed returning to a semblance of recovery, Russia invaded Ukraine, which reminded me of a grim cartoon I read somewhere decades ago about the weapons of the Fourth World War: a bow and arrow.

COVID-19 had one silver lining for me. Sheltered at home, I found it was a good time for reading and writing. Dr. Johnson's words to his future biographer, James Boswell—"Depend upon it, Sir, when a man knows he is to be hanged in a fortnight, it concentrates his mind wonderfully"—is no less true about life during a pandemic.

I admire many contemporary psychoanalytic scholars and clinicians, and it was a challenge to limit myself to a handful and then go into as much depth as possible in my discussions of their work. I chose the writers for several reasons. Sander Gilman, the late Allen Wheelis and Joan Wheelis, Nancy J. Chodorow, Christopher Bollas, and Adam Phillips are all genuinely interdisciplinary writers, spanning two or more fields, including my own, literary studies. All are deeply rooted in the humanities. All are highly controversial, in many cases lightning rods, challenging conventional psychoanalytic wisdom. All have spent a lifetime devoted to expanding and often critiquing psychoanalytic knowledge. And all regard themselves as outsiders, on the margins, despite the fact that they offer an inside view of psychoanalysis. Sometimes an outsider has unique insight into a group's inner workings.

A Brief Autobiographical Note

Like the authors I discuss in this book, I, too, am an outsider despite having spent more than half a century reading and writing about psychoanalysis and teaching graduate and undergraduate courses on literature and psychoanalysis. After receiving tenure in the late 1970s at SUNY-Albany, now called the University at Albany, I studied for three years at the National Psychological Association of Psychoanalysis (NPAP), the first non-medical psychoanalytic institute in the United States, founded in 1948 by Freud's student Theodor Reik. During the early 1980s, when I studied at NPAP, only medically trained psychiatrists could become candidates or members of the American Psychoanalytic Association (APsaA). It was not until 1989 that APsaA, under pressure of a lawsuit filed by four members of the American Psychological Association, permitted non-medical clinicians to study at APsaA-approved institutes. APsaA's exclusionary practice did not affect me. I had no desire to become an analyst. A handful of English professors have become practicing psychoanalysts, including not only Christopher Bollas but also Peter L. Rudnytsky and Vera Camden. My goal in studying at NPAP was to increase my understanding of psychoanalysis for my teaching and scholarship.

While studying at NPAP, I was probably the only person who was not in analysis. Going into analysis for several years, with two young children and a wife who was at the time a stay-at-home mother, would have involved incurring crushing financial debt, something I was unwilling to do (it would have made me more neurotic!), particularly since I didn't want to change careers. I was content to be a "research scholar" at NPAP and muddle through life without the benefit of analytic self-enlightenment. When the other NPAP students told me that I was missing the most valuable component of psychoanalytic education, a personal or training analysis, I shrugged my shoulders. The other students at NPAP spoke about their own personal analysis and what they learned from their patients; I joked that my clinical practice was limited to conflicted fictional characters, adding that I had inexpensive malpractice insurance because fictional characters seldom sue the psychoanalytic literary scholars who write about them. If I were beginning my life over again, I would make the same career decision, becoming an English professor and spending my life writing about literature and psychoanalysis.

In his late essay "Analysis Terminable and Interminable" (1937), Freud wrote about the difficulty of ending analysis. I don't usually believe in omens, but I had a near-death experience returning home from my final psychoanalytic classes that allowed me to read the handwriting on the wall. It was easy to study at NPAP when I was on sabbatical after I received tenure, but it became harder when I returned to full-time teaching. One morning each week, on a non-teaching day, I would drive from my home in the suburbs to downtown Albany and take a three-hour bus ride to Manhattan. After spending the afternoon visiting museums or the New York Public Library, I would take two back-to-back evening courses (all psychoanalytic institutes have their classes in the evening to accommodate clinicians' work schedules) and return to Albany exhausted, usually around 2:30 a.m., and then drive back home, collapsing into bed around 3:00 a.m., waking three or four hours later to teach my classes. At the end of the third year of psychoanalytic classes, I was so tired and disoriented as I was driving home that I couldn't understand why the few cars on the road at that time were furiously blinking their headlights at me—until I discovered, to my horror, that I was driving the wrong way on the interstate. Narrowly avoiding crashing into a car that was hurtling toward me, I took it as a sign that psychoanalysis was literally killing me and ended my formal education.

"The older I have become, the less I have understood or had insight into or known about myself." If the octogenarian C.G. Jung could write this without embarrassment at the end of his posthumously published memoir, *Memories, Dreams, Reflections* (358), so can I. An example of not knowing myself? I don't simply become teary eyed while watching a film in a theater or television at home; my body begins convulsing violently as I struggle to hold back a torrent of tears. Curiously, these intense filmic moments, which happen frequently, are not always about love and loss. Nor can I predict when these emotional eruptions will occur. I will tear up sometimes in the classroom when a student reads aloud a poignant essay, or when talking with a friend about a sad experience, but I'm not referring to these understandable situations. Rather, helplessly witnessing my body tremble during a film or television program is of a different magnitude. During these unbearable moments, I try to disguise my physical trembling lest I make a spectacle of myself.

Making a spectacle of herself is what Madelon Sprengnether does in her powerful film memoir *Crying at the Movies* (2002), where she traces her own weeping to the suppressed emotions following her father's accidental drowning when she was nine. Forbidden by her mother to display any emotions about her father's death, the bereft daughter, tongue-tied, escaped into fiction and film, where she read about and witnessed tales of orphans. Years later, partly as a result of being in analysis, Sprengnether learned that her fear of losing control in reel life betokened unresolved mourning in real life. Because of traumatic amnesia, the fragments of the story emerge like shrapnel, evoking piercing pain associated with sudden loss.

Is unresolved mourning the explanation for my own paroxysms of emotion while watching films? Have I failed to come to terms with the losses in my own life? I see myself as an emotional person, but have I not been emotional enough? I'm not sure. Would years of psychoanalysis help me understand this peculiar—*bizarre* might be a better word—behavior? Again, I'm not sure. All I know is that you wouldn't want to sit next to me in a movie theater.

Showing Authors How You Write about Them

I asked Sander Gilman, Joan Wheelis, Nancy Chodorow, Christopher Bollas, and Adam Phillips whether they were interested in reading my discussions of their work and responding to my questions. All generously agreed to do so. As Paul Roazen observes in *Freud and His Followers*, "In scholarship as in life, knowing the right questions is always the hardest problem" (xxx). Apart from Allen Wheelis, who was unusually self-disclosing, particularly in an age when psychoanalysts did not reveal much about themselves, the other writers in this book are not, and they did not always respond to my more personal (and intrusive) questions, such as "What did you learn about yourself from your analysis?" or "How did being a parent affect your psychoanalytic thinking?" Yet they were always forthcoming in the questions on which they did comment.

There are advantages and disadvantages of showing people in advance how you write about them. The advantages include their willingness to correct factual errors, point out interpretive differences, remark on authorial intentions, and sometimes offer additional information about their work that leads to new insights. The authors in this study knew from reading my chapters that I had profound respect for their psychoanalytic contributions, but I tried not to write "puff pieces" about them, which is the one disadvantage to showing authors how you intend to write about them. It is admittedly harder to criticize people when they read your evaluation of their work. Adam Phillips's observation in *Equals* that "writing about someone turns too easily into writing on their behalf" (228) is true. Most people react sympathetically to positive evaluations of their work; the corollary is that they may react unsympathetically to negative evaluations.

In my experience, the many advantages outweigh the single disadvantage. In the mid-1990s, I began writing about my students in *Diaries to an English Professor: Pain and Growth in the Classroom*, always with their written consent after they received their final grades and with permission of the university Institutional Review Board, which oversees human research. I showed my students in advance how I intended to use and contextualize their essays and diaries. I did this for their protection and my own. I have continued to follow this protocol in my later publications on teaching, such as *Surviving Literary Suicide* (1999), and in my books about spousal loss memoirs and death education. Paul Mosher and I followed this protocol when writing *Confidentiality and Its Discontents* and *Off the Tracks*, interviewing subjects and then showing them how we contextualized their words.

On Not Being Janet Malcolm

Investigative journalists like Janet Malcolm never do this. Two of her sensationalistic psychoanalytic studies, *Psychoanalysis: The Impossible Profession* (1981) and *In the Freud Archives* (1984), which first appeared in two essays published in *The New Yorker*, skewer her biographical subjects. In her acknowledgments in the 1981 book, Malcolm expresses gratitude to "Aaron Green," the forty-six-year-old Manhattan psychoanalyst whom she interviewed, for being a "remarkable and lovable man who opened his mind and heart to me and gave this book its life." Notwithstanding these laudatory words, the graduate of the New York Psychoanalytic Institute comes across as abrasive, snobbish, self-absorbed, insecure, envious, and narrow-minded. Malcolm has the ability to elicit her biographical subject's dangerous disclosures and then watch, to cite Hamlet's proverbial expression, as he is hoist with his own petard. Jeffrey Moussaieff Masson's promiscuity is perhaps the single most striking detail in Malcolm's 1984 exposé. "I knew there was something wrong," he recklessly confides to her; "I'd slept with close to a thousand women by the time I got to Toronto" (*In the Freud Archives* 39). But it's Masson's grandiosity that is most startling. Malcolm's portrait accentuates his egotism and overweening arrogance, his penchant for extravagant hyperbole, his narcissistic longing for success, and his betrayal of those who formerly befriended him.

Malcolm never acknowledges how she had ingratiated herself with Masson to extract his confessions. As Robert S. Boynton reported in *The Village Voice* in 1994, she interviewed Masson first in Berkeley, where he was living at the time, and then in her townhouse in New York City, where he and his girlfriend stayed with her for four days. Before her first article appeared in *The New Yorker*, she sent him a letter with the words, "I think you'll love it." He didn't. The outraged Masson filed a 13-million-dollar lawsuit in California against Malcolm and *The New Yorker*, alleging that she had fabricated five quotations, including, most notoriously, his statement calling himself an "intellectual gigolo" (*In the Freud Archives* 38). The lawsuit, which has been compared to the Jarnydce v. Jarndyce court case in Dickens's *Bleak House*, dragged on for years, eventually reaching the US Supreme Court.

The daughter of a psychiatrist, Malcolm was a brilliant writer who authored riveting books, but her journalistic ethics were highly problematic. As she declares in the opening paragraph to *The Journalist and the Murderer* (1990), indirectly commenting on her earlier books, the journalist is a "kind of confidence man, preying on people's vanity, ignorance, or loneliness, gaining their trust and betraying them without remorse" (3). Malcolm died in 2021 at age eighty-six. In her *New York Times* obituary, Katharine Q. Seelye cites Robert S. Boynton's warning in 1992: "Don't ever eat in front of Janet Malcolm; or show her your apartment; or cut tomatoes while she watches. In fact, it probably isn't a good idea even to grant her an interview, as your every unflattering gesture and nervous tic will be recorded eventually with devastating precision."

I'm a psychoanalytic literary scholar, not an investigative journalist, and I'm not interested in befriending biographical subjects only later to betray them. Only once have I had a problem when I sent a manuscript in advance to a person I was writing about—the psychoanalyst Hans J.

Kleinschmidt. By comparing Kleinschmidt's case study, ironically titled "The Angry Act: The Role of Aggression in Creativity," published in *American Imago* in 1967, with Philip Roth's highly autobiographical novel *Portnoy's Complaint* (1969), a chapter of which, "The Jewish Blues," appeared in 1967, I realized to my astonishment that Roth was Kleinschmidt's patient. Both analyst and patient were writing about the same biographical material.

Had I made this discovery solely on the basis of "The Angry Act" and *Portnoy's Complaint*, I would not have written about Roth, who would have been victimized twice, first by his analyst and then by a literary scholar. But in his 1974 novel *My Life as a Man*, Roth lightly fictionalizes this shocking breach of analytic confidentiality and leaves all the clues necessary for a psychoanalytically oriented literary critic such as me to make the connection. I decided to send my chapter "Philip Roth's Psychoanalysts," which was part of the book I was writing at the time, *The Talking Cure: Literary Representations of Psychoanalysis* (1985), to Kleinschmidt, asking him if he was willing to comment on it. Instead, he threatened to file a lawsuit against me. Kleinschmidt eventually backed off, however, and conceded that everything in my discussion was factually accurate.

In reading Adam Gopnik's wry essay "Man Goes to See a Doctor," first published in *The New Yorker* in 1998 and then reprinted in Jason Shinder's *Tales from the Couch: Writers on Therapy* (2000), I had a sense of déjà vu all over again, for I could tell from Gopnik's sly description that his German-born analyst, pseudonymously called Dr. Max Grosskurth, was none other than Kleinschmidt. Whenever the elderly Grosskurth fell asleep, which was often, all Gopnik needed to do was to refer to Roth's name and the analyst's head would immediately jerk straight up.

None of the chapters in this book contain any explosive revelations, but I didn't know whether the authors would be willing to take time away from their busy schedules to answer my questions. They did. They didn't always agree with my observations about their work, but no one asked me to delete any material. I did not ask the authors the same question (such as "Are you hopeful about the future of psychoanalysis?"), mainly because some of them had already answered the question in their books. Nor did I ask the authors to comment on each other's work. Some authors responded with brief answers, while others gave more expansive replies. I always thought of additional questions to ask after a "conversation" ended, but I didn't want to be a nuisance with another email query.

Discussing Authors' Scholarship before Interviewing Them

Several interview collections exist, including Peter L. Rudnytsky's excellent 2000 volume *Psychoanalytic Conversations: Interviews with Clinicians, Commentators, and Critics.* These collections, however, do not include in-depth discussions of the interviewed writers. My conversations with the writers were, with one exception, email exchanges. I sent my questions to the authors; they responded, and, in some instances, I added follow-up questions, hoping to achieve the illusion of the spontaneity of an actual conversation. I couldn't do this with Adam Phillips, however, because he doesn't use email. I would not have been able to contact him without the help of Christopher Bollas, who kindly gave me Phillips's London address and telephone number. Reluctant to telephone Phillips, mainly because I have a hearing problem, I mailed him a copy of my chapter about his work, and, to my delight, he agreed to read my chapter and responded promptly with his comments, which he snail-mailed me.

Throughout this book I take a chronological approach to their psychoanalytic writings, which allows me to point out the continuities and occasional discontinuities of their thinking. With a single exception, I comment on all of the books of each writer. Sander Gilman has authored or coauthored over ninety books (he can write a book faster than one can review it), and thus I limit myself to his psychoanalytic scholarship, which itself is vast. I also discuss the literary and psychoanalytic commentary surrounding the authors' writings. Whenever possible, I discuss how their work has influenced my own teaching and writing.

The Plan of This Book

Chapter 1 examines Sander L. Gilman, one of the great contemporary psychoanalytic cultural historians. He is, almost certainly, the world's most prolific psychoanalytic scholar. More than anyone, Gilman shows how Freud's unconscious feelings about his identity, particularly his ambivalence over being an Eastern European Jew, were inscribed into psychoanalytic theory. Demonstrating how the "poisoned" concept of race stands at the center of nineteenth-century science, Gilman offers radically new readings of Freud based on race, class, and gender. He analyzes how the "Jew" in Freud's Jewish jokes becomes the "woman" in psychoanalytic theory, embodying negative qualities of moral inferiority, weakness, and passivity. Gilman is the master interrogator of stereotypes and the rhetoric of differences, exposing the largely unconscious ideologies with which we structure the world. Like Michel Foucault, Gilman is interested in studying power, but unlike the influential French philosopher, Gilman focuses on the psychological dimensions of power. If we appear "smarter" than Freud, Gilman told me, we must remember that Freud developed the psychological tools by which we study him.

Chapter 2 focuses on Allen Wheelis, who, next to Freud and Irvin Yalom, was probably the greatest writer of psychotherapy tales. Like Yalom, Wheelis was a *dis*illusioner. I started reading Wheelis's novels in the 1980s and interviewed him in his elegant San Francisco home in the late 1990s, when I first began writing about him. Regrettably, I have little memory of what we discussed together. (Only later did I ruefully remind myself to write down everything important lest my poor memory betray me.) Wheelis at first fictionalized a traumatic childhood experience that he later wrote about in a nonfiction book, allowing us to see the lifelong humiliation he experienced as a child. He was a trenchant critic of his profession, to which he nevertheless remained devoted. Many of his fiction and nonfiction books describe the professional hazards of being a psychoanalyst. He was among the first analysts to write about the limits of insight, which does not always produce therapeutic change or relief from suffering. Like Chekhov, Wheelis believed that the role of the artist is to ask questions, not answer them. Fascinated with clinicians of despair, he is never despairing in his commitment to his twin passions, literature and psychoanalysis.

It is not common for a daughter to enter the same profession as her father and mother, and even less common for a psychoanalyst to write a memoir about her relationship to her parents. For this reason alone, Joan Wheelis's 2019 memoir, *The Known, the Secret, the Forgotten*, is noteworthy. Indeed, it is the only memoir of which I'm aware in which a psychoanalyst writes about her father and mother who were themselves analysts. Joan Wheelis offers a unique perspective on her parents, both of whom lived and practiced to their nineties. In her responses to my questions, she describes her complicated feelings about reading her father's books. She also writes about following in her parents' footsteps by becoming a psychiatrist and psychoanalyst but then going in her own direction by using a new therapeutic approach, dialectical behavior therapy, one that is especially valuable for "borderline" patients who usually are not helped by psychoanalysis. In her professional publications, Joan Wheelis displays the same modesty and humility when writing about patients as her father did.

Chapter 3 highlights Nancy J. Chodorow, whose first book, *The Reproduction of Mothering* (1978), has become a classic, profoundly influencing how two disciplines, sociology and psychoanalysis, theorize motherhood and child development. Despite the fame she achieved from the book, it was difficult for her to find a tenure-track academic position: psychoanalytically oriented feminist sociologists were not in demand in the 1970s. In her most recent book, *The Psychoanalytic Ear and Sociological Eye*, Chodorow offers a new psychoanalytic approach, intersubjective ego psychology, combining two antagonistic theoretical models, ego psychology (the study of defense mechanisms) and interpersonal psychology. She elaborates on two types of analysts: those who, driven by theory, listen *for* a patient's speech to confirm their own theoretical approach, and others who, by contrast, listen *to* a patient in an attempt to be more open-minded and inclusive. Chodorow's own preference is clear, and, following her lead, I listen to what she says. She proposes a new interdisciplinary academic department, "Individuology," to study human complexity. If such a department existed, Chodorow's books would most certainly be taught. In her responses to my questions, she offers excellent advice to psychoanalytic scholars beginning their careers.

Chapter 4 explores Christopher Bollas's writings, particularly how they reveal his psychoanalytic *literary* education. Bollas received a PhD in English literature before he became a renowned psychoanalyst. Evidence of his literary training is striking in all of his writings. Bollas is one of the most evocative psychoanalytic stylists, as can be seen in the theory for which he is best known, the "unthought known," named in the subtitle of his first and probably most influential book, *The Shadow of the Object*. Bollas is among the most stylish psychoanalytic theorists, with an uncommon knack for aphorisms and neologisms. He coins many new psychoanalytic expressions, such as a *sightophile*, a person who prefers seeing to thinking, reminding us that sight (and insight) without careful thought may be counterproductive. Bollas is also a talented creative writer; he has authored three novellas and a collection of plays, all of which dramatize his psychoanalytic vision. Bollas's fictional writings allow him to offer satirical criticisms of his profession in ways that would not have been possible in his nonfictional writings.

Chapter 5 considers Adam Phillips, regarded as one of Britain's greatest living psychoanalysts and literary critics. Freud loved literature and wrote, as he ruefully acknowledged, as a creative writer; nevertheless, he turned to literature mainly to confirm psychoanalytic theory. By contrast, Phillip reverses the process, arguing that psychoanalysis is a part of literature. A paradoxicalist and provocateur, Phillips is a masterful writer; his Wildean wit makes his books, to cite one of his titles, *Unforbidden Pleasure*. To cite another of his book titles, he is always *Attention Seeking* but never narcissistic or solipsistic. To avoid reading Phillips, we would be *Missing Out*, to quote still another book title. But if one had to equate Phillips with a single book title, it would be his coauthored *On Kindness*. He maintains throughout his many books a dual allegiance to literature and psychoanalysis. Challenging conventional psychoanalytic wisdom, he offers us, in his slender biography of the creator of the talking cure, a post-Freudian Freud, a disenlightener who, instead of solving the Sphinx's riddle with the discovery of the Oedipus complex, affirmed, perhaps without knowing it, mystery, ambiguity, and unknowability. Phillips's vision of psychoanalysis is uniquely his own—and, for me, irresistible.

In the conclusion I discuss psychoanalysis as a work in progress. Based on the differences among the writers in this book, one might refer to *psychoanalyses* to highlight the plurality of psychoanalytic visions. I raise several issues, including the extent to which psychoanalysis is scientific, the Dodo bird effect, the marital inequality between literature and psychoanalysis, the controversy over the new English translation of Freud's writings, and my impressions of my conversations with the authors in this study, including the realization of my own "unfinished business." Part of this unfinished business involves my transference to the authors, something of which I was not aware until it was pointed out by the anonymous reviewers of this book, who in effect became my "analysts." I end with a brief comment about the fate of psychoanalysis, looking forward to a time when the cataclysmic year 2020 will give way to a brighter future.

Had I world enough and time—and additional space in this book—I would have interviewed several other leading interdisciplinary psychoanalytic thinkers, such as Jessica Benjamin, Deborah Britzman, Glen Gabbard, Julia Kristeva, Thomas Ogden, and Peter Rudnytsky. I hope I have an opportunity to write about these seminal thinkers in future books.

"Every man I meet," Emerson observed in a letter in the late 1800s, "is my superior in some way. In that I learn from him." Sander Gilman, Allen Wheelis and Joan Wheelis, Nancy Chodorow, Christopher Bollas, and Adam Phillips are unquestionably superior clinicians, scholars, and theorists. All of them are, to use a social media word, *influencers*. I learned much from them, as I hope to show.

Chapter 1

Sander L. Gilman's Psychoanalysis of Freud

"How can we know the dancer from the dance?" Yeats famously asks at the end of his late, great poem "Among School Children" (1926). Yeats's rhetorical question, suggesting the impossibility of separating poet from poem, subject from object, is similar to Nietzsche's insight in *Beyond Good and Evil* (1886): "It has gradually become clear to me what every great philosophy has hitherto been: a confession on the part of its author and a kind of involuntary and unconscious memoir" (37).

Sander L. Gilman implicitly raises this question in his voluminous writings on Freud: how can we tell the theorist from the theory? The construction of Freudian theory is so inextricably interrelated to Freud's personality, the theorist's conscious and unconscious mind, that it is impossible to separate the man from his work. Biographies abound of the psychoanalyst who viewed himself as the disturber of the world's sleep; we know perhaps as much about Freud as about any other major twentieth-century thinker. And yet, as Gilman noted in his 1992 review of Yosef Hayim Yerushalmi's *Freud's Moses: Judaism Terminable and Interminable*, "Perhaps no writer has ever written more about himself and told his readers less than did Freud" (1179).

Many scholarly studies, beginning with David Bakan's kabbalistic speculations in *Sigmund Freud and the Jewish Mystical Tradition* (1958), have commented on Freud's "Jewishness," but no one has written more incisively than Gilman about how Freud's deep ambivalence became inscribed in his creation of psychoanalysis. Gilman realizes, of course, that analysts and non-analysts alike will be vexed by the idea that psychoanalysis is a kind of involuntary and unconscious memoir. Or as he pithily observes in *Love + Marriage = Death* (1998): "We all write autobiography (or we write to repress our autobiographies)" (vi). I suspect that Gilman's psychoanalysis of psychoanalysis would have initially agitated Freud, yet if he were the analysand, he might have overcome his resistance and begrudgingly granted the truth of Gilman's analysis. At the least, Freud would acknowledge the astuteness of Gilman's psychoanalytic approach.

"Why and How I Study the German"

Gilman rarely writes about himself, but he does in his 1989 article published in *The German Quarterly*, "Why and How I Study the German," parts of which are reprinted in his 1991 book *Inscribing the Other*, dedicated to the memory of his Jewish-Polish and Jewish-Russian grandparents. He is not "completely autobiographical," as he promises in the essay, but he is more self-disclosing than in any other work: "I am an Eastern Jew, an *Ostjude*, whose extended family vanished in the Holocaust. Indeed, the Polish fishing village in which my mother was born was so totally eradicated by the Germans and the Poles that only a cornfield marks the spot where it formerly existed. Of my father's family, only one aunt, out of six brothers and sisters as well as their extended families, escaped death and managed to reach the Mandated Territory [Palestine] in 1947" ("Why and How I Study the German" 200). Gilman's first language was Yiddish, and he realized when he began studying German that it was the language and culture produced by those who had destroyed his family. Germany would have destroyed him too had he not made it to the "*guldene medina*, the new paradise—so very distant and very different from the old." Being an outsider in this new land does not mean being "cool and clinical." Rather, "it must mean to burn with those fires that define you as the outsider." This is not the age of postmodernism, Gilman contends; "it is the post-Holocaust age," the "salient marker for our present world" (201). He ends the article by admitting that he doesn't wish to advocate his own point of view as the voice of choice for others. "My view works for me—as an American academic, a male, a Jew, an individual from a proletarian background with middle-class sensibilities (and pretensions)" (203).

Gilman's other self-disclosures are scattered throughout his writings. In *Smart Jews: The Construction of the Image of Jewish Superior Intelligence* (1996), a study in "'philo-Semitism' and its pitfalls," he describes himself as the "son of a truck-driver and the grandson of a junkman" (22). In *The Fortunes of the Humanities* (2000), he refers to his own humanistic education. He was the first in his family to graduate from high school in the United States, and the first to go to college. Tulane University admitted him at the age of sixteen, as a "wild card," he later learned, because the admission committee saw "some academic promise" (x). This surely ranks as the most understated remark in any of his writings. Had he not been granted a full tuition scholarship and loans, he would have gone to work immediately after high school—and we would have lost one of the world's most distinguished literary, cultural, and psychological historians, a polymath without equal in psychoanalytic scholarship.

"A Double Outsider"—and a Lightning Rod

Gilman acknowledged in a 1998 interview with Dinitia Smith in *The New York Times* that he felt as a "double outsider, between white and black" while growing up in New Orleans. Although he appeared white, he lived along a "fissure line because being a Jew in the South was not being white." As a teenager he was involved in civil rights sit-ins in New Orleans, which taught him "what ugly stereotypes could do." During the 1970s, he came across nineteenth-century photographic depictions of mental illness. The experience was a turning point in his life. "I started thinking about broader questions of stereotyping, the psychology of what happens when stereotypes begin to be internalized." Gilman's work on stereotypes, particularly his discussion of the image of the black woman in the nineteenth century, evoked knee-jerk criticism from some academics who believed he was perpetuating rather than critiquing stereotypes. "It's the 'kill the messenger's problem,'" Gilman told Smith. "I violate a lot of taboos. Academics have a very low threshold of anxiety. I've served as a lightning rod."

Gilman received his BA in German from Tulane in 1963, after only three years of college. He spent two years as a graduate student in German and English at Tulane on a fellowship, studied in Munich and Berlin, and then received his PhD in German from Tulane in 1968. He observes in *The Fortunes of the Humanities* that he was a beneficiary of the National Defense Education Act, which poured money into higher education following the Soviets' launch of Sputnik in 1957. Gilman began his teaching career at St. Mary's Dominican College, a now-defunct Catholic women's college in New Orleans, followed by teaching at Dillard, a traditional black private university, and then at Case Western Reserve, a large research university. He arrived at Cornell in 1969, when I first met him: I was a doctoral student in English, and he was an assistant professor of German. Born in 1944, Gilman was already viewed as a wunderkind. In 1973 he created the first interdisciplinary undergraduate German studies degree. Serving on both the humanities and medical faculties at Cornell, he held the prestigious Goldwin Smith Professorship of Humane Studies. One of the ironies of his endowed chair was that Goldwin Smith, the former Regius Professor of History at Oxford who later became a founder of Cornell, was the first biological anti-Semite in Britain.

After teaching at Cornell for twenty-five years, Gilman moved to the University of Chicago, where for six years he held the Henry R. Luce Distinguished Service Professorship of the Liberal Arts in Human Biology. Wishing to remain in Chicago, he moved a few miles away to the University of Illinois at Chicago, where he taught for four years as a Distinguished Professor of the Liberal Arts and Medicine. While there he created the Humanities Laboratory and founded its Program in Jewish Studies. In 2005 he arrived at Emory University, where he was a distinguished professor of the Liberal Arts and Sciences as well as professor of psychiatry at Emory's Medical School. From 2006 to 2010 he served as Director of Emory's Program in Psychoanalysis. He retired from teaching in 2019 but remains a prodigious writer.

Gilman has received many academic awards and honors. In 1995 he served as the president of the Modern Language Association. In 2008 he was selected as an honorary member of the American Psychoanalytic Association, one of a handful of non-clinicians to receive that recognition. In 2016 he was elected a fellow of the American Academy of Arts and Sciences, which noted that he helped create the field of medical humanities as well as Jewish cultural studies in the 1970s, from which the newer field of disability studies has evolved. He was awarded a Doctor of Laws at the University of Toronto, elected a Fellow of the Royal Society of Medicine in London, and is an honorary professor of the Free University in Berlin. Gilman's teaching, scholarship, and lecturing have earned him a reputation as a public intellectual who tirelessly champions the role of the humanities in society.

Despite his theoretical sophistication, Gilman uses lucid, jargon-free prose. "*Write in an accessible manner,*" he urges readers in "How to Get Tenure," a chapter in *The Fortunes of the Humanities* filled with pragmatic advice. "Every profession has its jargon, the verbal shorthand that makes it possible to communicate complex notions quickly to colleagues working on the same topic" (21). Yet great scholarship must be accessible to scholars in other disciplines, he insists, citing a remark the Princeton literary critic Elaine Showalter recently expressed to him: scholarly books must be readable books. Gilman's scholarship is always accessible. He writes for scholars in many different fields, and while his ideas are always complex and often controversial, his prose is never obscurantist.

"A Fraud"

Beginning in the 1970s, for many years, first at Cornell and then at the University of Chicago, Gilman taught an undergraduate course on literature and psychoanalysis. Offered in the departments of comparative literature, German studies, English, and psychology, the course had enrollment varying from 60 to more than 250 students. Students could write on a traditional academic subject or present an analysis of one of their own dreams. (Gilman generously credits my 1994 book *Diaries to an English Professor*, in which I discuss how students in my literature-and-psychoanalysis courses analyze their own dreams.) In *The Fortunes of the Humanities* he analyzes one of his own dreams, the "Airport Dream," a punishment dream in which he discloses his "load of sin" (46). He analyzes the dream in great detail, revealing his need to impose order on his life, his sexual attraction to a young girl, and his effort to dominate the dark aspects of his personality. The most fascinating detail about the dream is the statement that, working as a photojournalist for a local newspaper, he had a fight with his boss, who felt that one of Gilman's photographs was too subjective. Gilman's next comment is eye-opening. "I have a strong aversion to authority figures, often, I fear, because they are in positions to reveal that I am, in some way, a fraud" (48). As Dinitia Smith reported in the *New York Times* interview, Gilman once wryly called himself the "Trollope of the academy," a reference to the prolific nineteenth-century English novelist. Gilman's wife, Marina von Eckardt, aptly characterized him: "At one point, I decided if someone was going to do an autopsy on him, they would find a filing cabinet in his brain."

Few scholars have the depth and breadth of interdisciplinary knowledge to appreciate the extent of Gilman's contributions. It's not surprising that he read Freud in the original German and then in English translation. Nor is it surprising that he read all of Freud's books in the Freud Museum in London and then studied the marginalia glosses to discern the impact of the analyst's readings. But what is surprising, startling, is Gilman's observation in the preface to his 1993 book *Freud, Race, and Gender.* "At the National Library of Medicine, the Library of Congress, and the Library of the University of Maryland (College Park) I was able to examine all the materials that Freud cites in his references" (xiv). He says this casually, matter-of-factly, yet I know few scholars who would attempt to do this. I don't know if Gilman is a "monster of reading," as was Harold Bloom, who could read a 400-page book in an hour and remember it word for word, but Gilman's erudition is gargantuan. Indeed, I doubt that even the fastest reader could plow through the thousands of books and articles appearing in the bibliographical citations and footnotes in Gilman's books. No scholar has put his obsessions and compulsions, and perhaps private demons, to greater intellectual use.

"As I learned in the mid-1970s," Gilman writes in the preface to his coedited 1994 volume *Reading Freud's Reading*, "it is more than romanticization to read the books read by great thinkers. Reading their books gives you an insight to what they read and what they did not read; what they included in their reading of a text, and what they excluded" (xiii). Freud often scribbled the expression the "heart of the matter" in the margins of his books when he found what he thought was the essence of a text's meaning. Gilman, too, captures the heart of the matter of Freud's reading.

Wherever Gilman goes, he seems to read everything available and retain the contents of his reading—a photographic memory (which Freud also had) helps. He discloses in *Jews in Today's Culture* (1995) that while on a Berlin subway, he began, as was his usual practice, "to read my neighbor's newspaper over his shoulder (a practice that wins you as many friends in Berlin as it does in New York)" (32). What he read was unsettling enough to compel him to exit the train at the next station and buy himself a copy of the Berlin tabloid, which he then summarizes for us. Gilman is among the most generous and genial of scholars, qualities that enhance his writing and serve as a model to other scholars. To master one academic field may take a lifetime; but to master several—German studies, comparative literature, English studies, cultural studies, Jewish studies, history of science, disability studies, psychiatry, psychoanalysis— requires a large interdisciplinary faculty, and even then one wouldn't see the combined expertise that we see in Gilman. Henry James must have been thinking of Gilman when he spoke about the person "on whom nothing is lost."

Redefining "Science" as Ideology

What if psychoanalysis is not "scientific," Gilman asks in *Disease and Representation: Images of Illness from Madness to AIDS* (1988), but what if it "works all the same?" (182). That is, what if psychoanalysis is defined ideologically rather than scientifically, hermeneutically, or philosophically? Gilman's goal is to understand the origins of psychoanalysis by exploring its creator's hidden ideological assumptions about his racial identity, an approach largely ignored by other psychoanalytic scholars.

In what follows, I examine Gilman's profound contributions to our understanding of Freud's construction of psychoanalytic theory. "Sigmund Freud's own life," Gilman writes in "Why and How I Study the German," "bound by historical forces and stereotypical structures of his own perception—structures that he could not comprehend as constructions—remains the best argument for the basic validity of his own theories" (197). In the early 1980s Gilman began using psychoanalytic concepts, such as projection, identification, internalization, and transference—all largely unconscious phenomena—to study how stereotypes appear in Freud's writings. Reading Gilman's early psychoanalytic writings from the perspective of his later writings, we can see the evolution of his thinking. I focus in detail on the two books Gilman published in 1993: *Freud, Race, and Gender* and *The Case of Sigmund Freud*. Biographers have constructed and deconstructed nearly every aspect of Freud's life and work, but Gilman provides a new reading of the role of race and gender in the creation of psychoanalytic theory. In exploring the conscious and unconscious meaning of race and gender in Freud's life, Gilman adopts the interpretive insights of psychoanalysis, but he is also a cultural historian, explaining how larger sociological forces affected Freud's life and work.

Introducing Psychoanalytic Theory

Gilman's "Freud's *Three Essays on the Theory of Sexuality*: A Problem in Intellectual History," appearing in his 1982 edited volume *Introducing Psychoanalytic Theory*, represents one of his earliest forays into examining psychoanalytic theory in light of the history of ideas. Gilman begins the essay by citing the conundrum set by a "master puzzle solver," the Columbia literary critic Steven Marcus, who complained in his introduction to the American paperback edition of *Three Essays on the Theory of Sexuality* (1905) that it is impossible to understand why Freud associated a girl's polymorphous perversity with prostitution. Gilman then surveys medical attitudes toward childhood and literary portrayals of child prostitution in fin-de-siècle Vienna. Unlike most thinkers at the end of the nineteenth century who placed the prostitute in the category of the degenerate, Freud regards the prostitute as the natural extension of the female child.

To understand why the psychoanalyst held this view, Gilman cites Freud's analysis of a dream, conveyed in a letter to his confidant Wilhelm Fliess in 1897, in which he confesses feeling "over-affectionately" toward his ten-year-old daughter Mathilde. Freud conjectures that the dream fulfills his wish to blame the father as the originator of neurosis and end his doubt about the validity of the seduction theory, a belief that Freud held from 1895 to 1897, and then abandoned, that neuroses were caused by repressed memories of childhood sexual seduction. "Does the intense desire to see the seductiveness of the child," Gilman asks, "reflect a wish on Freud's part to resolve his own sexual projection concerning himself as the seducer?" (199). Regardless of whether Freud's controversial "seduction theory" was true in reality, as he believed in the mid-1890s, or true only in fantasy, as he later came to believe, it reveals a male's perception of female sexuality. "This in no way vitiates the validity of Freud's formulation of infantile sexuality," Gilman is quick to add, "but it does alter the rationale for its 'discovery'" (200). Gilman concludes by suggesting that the relationship between male projections of female sexuality and the realities of female sexuality is at best ambiguous. "The seductive child and the lower-class female are figments of the masculine imagination in turn-of-the-century Vienna, yet because they were articulated through works of art they became central metaphors for sexuality in Viennese society. They thus became the sexual fantasies, or nightmares, of an entire society" (201).

Difference and Pathology

Gilman's discussion of Freud's *Three Essays on the Theory of Sexuality* betokens a cautious beginning in placing the psychoanalyst on the couch. Gilman reprints a slightly revised version of the essay as the first chapter in his 1985 book *Difference and Pathology: Stereotypes of Sexuality, Race, and Madness,* a meditation on the power of stereotypes. The book spotlights Gilman's lifelong interest in exploring the ways in which myth and the unconscious deformation of reality combine to form stereotypes. The first section of *Difference and Pathology* focuses on stereotypes of sexuality, the second section on stereotypes of race. In both sections Gilman highlights the subjectivity of the human sciences, a position not likely to endear him to colleagues in those disciplines that claim objectivity. "Science creates fictions to explore facts, and an important criterion for endorsing these fictions is their ideological acceptability. Science, in spite of its privileged status in the West as arbiter of reality, is in this respect a blood relation of art" (28). He makes an even stronger statement in *Love + Marriage = Death*, where he observes that, having spent a year as a fellow at the Center for Advanced Study in the Behavioral Sciences in Stanford, California, he finds the stories humanists tell more compelling than those by social scientists. "If there is anything that differentiates the humanities, especially the study of literature and culture, from other endeavors in the academy, it is that we cannot expel our emotions from our work" (12).

Stereotyping, Gilman suggests, is a "universal means of coping with anxieties engendered by our inability to control the world" (*Difference and Pathology* 12). The need for stereotyping is so pervasive that it will never be thwarted. He hopes, however, that "education and study can expose the ideologies with which we structure our world, and perhaps help put us in the habit of self-reflection" (12). This remains Gilman's goal in *all* his books. Another goal is to indicate the degree of truth of contemporary psychoanalytic scholarship. Authoritative without being authoritarian, he can't resist critiquing Jeffrey Moussaieff Masson's sensationalistic 1984 book *The Assault on Truth: Freud's Suppression of the Seduction Theory*. "No credence can be given to any view, such as that of Jeffrey Masson, which attempts to isolate reality from fantasy. Freud himself never denied the possibility of actual seduction. What he stressed was the ubiquitousness of fantasies of seduction" (57).

Gilman's writings rely on the work of many psychoanalytic theorists, including two analysts closely associated with narcissism: Otto Kernberg and Heinz Kohut. Discussing the deep structure of stereotypes, Gilman uses ego psychology, object relations theory, and self psychology (which affirms the role of empathy in maintaining healthy self-esteem) to show how splitting and projection function. He traces negative stereotypes to infants' narcissism that compels them to split internal representations into "a good self" and "a bad self," projecting the latter onto other people. The result is a split between self and object, the latter of which becomes the "Other," a term he capitalizes. "The Other is thus stereotyped, labeled with a set of signs paralleling (or mirroring) our loss of control" (20).

This Other, often pathologized, is a central marker of difference. Gilman's racial rereading of Freudian theory rests on what Anna Freud called in *The Ego and the Mechanisms of Defense* "identification with the aggressor," a defense mechanism first formulated by Sandor Ferenczi. "By impersonating the aggressor," Anna Freud writes, "assuming his attributes or imitating his aggression, the child transforms himself from the person threatened into the person who makes the threat" (113). Gilman rarely refers to Jacques Lacan, largely because of the opacity of Lacanian theory and its ahistorical methodology.

Two of the chapters in the second part of *Difference and Pathology* focus on psychoanalysis: "Sigmund Freud and the Jewish Joke" and "Sexology, Psychoanalysis, and Degeneration." Gilman presents ideas in both chapters that undergird his later psychoanalytic writings. Freud was highly conflicted about his identity as an Eastern European Jew. "Jews assumed the status of the proverbial leper during the Middle Ages," an association that continued through Freud's age. Freud's Jewish jokes rely on mauscheln, speaking broken German, a macaronic language that conjures up laughter if not ridicule. Mauscheln is the language of failed cultural assimilation, spoken with the accent of Eastern European Yiddish along with a hint of Hebrew, the language of liturgy. A Jew's use of mauscheln was an insurmountable obstacle in being accepted into German society. Gilman identifies mauscheln, with its fantastic intonation, vocabulary, and grammar, as the hidden language of the Jews. Freud's Jewish jokes, Gilman demonstrates in *Difference and Pathology*, belie his efforts, largely unconscious, to distance himself from his humble religious and racial roots and ally himself with modern "scientific" discourse, the language of the cultural elite.

Race is ubiquitous in Gilman's writings, and because other scholars of history, medicine, and the social sciences use the word differently, he offers his own nuanced definition in *Are Racists Crazy?* (2016), coauthored with James M. Thomas. Race is a "set of historical and discursive practices that, in various forms, tether constructions of madness, disease, illness, and, fundamentally, *difference* to certain bodies" (9). Ideologies about innate racial differences are both the cause and effect of medical, behavioral, and social sciences. The concept of race is "unstable"; "shaped by historical, material, and discursive forces"; "without basis in human biology, anatomy, or physiology"; and yet "ontologically real" in that race remains a "fundamental organizer of political, social, and economic opportunities" (10).

Gilman highlights the impact of Otto Weininger's 1903 book *Sex and Character* on Freud's unconscious thinking. A misogynistic and self-hating Jew who converted to Catholicism and committed suicide shortly after the publication of his pseudoscientific book, Weininger regarded women's language as lies, similar to the Jews' inferior language of mauscheln. Freud read Weininger's writings and, threatened by his virulent anti-Semitism, sought to distinguish the language of science from the language attributed to Jews. In one of his most provocative insights, Gilman suggests that the Jew in Freud's Jewish jokes becomes the woman, embodying insecurity, weakness, and passivity, the opposite of the idealized German with whom he unconsciously identifies. Freud thus ironically allies himself with the non-Jew's caricature of the Jew. In Gilman's view, Freud exorcises his insecurities as an Eastern European Jew by creating a new discipline of study, psychoanalysis, and by inventing a new language, the discourse of the unconscious, a speech he alone mastered. Yet if Freud needed to distance himself from female lack, a subject Gilman explores in greater detail in his later books, Freud did not want to imply, as most of his contemporaries did, that sexuality was pathological. Rather, Freud asserted the opposite: sexuality was natural, normal, the opposite of degeneracy.

The University of Toronto medical historian Edward Shorter characterized Gilman's approach to the question of why nineteenth-century physicians believed that Jews were especially prone to disease as merely a matter of labeling. "Understanding these differences," Shorter avers, "means coming to grips with the complex interaction between culture and biology, rather than merely dismissing biology" (150). Gilman's argument, however, is more complex than this. Whether Jews had substantially higher incidences of mental illness than other groups, he states in *Love + Marriage = Death*, cannot be determined from the fragmentary and biased statistics used in such discussions. As a cultural historian, he claims to determine not the realities of difference but rather its representation, as seen in a close reading of the rhetoric of difference. In a review published in *Victorian Studies*, John R. Reed praises *Difference and Pathology* as a "fascinating examination of the propensity of human groups to agree upon fictions that deflect their guilt." Reed faults Gilman, however, for providing little information on "how those perceived as Other created stereotypes by projecting images of themselves on yet some other Other" (410). Reed's other criticism, that Gilman ignores positive stereotypes, is certainly not true in his later writings, where he remarks that positive stereotypes are as misleading as negative ones, a powerful means of control.

Jewish Self-Hatred

The rhetoric of difference appears in *Jewish Self-Hatred: Anti-Semitism and the Hidden Language of the Jews* (1986). It is not an easy book to read, especially if one is Jewish. Gilman's study awakens anxieties and ambivalences that one may not wish to confront. "Jews are not an invention of the anti-semite—or vice versa," Adam Phillips wrote in a laudatory review of *Jewish Self-Hatred* appearing in the *London Review of Books*. "It is a reciprocal relationship: each invents the other. Their identity is constituted, but never fixed, as Gilman's superb individual portraits show, by what goes on between them."

Gilman's thesis in *Jewish Self-Hatred* is that Jews could never escape their difference from non-Jews. "The more the Jews became like the Germans, the better their command of German, the more their existence within the body politic paralleled the existence of the non-Jew, the greater the need of some means to distinguish them from the non-Jew" (84). The problem of anti-Semitism for the Jew is not simply living in a world of rejection but avoiding internalizing the rejection. Gilman might have cited Walt Kelly's memorable phrase in his classic newspaper comic strip Pogo, "We have met the enemy and he is us."

I can give one personal albeit belated example of Jewish self-hatred. In rereading my review of *Freud, Race, and Gender* and *The Case of Sigmund Freud* published in *The Psychoanalytic Review* in 1995, I was struck by the following sentence: "European anti-Semitism comes as no surprise to European Jews, but to young and middle-aged assimilated U.S. Jews such as myself, who have been privileged to grow up in a relatively tolerant society, the degree and toxicity of this prejudice is startling" (779). The sentence is largely true (despite the confounding grammatical error in the last clause), but my desire to "pass" as a non-Jew was stronger than I was willing to acknowledge even in my early 50s. I was so uneasy about being Jewish that I remained silent in graduate school when Professor Arthur Mizener, F. Scott Fitzgerald's first biographer, lectured on *The Great Gatsby*, which contains one of the most virulently anti-Semitic characters in American literature, the predatory Jew Meyer Wolfsheim, whose cufflinks, made out of human molars, signify economic cannibalism, and who speaks mauscheln, referring to his "business gonnection" with Jay Gatsby. The novel's narrator, Nick Carraway, is fixated on Wolfsheim's stereotypical Jewish nose and nostril hairs. I seethed in mortification, too afraid to ask Mizener about the novel's (and novelist's) anti-Semitism.

Each time I teach *The Great Gatsby*, I ask my students, most of whom have read the novel in high school or in another college course, whether they recall discussing the story's prejudice against Jews. No one can.

Thanks to Gilman, I have a better understanding of Freud's ambivalence toward his own Jewishness. Ferociously ambitious, Freud was also fiercely anxious to be accepted by German society, which explains his refusal to use his first name, that of his grandfather, Schlomo Sigismund Freud, who died a few months before his birth. "In rejecting Schlomo, or at least in relegating it to his Jewish or private self," Gilman writes, "Freud followed the pattern set by [Heinrich] Heine, not in terms of conversion, but in the terms of separating himself from the world of Jewry rejected by the anti-Semite, whether the political or the scientific anti-Semite, and maintaining only his cultural affiliation" (266).

In *Jewish Self-Hatred*, Gilman applies his double-bind model of projection and identification to many German-speaking Jews, but he returns repeatedly to Freud. Gilman includes new material on the significance of Freud's Jewish jokes, particularly the way he often laced his letters to Fliess with Yiddishisms mocking *meschuge* ("crazy") Jews. Both assimilated Jews betrayed intense anxiety about their precarious status in Austrian or German society. Other scholars have commented on Freud's expression to Fliess in a September 21, 1897, letter, "Rebecca, take off your gown, you are no longer a bride" (a suggestive line Adam Phillips used in the title of his review article), but Gilman uncovers a hidden meaning. "The punch line is made even more telling by the use of the Yiddishism *Kalle*, which is itself a sexual double entendre meaning both 'bride' and 'prostitute'" (263).

Gilman remarks astutely on Freud's rhetorical strategies when narrating Jewish jokes. Part of this strategy involved compelling the reader's identification with him. "Freud allies himself with a reader, whom he expects to be conversant with the 'modern' scientific discourse on the unconscious, that is, Freud himself. This is, of course, a projection that reveals to us the identification that Freud, the provincial, has with those Eastern Jews who speak only in *mauscheln*" (264). In analyzing the hidden meaning of Freud's language, Gilman plays the role of psychoanalyst—or pathologist, having "autopsied," as he ruefully says, the language of self-hatred.

Freud never rejected his religion, as did other German-speaking Jews such as Henrich Heine, who was forced to convert to compete for a government position. Nor did Freud become a vitriolic self-hating Jew like Otto Weininger or Karl Kraus. But as a member of a persecuted minority, Freud could not help feeling burdened by his Jewish identity. One of the best examples of this occurs in *The Interpretation of Dreams* when Freud recalls being taken on a walk as a young boy by his father, who told him the following story of walking with a new fur cap on his head: "A Christian came up to me and with a single blow knocked off my cap into the mud and shouted: 'Jew! Get off the pavement!' 'And what did you do?' I asked. 'I went into the roadway and picked up my cap,' was his quiet reply. This struck me as unheroic conduct on the part of the big, strong man who was holding the little boy by the hand" (*SE* 4: 197). Freud never forgot this humiliating story and vowed to be heroic like Hannibal, not cowardly, as he perceived his father to be. Freud never repudiated his Jewishness. On the occasion of his seventieth birthday, in 1926, Freud was honored by the Viennese lodge of the Jewish fraternal order of B'Nai B'rith, to which he had belonged since 1895. Illness prevented Freud from appearing in person, but he wrote a two-page statement, described by Gilman as a *confessio judäica*, in which he sought to summarize his Jewish identity.

Gilman ends *Jewish Self-Hatred* with an overly optimistic sentence, claiming that "after a thousand years this chapter of Jewish identity formation for the Jewish writer has been closed" (392), a statement Jacob Neusner also found puzzling: "Only time will tell whether Gilman's judgment proves sound" (151). Neusner nevertheless calls the study a "landmark book, the best ever written on Jewish self-hatred," and ends his review with the highest praise. "Gilman's profound and important book will serve as the first, and the classic statement on the impact on writing by Jews, of the negative image imputed to them by their circumstances" (151). George Mosse similarly hailed *Jewish Self-Hatred* (and *Difference and Pathology*) as innovative and important. Mosse concludes his review by noting that in *Jewish Self-Hatred* Gilman "has had the courage to tackle the complex reactions of those victimized, to open up a Pandora's box of prejudice and hurt feelings. Gilman remains one of the most fascinating, competent, and learned guides to a subject none of us can afford to ignore" (168).

Disease and Representation

The same model of the internalization of cultural stereotypes used in *Jewish Self-Hatred* appears in *Disease and Representation*. Gilman argues that those who "deny the reality of the experience of disease marginalize and exclude the ill from their own world" (9). Of the fourteen chapters, "Constructing the Image of the Appropriate Therapist: The Struggle of Psychiatry with Psychoanalysis" reveals Gilman's prescient criticisms of the medicalization of American psychanalysis. Despite Freud's strong recommendation against medical training for psychoanalysts in *The Question of Lay Analysis* (1926), American psychoanalysts rejected the advice, insisting that analysts be physicians. Gilman analyzes the conscious and unconscious motives of both warring parties.

One of Freud's hidden motives, Gilman suggests, was the wish for his daughter Anna, the heir apparent who had minimal professional credentials, to practice psychoanalysis. She never challenged the British regulation that required non-medical analysts to practice only under medical supervision. Another motive, a subtle racial one, was the belief that the Eastern European Jew was a "money-grubbing Jew" in European anti-Semitic discourse. "The status of the Jewish psychoanalyst was tied to the status of European science, and Freud's attempt to loosen these bonds ran counter to the need of the exiled or emigrant psychoanalysts to call upon the status of European science to establish themselves within the closed world of American medicine" (198–199).

Proponents of medical psychoanalysis had their own hidden agenda, beginning with the prestige of medicine in the United States and the obvious financial incentive of charging higher fees. Gilman cites Robert Michels, chair of the Department of Psychiatry at the Cornell Medical College, who recognized that requiring psychoanalysts to be physicians represented the wish to return the psychiatrist to the hospital and the medical community, "in many ways playing the same sociological role in the 1940s," in Michels's words, "that neurobiology and psychopharmacology played in the seventies" (199). Michels realized at the time, as did Gilman, that allowing non-physicians to become analysts would be a potential watershed marking the end of the relationship between psychiatry and psychoanalysis in the United States. The question of who is or is not considered a psychoanalyst would require a book-length history of modern American psychoanalysis, Gilman states, adding that the objections to non-medical analysis are slowly being overcome despite predictably sharp opposition from the medical establishment.

Gilman was right. Responding to a lawsuit, the American Psychoanalytic Association changed the requirements for admission to psychoanalytic institutes in 1989, allowing non-physicians entry. As I was writing this chapter, in early 2020, Lee Jaffe, the first clinical psychologist in a century to be president of the American Psychoanalytic Association (APsaA), commented on the reasons the organization needed to apologize to non-medical psychologists:

> During the years that training was restricted to physicians, it was difficult if not impossible in most cities for others to become psychoanalysts. Some interested in analytic training were rejected outright, while others no doubt were aware that they were not welcomed and did not even apply for training. Since APsaA had a near monopoly on analytic training in the United States, there were no alternatives for many who were not medical doctors. Consequently, career choices were restricted, and some mental health professionals were denied their desire to become psychoanalysts. Feelings were hurt and grudges against APsaA festered. Moreover, these restrictive policies contributed to an atmosphere in our field that did not value the contributions to psychoanalysis from other disciplines. (1)

Jaffe then ends with a formal apology: "We unreservedly apologize for unfairly discriminating against our colleagues, devaluing their expertise, and causing them difficulties or harm" (4).

Freud, Race, and Gender

One of two books Gilman published in 1993, *Freud, Race, and Gender* reconstructs the racism and anti-Semitism present in fin-de-siècle Vienna, showing how racialized science affected Freud's thinking. "There was a seamlessness to all aspects of the biology of Freud's day that made the biology of 'race' a vital part of the arguments of biological and medical science" (5–6). Gilman is relentless in documenting the racial implications of medicine and psychology in fin-de-siècle Vienna. His position as an outsider gives him, paradoxically, insight into Freud's inner reality.

Chapter 1, "Sigmund Freud and the Epistemology of Race," shows how being Jewish meant to Freud being a member of the Jewish *race* rather than the Jewish religion, an insight that Peter Gay ignores in *A Godless Jew: Freud, Atheism, and the Making of Psychoanalysis* (1987) and in his 1988 biography *Freud: A Life for Our Time*. Indeed, the word *race* does not even appear in the biography's index. In a review published in the *Jewish Quarterly Review*, Gilman praises Gay's biography as "extraordinary" but offers a major caveat, calling it "too clear, too clean, too organized," concluding that it "avoids many ambiguities which would complicate Gay's image of Freud as the great rationalist" (253). Race is also ignored in two later biographies: Louis Breger's *Freud: Darkness in the Midst of Vision* (2000) and Joel Whitebook's *Freud: An Intellectual Biography* (2017). When Freud, in a letter to the Lutheran pastor Oskar Pfister in 1918, called himself a "completely godless Jew" (Freud and Pfister 63), he regarded his Jewishness not as a religious category but as a racial one. Sharing the mistaken Lamarckian assumption that "ontogeny recapitulates phylogeny," the inheritability of acquired characteristics, Freud assumed the existence of a racial memory that affected every generation. As in his earlier writings, Gilman argues that fin-de-siècle medical science viewed the Eastern European Jew as diseased.

The centerpiece of Gilman's new argument is that Freud excised the rhetoric of race from his scientific writings but converted it into the construction of gender. Freud regarded the sexual life of adult women as psychology's "dark continent," an image he expressed, in English, in *The Question of Lay Analysis* (1926):

> We know less about the sexual life of little girls than of boys. But we need not feel ashamed of this distinction; after all, the sexual life of adult women is a "dark continent" for psychology. But we have learnt that girls feel deeply their lack of a sexual organ that is equal in value to the male one; they regard themselves on that account as inferior, and this "envy for the penis" is the origin of a whole number of characteristic feminine reactions. (*SE* 20: 212)

Many scholars have tried to explain what is probably the most troubling and contested aspect of psychoanalytic theory, but Gilman offers a new theory for why Freud transformed the dark Jewish body (Jews were considered a dark race), which in Freud's discourse is the male Jewish body, into the female body. Gilman cites the following passage from *Introductory Lectures on Psycho-Analysis* (1915–1916): "Women possess as part of their genitals a small organ similar to the male one; and this small organ, the clitoris, actually plays the same part in childhood and during the years before sexual intercourse as the large organ in men" (*SE*

15: 155). Gilman then informs us that the clitoris was known in fin-de-siècle Vienna as the "Jew" (*Jud*); the phrase for female masturbation was "playing with the Jew" (39). Gilman adds, parenthetically, a reference to an article published in *The American Journal of Diseases of Childhood* in 1987, only a few years before the publication of *Freud, Race, and Gender*:

> The "small organ" of the woman became the *pars par toto* for the Jew with his circumcised organ. This pejorative synthesis of both bodies because of their "defective" sexual organs reflected the fin-de-siècle Viennese definition of the essential male as the antithesis of the female and the Jewish male. (This feminization of the Jewish male continues into the present. In 1987, circumcision was attacked as the "rape of the phallus," a choice of language that reflects the sense of the feminization of the procedure.) (39)

It is characteristic of Gilman's scholarship to trace the image of the "dark continent" in Freud's writings to an anti-Semitic reference to the dark castrated (diseased, deformed, inferior) Jew; recognize that the truncated circumcised penis was Viennese slang for the clitoris; and then find an obscure reference in a contemporary medical journal that perpetuates the stereotype for the feminized Jewish male.

In chapter 2, "The Construction of the Male Jew," Gilman interprets the complex meaning of infant male circumcision, an act that not only *made* the Jew but also made the Jewish body different from the non-Jewish body. "Christendom practically holds circumcision in horror," the anti-Semitic British explorer and writer Richard Burton was quoted as saying (49), a view that characterized Aryan stereotypes of the Jew. Among the many meanings of circumcision, Gilman points out, was that of self-mutilation, resulting in the Jew becoming a pariah. Another meaning of circumcision was that it resulted in a damaged penis, leading to the potential ravages of sexually transmitted diseases, a fear that haunted the syphilophobic age. Yet some medical fin-de-siècle theorists saw circumcision as a prophylactic against sexual disease. In either case, Gilman reports, circumcision was a Jewish marker of difference—and of everything fraught, including the feminization of the male Jew. "The castration complex is the deepest root of anti-Semitism," Freud writes in his case study of the five-year-old Little Hans, and Gilman proceeds to show how Freud viewed castration as a symbolic act of circumcision. "It is important to follow Freud's stated train of thought: if—says the child—I can be circumcised and made into a Jew, can I not also be castrated and made into a woman?" (77).

In chapter 3, "Jewish Madness and Gender," Gilman shows how Freud sought to counter the anti-Semitic association of Jews with illness that racial science held at the time. Gilman offers close readings of Daniel Paul Schreber's 1903 *Memoirs of a Neuropath* and Freud's 1911 case study based on it, *Psycho-Analytic Notes on an Autobiographical Account of a Case of Paranoia (Dementia Paranoides)*. Schreber, the chief judge of a provincial court in Saxony, used the rhetoric of the diseased Jew throughout his memoir, implicitly associating his overt fear of emasculation and devirilization—in other words, castration—with circumcision, a conflation common in the age. "The exclusion of the parallel between the female and the Jew from Freud's reading of the Schreber case provides an insight into Freud's defensive mechanisms" (146). As evidence, Gilman notes from a study of Freud's marginalia comments that Freud underlined every reference to castration, and at one point wrote "Fantasy of feminization" (154).

Gilman shows throughout *Freud, Race, and Gender* how madness was racially charged. In the conclusion, "Systemic Diseases: Cancer and Anti-Semitism," he examines how organic diseases were also ideologically structured. Freud struggled with cancer from 1923 to 1939, undergoing dozens of surgical procedures for oral cancer. "Freud's cancer occurred during the period when there was an intense debate about why Jews do or do not develop certain forms of cancer." In Gilman's alliterative words, Freud and his Jewish colleagues, including his two physicians, Felix Deutsch and Max Schur, saw his cancer "not as a disease of the Jews but as a disease of the jaw" (179). Freud started his final book, *Moses and Monotheism*, in 1933, but it was not published until 1939, the year of his death. Unlike other scholars, who view the murder of Moses in Freud's story as a mythic rather than actual event, Gilman conjectures that Freud needed to mark a traumatic moment in the history of the Jew. Translating the biology of race into psychology, Freud, in Gilman's view, saw the killing of Moses as revealing the universal wish to slay the primal father.

The Case of Sigmund Freud

A companion piece to *Freud, Race, and Gender*, *The Case of Sigmund Freud: Medicine and Identity at the Fin de Siècle* continues Gilman's interrogation of the impact of racially charged ideology on Freud's thinking. "My thesis is rather simple," he writes in the introduction: "given that the biology of race stands at the center of the nineteenth-century 'science of man' (which would include biology, medicine, and anthropology), it is extraordinary to imagine that anyone who thought of himself as a 'scientist' during this period could have avoided confronting this aspect of science" (5). Yet there is nothing simple about Gilman's thesis, for he shows how the concept of race is not only problematic but also fatally poisoned.

Chapter 1, "Psychoanalysis, Race, and Identity," examines one of the central yet unspoken epistemological problems of late nineteenth-century biological science: How can one be a subject of a scientific study while at the same time occupy the role of observer? Freud sought to be the objective or neutral scientific analyst of his patients' illnesses, yet he also recognized the analyst's own subjectivity, which he called countertransference, paralleling the patient's subjectivity, transference. Transference and countertransference are among Freud's greatest discoveries. The patient sees in the analyst, Freud writes in *An Outline of Psycho-Analysis*, the "return, the reincarnation, of some important figure out of his childhood or past, and consequently transfers on to him feelings and reactions which undoubtedly applied to this prototype" (*SE* 23: 174). The psychic mechanism behind transference is projection, in which a fear or desire is first denied and then displaced upon another person. The analyst must guard against the tendency toward countertransference, his or her own projective tendencies. Freud never felt comfortable writing about countertransference, which he feared would undercut his scientific objectivity. The question of observing and being observed, seeing and being seen, was so bedeviling to him that he did not want his patients to stare at him directly: hence, he requested patients to lie on the analytic couch.

Other psychoanalytic scholars have commented on Jewish difference, but Gilman offers a new interpretation, presenting dozens of examples (and photographs) of how Jews not only looked different to other people but also how the Jewish gaze struck non-Jews as pathological. To give only one example, Gilman cites the eugenicist Francis Galton, Charles Darwin's cousin, who maintained that the Jew's gaze betrays the pathological Jewish soul. Freud sought to change this belief by transforming the Jewish gaze of psychoanalysis (deemed the "Jewish science") into a quality of therapy, positive, productive, and universal. Freud used four strategies, Gilman suggests, for resisting negative stereotypes: reversal, rejection, recontextualization, and universalization, all of which became part of his armamentarium.

Gilman must have been aware that he was confronting the same epistemological problem as Freud, offering interpretations of the psychoanalyst's life and work that also reveal aspects of the interpreter's own life and work, Gilman himself. His immense scholarship is apparent on every page, as is his empathy, his effort to understand Freud rather than to judge him.

Chapter 2, "Conversion, Circumcision, and Discourse," connects Freud's "discovery" of the Oedipus complex to a new source. He analyzes the rhetoric of conversion Freud used to discuss the origins of the Oedipus complex, tracing it to mid-nineteenth-century discourse on infant baptism: "The baptism of a Jewish child by a Christian nursemaid is a topos in the conversion literature of that period" (77). Gilman suggests, counterintuitively, that it was not Freud's mother who was the source of his Oedipal feelings but his elderly Czech Catholic nursemaid, Theresa Wittek. Other scholars have commented on the significance of this shadowy figure in Freud's early childhood, but Gilman offers a new theory of the origins of the Oedipus complex:

> Freud's statements about her attempts to "seduce" him through the attractions of Christianity were formulated within a month (October 1897) of the abandonment of the seduction theory. And Freud converted this experience, his own fantasy about the body and soul of the Christian Other, into the universal language of the Oedipus theory. The Oedipus myth has its origin in the tale of the seduction (through conversion) of the male Jewish child by the old Catholic servant rather than in the seduction of the mother by the male child. (76)

Chapter 3, "The Degenerate Foot and the Search for Oedipus," is the oddest to me, mainly because, although I've always been self-conscious about my pronounced Jewish nose, I'm proud of my feet. Who knew that the Jewish foot has long been a marker for Jewish degeneracy? Gilman examines a "footnote" to the language of the Jews' pathophysiology. Noting that in fin-de-siècle Vienna the images of the limping devil and the limping Jew were interchangeable, Gilman observes that the gait of the Jew, particularly flat feet, was connected in Aryan discourse to military service. Jews were considered unfit for military service because of their defective feet. Additionally, Gilman draws a connection between feet and hysteria, remarking how Freud stressed in his discussion of sexuality the meaning of the hysteric's foot fixation. Scholars have noticed Freud's omission of the early history of Oedipus, whose name meant "swollen feet." Why did Freud omit any discussion of Oedipus's father, Laius, who pierced his son's ankles before abandoning him, so that his ghost would not walk? It was not because Freud was unaware of this detail, Gilman assures us. "Freud knew this etymology from his primary reading of the Oedipus myth and closely marked much of the chapter in his source" (136). In Gilman's view, Freud did not want to associate the act Laius wished to avoid, the incestuous marriage of his son, with Jewish sexual selection, understood as "dangerous inbreeding" in the racialized science of the time, Jews marrying other Jews, endogamous marriage.

Gilman then deftly traces the foot imagery in Wilhelm Jensen's 1903 novella, *Gradiva*, which compelled Freud to write his 1907 essay, "Delusions and Dreams in Jensen's *Gradiva*," his first complete study of a literary work. Gilman adds a fascinating detail about Freud's curious 1912 postscript to the second edition of the essay, in which the analyst conjectures, based on a review he read of Jensen's last novel, that the illegitimate Jensen, who died in 1911, may have had an "intimate" relationship with his sister—despite the fact that the novelist had written a 1907 letter to Freud stating he had no blood relatives. Gilman's explanation for the Freudian slip? "In Freud's reading, Jensen becomes nothing more than an incestuous Jew" (153).

Freud maintained that creativity depended upon sublimated sexuality, yet what's perhaps most striking about his belief in artistic creativity—and Gilman was the first to point this out in *Smart Jews*—is that from 1900 to 1919, he never cites any Jewish writer or painter: "not his contemporary and neighbor, the playwright Arthur Schnitzler, or the best-known German artist of his day, the Impressionist Max Liebermann, or the classic examples of Jewish creativity, Spinoza and Heine—in his discussions of 'creativity' and the nature of the 'creative.' 'Creativity' is universal; Freud's examples are not. They self-consciously eliminate the 'Jewish' component in European culture" (118).

Chapter 4, "Seduction, Parricide, and Crime," documents the perceived greater rate of "inbreeding" among the Jews, defined as endogamous marriage. Gilman shows the Christian preoccupation with the Jewish custom of the levirate marriage, in which a man was obliged to marry his brother's widow, an act that was viewed as incestuous, therefore criminal. Freud's efforts to universalize incest and patricide, in the form of the Oedipus complex, represent his attempt to answer the charge of inbreeding lodged against the Jews. In *Totem and Taboo* (1913) Freud projected the sexual charges made against the Jews into primeval history, viewing the son's desire to murder the father and marry the mother as the psychological origins of human nature.

Gilman reminds us, in the conclusion to *The Case of Sigmund Freud*, that the origin of a theory does not undercut its ultimate validity. He never tells us which aspects of psychoanalytic theory he does *not* regard as clinically valid. This may frustrate some readers who seek to know what is true and not true about the twentieth century's dominant psychological theory. There is little doubt, however, that Gilman believes psychoanalysis will survive because of its adaptability. Neither a hagiographer, like Ernest Jones and Max Schur, nor a Freud-basher, like Frederick Crews, Gilman offers a sympathetic portrait of a man who struggled with his inner demons that became inscribed in his theory.

Reviews

After reading *Freud, Race, and Gender* and *Freud, Race, and Class*, I find that the two books merge into one, raising the question, could they have been combined into one? This was Judith M. Hughes's impression in *American Historical Review*: a single volume would "not only have been more economical but it would also have been more effective" (1285). Paul Roazen believes that there is a "certain overlap between these two books, and yet they are distinct entities" (*The Historiography of Psychoanalysis* 381), a statement with which I agree, as well as with Roazen's conclusion. "Students in the field should be studying his citations and notes for a long while, since Gilman has brought to this field a cosmopolitan scholarship that is richly rewarding" (383).

Other reviewers, while generally sympathetic to *Freud, Race, and Gender* and *The Case of Sigmund Freud*, offer different caveats. Naomi Seidman suggests that although *Freud, Race, and Gender* and *The Jew's Body* owe much to the women's movement, of which they are an outgrowth, they nevertheless "often stand in uneasy relation to feminism," partly because of Gilman's reluctance to "pursue a psychology of Jewish femininity as a true reflection of the material" (122). Jay Geller conveys a related criticism. Gilman "has perhaps more than anyone inventoried the leavings of European modernity's pandemic of antisemitic discourses," but he "has let the indigenous misogynist discourses of Europe off the hook by 'explaining' Freud's discourse on women as his defensive displacement of the discourses of racial antisemitism" (8–9). Judith Hughes describes Gilman's technique in the two Freud books as "pointillist: with myriad details, selected not at random, but with no announced methodological guidelines." Had Hughes read Gilman's earlier books, though, she would have been aware of his methodological approaches. H.L. Malchow calls *Freud, Race, and Gender* a book "full of suggestive insight" but questions whether Gilman's methodology, exploring the "correspondences and homologies of disparate discourses," will convince those who are skeptical of such techniques (899). Despite this criticism, Malchow is impressed with Gilman's achievement. "No one writing on the history of scientific thought at the turn of the century, or on Freud, can now afford to neglect the relationships between race and gender which Gilman traces" (899). In a generally positive review appearing in *The New York Times*, Howard Eilberg-Schwartz faults Gilman for not making it clear whether psycho-analytic theories of the unconscious and penis envy "are the products of Freud's Jewish anxiety or not."

In the same year his two books on Freud appeared, Gilman con-tributed an essay on "Psychotherapy" to the *Companion Encyclopedia of the History of Medicine*. The essay is a remarkably non-tendentious account of the history of psychotherapy, which he defines as the "non-invasive treatment of those mental or emotional states understood by the patient and the therapist as pathological or maladaptive" (1029). Gilman shows how the roots of psychotherapy may be traced to the sacrament of con-fession in the Catholic church. He ends the essay by noting that in the 1980s, psychotherapy fragmented into many different approaches, none of which can be understood as primary. He provides insights without judgments, as when he comments on the rise of psychopharmacology: "Indeed, one of the ironies is that Freudian psychotherapy, stripped of its theoretical basis, comes by the 1970s and 1980s to be a substantial addition to the chemotherapy of emotional and psychic illness as 'sup-portive psychotherapy'" (1046).

Franz Kafka

Had Gilman written *only* on Freud, he would have been known as a prolific scholar, but he has continued to author book after book at an astonishing pace. After writing about Freud, Gilman turned his atten-tion to Franz Kafka, penning two books on the Prague writer over the course of a decade: *Franz Kafka: The Jewish Patient* (1995) and *Franz*

Kafka (2005). Both books rely on the same psychoanalytic methodology. Always intrigued by literary identity formulation, Gilman explores how Kafka's internalization of Jewish physical and mental difference shaped his life and art. Kafka's bedrock belief, as disclosed in a letter, that he was a "mendacious creature," had much to do, Gilman argues, with the fear of becoming an Eastern European Jew, whom he imagined as poor, ill, and inarticulate. "It is the anxiety of becoming what one is condemned to become. It is a fear engendered by the images associated with the Jewish male in Kafka's world" (8). Gilman's task in the 1995 study, he declares, using a Nietzschean expression, is to disclose the "secret alphabet-script" of Kafka's bodily self in his work (9).

Gilman continues his analysis in *Franz Kafka*, examining the writer's unpublished papers, where Kafka admitted that it "is not a pleasure to deal with psychoanalysis and I stay far away from it, but it is certainly manifest in this generation. Judaism has always brought forth its sorrows and pleasures with the necessary 'Rashi-commentary' [a reference to the renowned Middle Ages Jewish Biblical commentator], so too in this case" (23). Gilman offers a convincing psychoanalytic reading of two of Kafka's most celebrated stories, "The Judgment," his first published fiction, and *The Metamorphosis*, perhaps his most famous tale. "No deep knowledge of Freudian psychology was necessary for Kafka to write in this encrypted manner," Gilman observes. "You only had to know enough psychological theory from the daily newspapers or contemporary literature" (94).

I have long taught these two stories in my literature-and-psychoanalysis courses, believing that psychoanalysis offers us unique insight into the psychological meaning of Kafka's fiction. Gilman takes a more detached view, however, maintaining that Kafka used Freudianism largely as window-dressing in *The Metamorphosis*, passing the story's depiction of family dynamics "through Freud's Oedipus with a bit of sibling incest and Jewish self-loathing thrown in for fun" (*Franz Kafka* 94). What came repeatedly to Kafka's rescue, Gilman contends, was neither psychoanalysis nor writing but rather his neurotic anxiety over his health. "His hypochondria was his salvation. It rescued him from jobs he did not like and relationships with those, especially women, whom he feared" (95).

Reading as an On-Going Process

Gilman never pretends that his reading of Freud will be either definitive or complete. In his 1983 review of the French psychoanalyst Marie Balmary's book *Psychoanalyzing Psychoanalysis: Freud and the Hidden Fault of the Father*, Gilman makes several observations that apply to his own books as well. His statement about Balmary's approach, "one can use Freud's method, his theory, to examine Freud as one would examine an analysand" (214), is exactly what he does in his own work. Gilman welcomes rather than deplores the raft of new readings of Freud. "One sees not the fossilization of Freud within strict Freudian readings of the psyche, but Freud as the originator of a theory flexible enough to be turned on itself" (214). Like other scholars who write about Freud but who seek independence from him, he places Balmary (and himself) in a critical position in which the critic's insight is greater than Freud's—without implying intellectual arrogance. "This is a necessary stage in the history of any theory which is accepted as important." He offers an excellent historical example. "One can imagine the third generation after Socrates, Plato's students, doing much the same thing to Socrates' views" (214). The best scholars can do, he suggests, is offer readings reflective of their own times, realizing that future times will require different readings. "Reading texts, especially meaningful texts, is an on-going process, a process which amalgamates prior readings with present needs" (215). One can only wonder, he muses at the end, the truths of the next generation of Freudian scholars. Whatever these new truths may be, it's certain that Gilman's own books will remain for Freudian scholars the heart of the matter for years to come.

JEFFREY BERMAN. I begin my discussion of your work by suggesting that although Freud would probably have resisted initially your interpretation of the extent to which his unconscious attitudes about being Jewish affected the construction of psychoanalytic theory, he might have agreed with your conclusions. Have you wondered about Freud's reactions to your work? How have other psychoanalysts responded to your work?

SANDER GILMAN. One of the truisms of being an intellectual and cultural historian is that we are always "smarter" than our subject because we don't see our own limitations. That is the problem I have had with my work on Freud. Freud, indeed, most of the medical faculty I have taught with over the years, was "smarter" than I am. He developed tools to examine areas that were not only impossible to study, such as the unconscious, but he also developed theories that helped frame how and why these tools were effective. I have always had enormous respect for the well-designed experiment, and Freud knew how to generate such experiments. Freud would have had to live *after* Freud to respond to my insights, and if he had that capability, I am positive he would have seen himself as his best object of study, as indeed, he had during his lifetime. As for the responses from my contemporaries: they have ranged from dismissing me as an anti-Semite or a self-hating Jew for my studies of Freud to acknowledging and using my insights. Some of my best students, such as George Makari, have approached analogous questions from the standpoint of intellectual history or the history of ideas even though they are trained psychoanalysts. That too is a fascinating phenomenon.

JB. You've never written about your fascination with psychoanalysis. Would you describe what led you to psychoanalytic theory and to Freud in particular.

SG. Many decades ago I had an exchange with Michel Foucault about "power" as the moving concept in history. For Foucault, in answer to his Marxist contemporaries, power was a social but not necessarily an economic phenomenon. I thought that one could never speak of power unless one understood it as a psychological phenomenon, and Freudian psychoanalysis, including object relations theory, seemed to me to provide a model that could be used not only to understand the specific nature of individual responses, but, as Freud himself did, to examine cultural and historical ones.

JB. Psychoanalytic theory is central to your work on stereotypes and difference, particularly projection, identification, internalization, and transference, all of which are part of the unconscious. Are there other aspects of psychoanalytic theory that you find helpful to your work? You often write about "pseudoscience," but you never refer to psychoanalysis in this way. Of what aspects of psychoanalytic theory are you skeptical?

SG. Karl Popper in 1935 Vienna used psychoanalysis and astrology as his examples of "pseudoscience." I think you need to examine in any given moment in science the boundary between what is defined as science and that which is not. For me psychoanalysis, as with all science, is in constant revision and refinement, with new additions, reshaping arguments, and approaches. Pseudosciences like astrology by definition are fixed systems, or at least make the argument about their inalterability no matter how their relationship to the flow of knowledge changes.

JB. In *Diseases and Diagnoses* you suggest the difficulty if not impossibility of testing the scientific basis of psychoanalysis. The "claims of efficacy through empiricism rest on a set of assumptions about 'evidence-based medicine' that reflects the ideological bias of the twenty-first century" (198). Should psychoanalysis, or any other psychiatric or psychological approach to mental illness, seek "scientific credibility?"

SG. What recent studies of psychoanalysis and brain science, such as those by Peter Fonagy, have shown is that we may be entering the moment, which Freud foretold, that our basic knowledge of brain structures on the molecular level can provide a bridge between brain, behavior, and mind. This is a very early stage now, but I am interested in this as a potential pathway. But what it recalls is that Freud was clear that we cannot differentiate brain from mind, behavior from motivation, action from cause.

JB. If, as you suggest, psychoanalysis is mainly an ideology rather than a science, hermeneutic, or philosophy, how do you explain its healing power, at least for some people?

SG. Ideology is how we understand the world, and if I am correct, it is our process of understanding the world that has within it the potential for individual transformation. Here Nietzsche and Freud are linked. I refuse to use the term "healing" as it demands a sense of ultimate ends rather than an on-going process.

JB. Writing about the difficulty of expressing his feelings about being a Jew, Freud compares his torment in *Moses and Monotheism* to that of an "unlaid ghost" (*SE* 23: 103). You use a different metaphor to describe your own writing: "burn[ing] with those fires which define you as the outsider" ("Why and How I Study the German" 201). Which of your books were the most difficult to write?

SG. Every single thing I have ever sat down to write has been both an effort and a pleasure. Bigger projects from *Jewish Self-Hatred* to my recent *Stand Up Straight!* have been all-consuming in terms of my emotional as well as my temporal life. One of the things that I now understand is that my procrastination in beginning projects has to do with this emotional excavation. Which may be why I begin many projects and deal with them simultaneously.

JB. Are you hopeful about the future of psychoanalysis?

SG. Yes: as a historian I have seen interest in psychoanalysis both as a means for examining human activity and for therapy wax and wane. Recently, the interest of psychiatric residents in at least being exposed to psychoanalytic therapeutic methods as a counter to the pharmaceutical end of psychiatry has been notable. What the future can bring will only puzzle and interest us, and for that psychoanalysis is the perfect venue.

Chapter 2

Allen Wheelis's Depiction of Remediable and Irremediable Suffering and Joan Wheelis's *The Known, the Secret, the Forgotten*

Not many psychoanalysts call themselves "technicians of loneliness" or "clinicians of despair," but then again, Allen Wheelis (1915–2007) was no ordinary psychoanalyst. A maverick, he remained unique in his distinctive analytic and novelistic voices. He was among the handful of clinicians who wrote riveting psychotherapy tales; he practiced psychoanalysis in San Francisco for more than half a century while at the same time penning fifteen books on a wide range of subjects, including psychology, psychoanalysis, philosophy, fiction, biography, and memoir. He remains best known to the psychoanalytic community, but he was also honored as a creative writer who explored, with unflinching honesty and courage, dark subjects that most analysts would not dare divulge in public. Joan Wheelis followed in her father's (and psychoanalyst-mother's) footsteps, but then she turned in a different professional direction.

Allen Wheelis was born in 1915 in Marion, a small town in northern Louisiana, and attended the University of Texas, Austin. He received his medical training at the College of Physicians and Surgeons of Columbia University, served for three years in the navy during World War II, studied psychiatry at the Menninger Foundation in Topeka, Kansas, and completed his professional training at the New York Psychoanalytic Institute. He began as a staff psychiatrist at the Austen Riggs Center in Stockbridge, Massachusetts, and then moved to San Francisco in 1954, where he continued to practice psychiatry and psychoanalysis.

As Stephen L. Tanner observes in a 1999 issue of the interdisciplinary journal *Explorations* devoted to an appreciation of Wheelis's work, "Wheelis's books are not widely known, despite being issued by prestigious publishers. Part of the reason for this neglect is that Wheelis is a psychiatrist who thinks like a philosopher, remembers like an interpretive autobiographer, and writes like a poet" (2). Tanner adds that Wheelis has tended to "remain ahead of his time in his critique of psychoanalysis, rationalism, and determinism, frequently anticipating the currently unfolding issues of postmodernism" (6).

The Quest for Identity: "Behind the Abstractions Lurks a Shadow"

Wheelis's fiction career began in 1951 when his story "Goodbye, Mama" was published in *The New Yorker*. Before then, he had published several psychoanalytic papers, including "The Place of Action in Personality Change" (1950). His first book, *The Quest for Identity*, appeared in 1958. One might have expected Wheelis, with his impeccable credentials, to remain in the orthodox Freudian tradition in which he had been trained. Not so. He acknowledges in the beginning of his book that psychoanalysis is no longer a force for cultural change, as it was decades earlier. We can already see Wheelis's disillusionment with psychoanalysis, to which he nevertheless remains committed. *The Quest for Identity* is one of his most important books, one of the few that have remained in print, partly because of its powerful moral vision. Wheelis argues that insofar as the "decline of the superego" has contributed to social and cultural unrest, it is time for humankind to cast off its old identity, which it has outgrown, and create a new one that is better suited to the age. The book's discussion of the emergent social character and value system is also valuable. *The Quest for Identity* is noteworthy for another reason, as Wheelis hints at cryptically in the foreword, because "interwoven with the abstractions is a thread of personal narrative" (10). In one of the most suggestive lines in the book, he observes that "behind the abstractions lurks a shadow. Only by a sudden metaphor, a wry twist of phrase, does the reader sense that what he reads was wrought in conflict and sometimes anguish."

Where is the personal conflict and anguish in *The Quest for Identity*? Wheelis does not elaborate, but he enlivens his theoretical discussions with six extended clinical vignettes about a young man named Larry Hunt and his parents, Morris and Carolyn. These vignettes, which focus on Larry's quest for identity, constitute the most intriguing sections of the book and indicate Wheelis's preoccupation with the inner world of character. The first three vignettes, "Leeville," "Family Prayer," and "Sunday," portray Larry's family: his strict, pietistic physician-father, who has become an invalid as a result of tuberculosis; a loving and doting mother, unable or unwilling to countermand her husband's harsh commands; and a sister named Helen, who does not figure prominently in the story.

The fourth vignette, "Grass," is the most compelling. Wheelis depicts an embattled father-son relationship that readers are not likely to forget. Larry brings his report card home on the last day of school and excitedly shows it to his mother, who praises his high grades. The boy is eager to play baseball with his friends, but before he can do so, he must show the report card to his bed-ridden father, who has been forced to give up his medical practice. The father reprimands his son for receiving only a seventy-five percent in conduct and orders him to cut the grass on their farm, not with a hoe, scythe, or sickle, as is customary, but with an old, ivory-handled single-edged razor. To further his humiliation, the father insists that his son cut the grass level with the ground and pick up every stone in the cleared area.

Not grasping the enormity and cruelty of the Sisyphean task, Larry dutifully obeys his father, but as the weeks pass, he begins to protest, at first meekly, then more defiantly. His complaints fail to soften his father's intransigence. Wheelis captures the father's ability to rationalize his behavior by claiming that he is acting on his son's behalf. "'Remember, son,' he said in a husky voice, 'whenever it seems I'm being hard on you . . . it's because I love you'" (124). The father never misses an opportunity to shame his son, as when he rhetorically asks: "Do you want to be a lazy, no-account scoundrel?" (109). Wheelis suggests that this tortured father-son relationship is more characteristic of the nineteenth than the twentieth century, but it seems strikingly Kafkaesque in its dynamics of guilt, self-punishment, and internalized aggression:

> He became inured to the work but not reconciled to it, and throughout the summer continued to resist. Whippings—which had been rare before—were now common, and after each he would, in the evening, be required to apologize. He would go out on his father's porch, say he was sorry, and then listen guiltily to a restatement of the principles involved. Tirelessly

> Morris would explain what he had done wrong, the importance of learning to work, and the benefit to his character which this discipline would eventually bring about. After each of these sessions Larry would feel that he was innately shiftless, lazy, and impulsive. Each time he would resolve to try harder, but each time would relapse. After two or three days he would again become sullen or rebellious and again would be punished. Sometimes he saw his mother in tears and he knew that often she interceded in his behalf, but her efforts were ineffective. (*The Quest for Identity* 117)

Wheelis's traumatic experience recalls the one described by Charles Dickens, who was ordered at the tender age of twelve to paste labels on blacking pots at Warren's Blacking Warehouse. Dickens later wrote about his piercing shame, first in the unpublished "Autobiographical Fragment" and then in *David Copperfield*. "My whole nature was so penetrated with the grief and humiliation of such considerations," Dickens confided near the end of his life to his friend and biographer John Forster, "that even now, famous and caressed and happy, I often forget in my dreams that I have a dear wife and children; even that I am a man; and wander desolately back to that time of my life" (Forster 26–27).

Larry finally summons the courage to curse his father—"You're the meanest man in the world. You lie up there in bed and are mean to everybody. I hate you!" (119)—but either the father does not hear these words or refuses to give him the satisfaction of defiance. Larry finishes his task shortly before school begins, prompting his father to proclaim the dignity of work and express the hope that his wayward son has now learned something positive from the experience. Wheelis ends the clinical vignette with an ironically understated sentence revealing the father's tyrannical power over his broken-spirited son. "He was more quiet than before and better behaved, and when next the report cards were distributed he had a nearly perfect score in conduct" (125).

Wheelis describes in the fifth vignette, "Goodbye, Mama," Larry's departure for college and his mother's reluctant decision to return to Leeville to live with her parents. She is now forty-five, a widow for nine years. Yet Carolyn cannot bear to be separated from her son, who is the only man in her life. If Wheelis's purpose in depicting Larry's relationship to Morris is to show the dangers of a punitive superego arising from a castrating father, he now dramatizes the son's struggle to distance himself from a mother's all-consuming Oedipal love. The final vignette in *The Quest for Identity*, "Impasse," depicts Larry's awakening interest in creative writing, which compels him to drop out of college, over his mother's objections, and move to a San Antonio YMCA, where he devotes himself entirely to writing a novel embodying his idea that physical love brings about the death of spiritual love. He writes month after month, often spending twelve hours a day, but as his manuscript grows, so do his doubts about its worth, and he cannot complete the final two chapters. His physical and psychological health deteriorates, and he can neither sleep nor eat. Unable to concentrate, he visits a brothel and has his first carnal experience, but his sexual initiation brings no relief. His words have dried up.

Fearing he is losing his sanity, Larry goes to the library and begins randomly reading medical and psychology books in an effort to heal himself. Nothing helps until he picks up a copy of Alfred Adler's *Understanding Human Nature*. The book is a revelation: suddenly he realizes that his insomnia has been a symptomatic defense of his fragile self-esteem. "If he couldn't sleep he couldn't work; if he couldn't work he couldn't finish the novel; if he could not finish the novel, then no one would be able to say definitely that it was a failure" (221). Larry realizes that he is not yet ready to become a creative writer and soon returns to college to complete his education.

Wheelis doesn't cite any particular passages in Adler's *Understanding Human Nature*, first published in English in 1928 and reprinted frequently. It's not likely he was impressed by Adler's grandiose title, which claims a wisdom that Wheelis always mistrusted. Nor is it likely that Wheelis would be sympathetic to the title of the second part of Adler's book: "the science of character." But Wheelis would have agreed with Adler's assertion that the "basis of educability lies in the striving of the child to compensate for his weaknesses," as well as the statement that a "child who desires to adapt himself to his environment suddenly finds difficulties lying in his way, especially where he grows up in an environment which has itself lost its courage and is imbued with a pessimism only too quickly transferred to the child" (35). These insights would have resonated in Wheelis because of his father's wounding words. Wheelis would also agree with Adler's remark that sometimes one becomes a "model child" as a way to regain parental love (40). Adler's emphasis on the "inferiority complex" and on the striving for recognition would likely meet with Wheelis's approval. "Ridicule of children is well-nigh criminal. It retains its effect upon the soul of the child, and it is transferred into the habits and actions of his adulthood" (71).

Wheelis mentions Larry's name infrequently in the remaining twenty-five pages of *The Quest for Identity*, but he has his protagonist in mind as he chronicles the "vocational hazards of psychoanalysis" in the last chapter of the book. Wheelis intimates that Larry's insight into his psychological crisis, and the self-mastery arising from having penetrated a mystery, enable him to abandon creative writing without feeling an overwhelming narcissistic injury. Additionally, the shock of recognition upon reading Adler's text is the principal determinant of his choice to become an analyst. Fascinated by the life of the mind, the young man first becomes a psychiatrist and then a psychoanalyst. He learns a great deal about himself in the course of his self-analysis. The counterphobic motivation behind Larry's decision to become a psychoanalyst undercuts neither his professional commitment nor his therapeutic effectiveness.

The Limits of Insight

The reader might expect Wheelis to end his book here, with Larry's successful resolution of his psychological conflict. But Wheelis goes on to show, from an insider's point of view, the young psychoanalyst's keen disappointment with his new profession. He discovers that insight, while valuable in itself and sometimes transformative, is not always sufficient for psychological change and happiness. Knowledge does not always lead to power, as he had been trained to believe. An analyst's interpretation of a patient may be accurate, Wheelis told James M. Glass in 1993, but the patient may respond, "so what," meaning, "all right, that may be true, but it doesn't help me" (101). The analyst must then search for another available truth that may be more helpful. The primary objective of therapy, Wheelis adds, is to mitigate a patient's suffering.

Wheelis's most valuable contribution to psychoanalysis, C. Fred Alford suggests in a 1999 volume of *Extrapolations* devoted to Wheelis's work, is the recognition that self-knowledge does not always lead to recovery. "Analytic insight leads to analytic insight, not necessarily a better life. Mysterious things like will and spirit remain more important" (223). Larry is not radically transformed as a result of his long self-analysis and professional work—he is still anxious about certain subjects. Nor are his great expectations about his role as healer fulfilled. He cannot work wonders with his patients; he is no minister who can invoke God's power to cure a patient. Over time Larry begins to suspect that psychoanalysis may be a more effective explanatory system than a vehicle for therapeutic cure.

The Quest for Identity demonstrates how the analyst's disillusionment may lead to two different responses, neither of which is personally or professionally healthy. One response is to retreat into rigid dogma, thus denying the cancerous doubts about the value of his work. This escape into orthodoxy, a reaction formation, a defense mechanism in which a person unconsciously replaces an anxiety-producing thought or feeling with its opposite, undermines the healthy skepticism, freedom of inquiry, and tolerance of doubt necessary for the advancement of truth. The opposite response is to retreat into cynicism and transform doubts into a counter-dogma. Professional dissidents may spend all of their time attacking colleagues rather than pursuing knowledge. "If unusually gifted and skillful," Wheelis observes wryly, "he may have the good fortune to be expelled from the ranks and thereby achieve martyrdom. If but a run-of-the-mill deviant, this honor will be denied him. He will simply be ignored, left in the rancorous position of being a rebel of whom no one is afraid" (234).

Wheelis provides no solution to the analyst's loss of faith. Rather, he shows how the analyst experiences a double vulnerability: one enters the profession because of a heightened sensitivity to psychic conflict, and once in the profession, the analyst must bear his patient's traumas that can be overwhelming. Freud argued that artists are neurotic and retreat into art to escape the pressures of the real world; Wheelis counterargues that psychoanalysts are the neurotic ones, beset by loneliness and driven by unfulfilled desire. Unlike artists who can achieve a profound closeness with their fictional creations, analysts have greater difficulty struggling to maintain boundaries. Analysts' desire for closeness with their patients must be balanced by the need to remain appropriately detached. Analysts motivated by the desire for love and passion may gratify their own needs but subvert their patients' therapy. Is Wheelis speaking about Larry when he offers the following description of an analyst who fails to achieve serenity in his work? "I am a technician of loneliness, but suffer from the malady I treat and spend my days alone, silent, listening. I am tormented by an ineludible yearning to lose myself in the inner life of another. And yet I never dare" (238).

The final pages of *The Quest for Identity* contain one of the most devastating inside critiques of psychoanalysis found anywhere. Switching from the analyst's to the analysand's point of view, Wheelis suggests that the former's "contribution to mankind" is perhaps to "slightly rearrange the neurotic ingredients in the lives of a total of about ten wealthy and self-centered people" (242). In a torrent of words, the analysand accuses his analyst of verbal duplicity, intellectual dishonesty, inhumanity, and self-indulgence—criticisms that the discerning reader suspects are Wheelis's self-criticisms.

The Quest for Identity nonetheless ends hopefully. Wheelis implies that if analysts are the target of their patients' hatred, they are also recipients of their love—a love that most analysts do not exploit. The final sentences portray an affirmative vision of psychoanalysts, who, in a Faulknerian sense, not only endure but prevail:

> Living out their years in a climate of hatred and dependence and torment, they nevertheless maintain that the life of man has meaning, can be understood, and that his suffering is in part remediable. Though perhaps always slightly out of reach for themselves, they believe love and closeness to be achievable. They hold no brief for the greatness of their hearts—they are among the least of those who work beyond themselves—but to some extent they lessen the man-made misery of man. They stand by. Hatred they endure, and do not turn away. Love comes their way, and they are not seduced. They are the listeners, but they listen with unwavering intent, and their silence is not cold. (246)

How People Change: The Shadow Revealed

The 1973 publication of the nonfictional *How People Change* dispelled whatever doubt readers might have had that *The Quest for Identity* represents Allen Wheelis's *Bildungsroman*. He reprints in this slender volume the vignette "Grass" but dispenses with the fictional name Larry. Now he simply uses the pronoun *I* to discuss the humiliation he experienced when he was forced to spend the entire summer cutting his lawn with a single-edged razor blade. The son could hear his father's brutal words long after his death: "Do you want to be a lazy, no-account scoundrel?" The father's words reverberate in his son's ears, drowning out his ineffectual protests. The judgment haunts Wheelis's imagination and seems to be the underlying motivation behind his need for achievement. "His denunciation yields guilt and anxiety, tends to drive me out of human society into the wilderness alone, thereby to confirm even more deeply the image of myself as unworthy to live with others, having nothing to say, deserving of any recognition" (*How People Change* 73). Wheelis notes ruefully the paradox that even as he writes book after book in an effort to reject his father's words, he cannot help wondering whether his crusade to destroy the credibility of determinism to affirm freedom may indicate the extent to which he remains a psychological slave, unable to exorcise the specter of his father's judgment.

It is rare for a psychoanalyst to confess publicly that he still feels traumatized by his father's ancient accusation. Wheelis experiences the memory of his father as "steel fingers" closing around his heart. The healer cannot entirely heal himself; the realization that he has internalized his father's judgment, and therefore must battle an inner adversary who remains alive long after his father's death, diminishes but does not entirely eliminate his feeling of humiliation. Wheelis's acknowledgment of the difficulty of change is thus born from painful self-awareness; he never exempts himself from the conflicts he sees in his patients. Nor does he shrink from divulging his own countertransference issues that other analysts might record only in a professional journal. This was also true of Freud. In describing his patients' illnesses in *The Interpretation of Dreams*, Freud was revealing much about his countertransference, but he never admitted in his dream book that he was writing about himself; moreover, he vowed he would never again write autobiographically. Not so with Wheelis, who dares to write personally regardless of the consequences.

The single most formative experience in his life, Wheelis confided to Glass, was his father's punishment of him. "I am sure psychoanalysts are right when they say one identifies with the more strict and forbidding of the two parents although it is not quite that simple; for sometime the outcome is a negative identification, a wish to be just the opposite of the father" (89). Wheelis's negative paternal identification was the lifelong belief he was worthless, an accusation that he struggled to reject; his positive paternal identification was consistency and control. Wheelis doesn't speak about his own modesty and compassion, but they are two of his most endearing qualities, visible in all of his writings.

Wheelis begins *How People Change* by admitting that the "older I get the less I know, the darker the well of time" (6). He values intellect but sees its limitations everywhere. He remains devoted to his patients but concedes that the analyst serves only as a catalyst in the process of personality change. "As a cause he is sometimes necessary, never sufficient" (7). He believes that analysts are no different from other people and are not immune to the problems of life. "The surprise we feel when a 'well-analyzed' person breaks down derives from our wish to view man as a machine" (114). Wheelis remains under no illusions about his colleagues. "Psychoanalysis does not qualify anyone to live in the kingdom of heaven," he dryly confesses. "Indeed, since we who undertake analysis are those who have more than average trouble with inner conflict, we may receive considerable help—quite enough to justify the undertaking—and still end up with more misery than those who have not been analyzed" (*How People Change* 114–115).

Not surprisingly, Wheelis's fictional protagonists are mainly psychoanalysts, and they live in the same affluent section of San Francisco as he did. They are highly intelligent, steeped in existentialist philosophy (particularly the writings of Nietzsche and Camus) and poetry and fiction. They spend a good deal of time writing on clinical and theoretical subjects. They are also highly cultured, valuing Mozart, Beethoven, and Mahler, and drawn to expensive paintings and sculptures that tastefully adorn their offices. They are dashing and debonair, as Wheelis himself was. And many of Wheelis's fictional analysts are the same age that he was when creating them.

Yet however much they may resemble their creator in their age, surroundings, theoretical orientation, and sensibility, Wheelis's fictional psychoanalysts choose different paths from his own. From their mistakes and failures derive the plots of Wheelis's novels. Many of his fictional analysts are distinctly unlikable characters: self-absorbed, arrogant, unself-critical, and highly libidinous. They also transgress patient-therapist boundaries. Wheelis's novels are cautionary tales, not simply for psychoanalysts struggling with despair, but for all people searching for an answer to the question Joseph Conrad raises in *Lord Jim*: "how to be."

The Seeker: "The Dynamics of Disillusion"

Wheelis began his first novel, *The Seeker* (1960), with an obligatory disclaimer: "The persons and events of this novel are imaginary. Any resemblance to actual persons or events is accidental and unintended." Yet his first-person narrator, a psychoanalyst named Oliver who is on the staff of a small Vermont mental hospital that bears an uncanny resemblance to Austen Riggs, the psychiatric hospital in western Massachusetts where Wheelis himself worked (and where, as we shall see, Christopher Bollas also worked), echoes many of the statements that appear in *The Quest for Identity* and *How People Change*. "In my experience analysts are not rebels but cautious liberals and tend to be anxious and passive" (*The Seeker* 108). Oliver has not found in psychoanalysis the meaning that he seeks; he seems to be drifting through life, saddened by the inability to discover anything worth pursuing. "I function as guide to the lost, but do not myself know the way" (43). The awareness of his own bruised narcissism does not make him less self-absorbed. One thinks of T.S. Eliot's rhetorical question in his 1920 poem "Gerontion": "After such knowledge, what forgiveness?" (22).

Like his creator, Oliver is a writer and wonders whether he can work through his conflicts by transfiguring them into art. "I tried to imagine how I would accomplish this in fiction. Suppose I were writing a novel about a person exactly like myself and wanted to portray a change in him from narcissism to social commitment. How would I do it?" (170). Yet when he tries to write, he discovers that the result is not convincing. "It sounded like the transformation of character at the moral behest of the author rather than in accordance with the reader's experience of the slowness and ambiguity of personal change" (171).

The character who helps Oliver achieve a convincing transformation at the end of *The Seeker* is another psychoanalyst named Stanley Nichols, who has served as Oliver's personal therapist and supervisor at the clinic. Oliver is too embarrassed during his personal crisis to seek counsel from his former mentor, but he comes across some of Stanley's clinical notes after his untimely death and is struck by their pragmatic truth. "'O. is right,' he wrote. 'There *is* a kind of nameless sorrowing. I might have told him, but he makes too much of it. We can't get at it, so better not dwell on it. It's not so bad. It can be endured. Anyway, there's nothing to be done but accept it and carry on'" (215). Stanley dies before he can develop this thesis in a paper tentatively titled "The Dynamics of Disillusion," but his notes about Oliver's mid-life crisis suggest two types of suffering, one remediable, the other irremediable. "Much of the misery of life is actually or potentially remediable, and he who is driven to relieve it may succeed; but there is also an elusive anguish for which there is no help, and he who is driven to relieve this will—however much else he may accomplish—be disillusioned" (216).

Without reducing the complexity of a writer's work to a single thesis, one cannot exaggerate the importance of this idea in Wheelis's fiction and nonfiction books. Psychoanalysis can indeed diminish certain forms of pain, but it is helpless against the larger existential and spiritual questions. Freud acknowledges the insight in the final paragraph of his first psychoanalytic book, *Studies on Hysteria* (1893–1895), coauthored with Josef Breuer, in which he anticipates a patient's objections to the talking cure:

> When I have promised my patients help or improvement by means of a cathartic treatment I have often been faced by this objection: "Why, you tell me yourself that my illness is probably connected with my circumstances and the events of my life. You cannot alter these in any way. How do you propose to help me, then?" And I have been able to make this reply: "No doubt fate would find it easier than I do to relieve you of your illness. But you will be able to convince yourself that much will be gained if we succeed in transforming your hysterical misery into common unhappiness. With a mental life that has been restored to health you will be better armed against that unhappiness." (*SE* 2: 305)

No one familiar with the twenty-four volumes of the *Standard Edition* can accuse Freud of being an optimist, for he consistently reveals a tragic vision of life in which there is no consolation, religious or otherwise, for inevitable suffering, loss, and death. Wheelis's vision is bleaker. Unlike the atheistic Freud, whose faith in his creation, psychoanalysis, approached religious dimensions, Wheelis was unable to sustain the same hope in the profession to which he devoted his entire life. Oliver's last words in *The Seeker*, as he enters the final stage of terminal cancer, reveal little of Freud's Promethean defiance against the forces of darkness: "This, I think, is a conflict for which there is no solution. It has simply to be endured. To be human depends upon the awareness of an incommunicable self; to be civilized depends upon an identification of self with the social process. The meaning of my life lies in my contribution to this process, but it is with the interior life that I feel identified. I can endure its destruction, but cannot be reconciled to it" (239). Wheelis viewed all his writings, he told Glass, as an implicit critique of the "mystique" of psychoanalysis. "In the 1950s and '60s, this mystique acquired great authority and prominence in our culture; it was the key to unlock the unconscious which in turn would put you on the royal road to a fulfilled life. It was over-sold and over-played and over-marketed, and I was always in skeptical and derisive opposition" (92).

The Seeker is an impressive first novel, betraying little of the difficulty that its author had in creating it. Wheelis recounts in his 1990 book *The Path Not Taken* a brief anecdote about the struggle to complete *The Seeker*. He showed the manuscript, which he described as "that cross on which I had been hanging for years," to Robert Knight, the renowned analyst and director of the Menninger Foundation and Wheelis's training analyst. When offered the directorship of Austen Riggs in 1947, Knight asked Wheelis if he wanted to come with him to join the staff. Knight read the manuscript and then called Wheelis into his office. "'I don't think you can correct what's wrong with this book,' he said, 'until you are analyzed.' Whatever else he said is forgotten, but there it was, in that one sentence, the mysterious glittering promise: Effort is unavailing; the underlying psychic mechanism must be modified. Then, then! all will be possible" (78).

Wheelis's training analysis may have played a salutary role in his development as a novelist, enlarging his insight into the dynamics of anxiety, guilt, and repression, and helping him understand the reasons for becoming a writer. His analysis may have also given him the self-confidence to deal with the psychological pressures and inhibitions that impede writing. Wheelis became an analyst, he told Glass, as part of a "private endeavor to heal myself by understanding myself" (108). But psychoanalysis by itself cannot develop a writer's creative skills. Therapy cannot help a writer forge the distinctive vocabulary, style, and voice that constitute an aesthetic sensibility. Only talent, experience, and hard work can do that, qualities that Wheelis demonstrated over a lifetime.

The Illusionless Man: Thanatotherapy

The psychoanalysts in Wheelis's other stories fare no better than Oliver in transforming their patients' or their own neurotic misery into common unhappiness. *The Illusionless Man* (1966) consists of four comic short stories. In the first, "The Illusionless Man and the Visionary Maid," Lorabelle sees a psychoanalyst named Dr. Milton Tugwell, who invokes the familiar Freudian psychosexual interpretations of orality, anality, penis envy, and Oedipus complex to explain his patient's character, but these abstract theories have little impact on her life. She abruptly terminates five years of analysis when her husband decides he will no longer pay for her treatment. Dr. Tugwell displays no regret at her decision and quickly finds another wealthy patient to fill the vacant hour. Another story in *The Illusionless Man*, "The League of Death," contains a glib-speaking psycho-therapist-lawyer whose existential malaise conceals terminal boredom with life. He consults an analyst despite his belief that he knows too much to be helped. The story is written in the form of a psychoanalytic monologue in which the cynical first-person analysand frequently interrupts himself to comment on the rituals of analysis. "It's such a bore to be watched—don't you agree?—and such a strain. That's the great advantage of the couch. All psychotherapies tend toward the couch, not just Freudian. It's the weariness of the therapist not the requirements of his theory that lays a patient on his back" (61).

Wheelis's narrator makes two "revolutionary discoveries" in the course of his five analytic sessions with his mute analyst. The first is the Keatsian idea that to appreciate life, one must apprehend death—an idea to which Wheelis would ordinarily be sympathetic were it not for his narrator's intoxicated language and fraudulent motivation. The narrator creates a new school of psychology called "Thanatotherapy" and, along with three of his former patients who are now colleagues, a professional organization, the American Thanatology Association. The collapse of the organization does not prevent him from reaching his second revolutionary insight: "death must be courted. Recognition is not enough; pursuit is mandatory" (82). These two insights momentarily energize the narrator and his associates, "pioneers in the wilderness of nihilism, struggling to infuse meaning into the pallid life of our times" (87). But as his fellow thanatologists violently die, each pursuing the death of his choice, the narrator finds himself professionally discredited and once again confront-ing his old nemesis, boredom. Wheelis's poet laureate of death reveals in his final therapy session a new "love affair": each night he sleeps with a loaded Smith & Wesson revolver, .357 Magnum, which he places in his mouth and then caresses. Wheelis ends his Liebestod with the narrator conceding that he is now ready for the final climax with his silent partner. "This frantic lovemaking has gone on too long. Maybe tonight we'll not make love, but lie down in each other's arms and drop off together" (95).

Of the four stories in the volume, "The Illusionless Man and the Visionary Maid" may contain disguised autobiographical elements. Lorabelle's husband, Henry, is a termite inspector, crawling in darkness under old houses, seeing decay everywhere. "The metaphor of a termite inspector for a psychoanalyst who sees illusions and roots around in the dark underpinnings of people's minds is too perfect to resist," observes psychoanalyst Paul Mosher (personal communication, May 9, 2019), who loved the story when he first read it. "Lorabelle is a typical analyst's wife because of the gulf that appears between someone with the necessarily cynical termite exterminator outlook on life and the likelihood of such an obsessive man being married to a somewhat hysterical woman. Henry is all of us!" Wheelis's story was the basis for the low-budget 1966 feature film *The Crazy-Quilt*, directed by John Korty and narrated by Burgess Meredith. The film received rave reviews: the *New York Times* reviewer Vincent Canby called it a "wonderfully funny—curiously fey—comedy." *The Crazy-Quilt* was on Judith Christ's top ten movies for 1966.

The Moralist: Clinicians of Despair

Clinicians of despair have long intrigued Wheelis. He would no doubt agree with the Conradian idea that the person who believes he has no illusions has precisely that one. Cynicism is more dangerous than idealism in Wheelis's world; the latter merely distorts life, but the former destroys it. Intellectuals are more vulnerable to cynicism or, worse, nihilism, particularly those who claim to seek authenticity and unmask the pretenses of life. Wheelis's detestation of these intellectuals who lack humility and empathy inspires one of his most eloquent modest proposals in his 1973 meditation *The Moralist*. "Let nihilists be required to earn a license. Each and every candidate for nihilism who acts to relieve suffering, to better the human lot, who takes all the risks of a life given over to such action—not just the risk of failure but the risk of making things worse, not just the risk of being shot but the risk of being a fool, of falling on one's face—will be given a license to teach us his vision of life as meaningless. All other candidates will be rejected as unqualified" (14).

The Scheme of Things: "The Subject of My Work Lies Beyond Psychology"

The protagonists in Wheelis's subsequent novels are licensed to practice psychoanalysis, but they do not serve their profession well by espousing nihilistic creeds. The 1980 novel *The Scheme of Things* contains an analyst who embodies many of the ideas and life situations of Wheelis's earlier characters. As the novel opens, Dr. Oliver Thompson recalls a moment twenty years earlier, when he was living in a San Antonio YMCA in 1935, writing a novel about spiritual and carnal love. He was eighteen years old at the time—Wheelis's age when he was struggling to write his first novel. Sections of *The Scheme of Things* exactly parallel *The Quest for Identity*, as if Wheelis is replaying his past, offering a portrait of the psychoanalyst as a young man. Like Larry, Dr. Thompson's motive in writing a novel about the superiority of spiritual love is to shore up a shaky defense against sexuality, which his puritanical father has taught him to regard as sinful. Again like Larry, Dr. Thompson finds himself suffering from headaches and nausea while writing. He finds relief neither from a physician who removes his tonsils nor from a prostitute who takes away his innocence.

Oliver recovers from his early breakdown, succeeds in his chosen profession, but experiences a growing sense of disillusionment and dread. Like the thanatologist in *The Illusionless Man*, he grows obsessed with death. As he meditates on the shadow of death, which he regards not merely as a private terror but as the unchanging backdrop of existence, he makes a distinction between "the way things are" and "the scheme of things." In his formulation, which describes the meaning of the present novel's title and foreshadows the title of a later novel, *The Way Things Are*, the "unchanging backdrop" is the "raw nature of existence, unadorned, unmediated, overwhelming us with dread. What should that be called? Perhaps simply the way things are. The other is that changing succession of stage sets which we put up in front of the backdrop, blocking it from view. What should they be called? They are the schemes of things, the systems of meanings, within which we live" (*The Scheme of Things* 28).

In Dr. Thompson's view, psychoanalysis is valuable in that it helps to correct those problems that have come about as a result of mistreatment in childhood—remediable pain. Psychoanalysis, alas, can do nothing to alleviate the misery associated with the human condition—irremediable pain. "The subject of my work lies beyond psychology," he declares (33). His preoccupation with irremediable suffering reflects Wheelis's own preoccupation. Thompson rejects psychoanalysis because of his belief that it is an arrogant attempt to know a mystery that remains beyond its reach. He discovers, through his growing relationship with his orphaned niece, whom he has reluctantly adopted after his sister's death, and her dog, Barney, the sense of attachment that is, for Wheelis, a transcendent value.

Wheelis's doctor does not mention the eminent psychoanalyst John Bowlby, whose work on attachment theory might have proved to be a revelation to the beleaguered character. Yet one senses that Dr. Thompson has given up on his profession. *The Scheme of Things* closes with the psychoanalytic community censuring the apostate for his reliance upon spirit, sin, and redemption—religious concepts that the novel affirms nondogmatically.

The Doctor of Desire and *The Way Things Are*: "No One Becomes a Psychoanalyst Without Worms Gnawing at His Soul"

Wheelis's next two novels, *The Doctor of Desire* (1987) and *The Way Things Are* (1994), continue his exploration of character, once again analyzing the psychoanalyst and finding him sadly deficient. But now Wheelis's chief concern is with erotic desire, a subject he deftly anatomizes with the precision of a psychic surgeon. *The Doctor of Desire* reminds readers of Philip Roth's 1969 tour de force *Portnoy's Complaint*, as well as perhaps his later novel *The Professor of Desire* (1977). Both writers investigate the nature of passion, which is invested with ancient Oedipal taboos, and both explore the tension between the demands of an insatiable id, on the one hand, and a punitive superego, on the other. Both writers suggest that a man's obsession with a woman is kept alive by her unattainability. The novelists' characters seem to be in love not with specific women but with love—or lust—itself. Both novelists portray male desire and have little to say about female desire. The psychoanalytic authenticity of *The Doctor of Desire* and *Portnoy's Complaint* is beyond question; the former is written by a practicing analyst, and the latter is written by a novelist who gives the impression that he has read—and written—the last word on narcissism.

The many similarities between Wheelis and Roth, however, should not blind us to their differences. The manic energy of *Portnoy's Complaint* never falters, not even when Alex Portnoy finds himself entrapped in his masturbatory fantasies. He may not be able to "put the id back into Yid," as he exclaims, but he seems to enjoy all of his neuroses, including those that leave him unmanned in his "mother country," Israel. *The Professor of Desire* is a somber novel, narrated by a speaker who is tormented by guilt for his sins and by regret at missed opportunities for sinning. Roth is interested in the analysand's point of view, about which he has vast experience; by contrast, Wheelis is interested in the psychoanalyst's per-spective, of which he is an authority. The portrait of Dr. Henry Melville is flattering neither to himself nor to his profession.

The Doctor of Desire probes the relation of desire to despair and consists of two unequal parts. The first, simply called "Story," is narrated in third person and focuses on a fifty-three-year-old analyst's entanglement with a beautiful musician from Venice, Lori Savella, who is young enough to be his daughter. One of Dr. Melville's patients, Charles Morgan, is also attracted to Lori. The situation injects comic relief into the novel as the analyst glumly hears Morgan's sexual progress with Lori. The second part, "Meditation," is much shorter in length and is narrated in first person as Dr. Melville tries to make sense of his fatal attraction to his patient. If the first part of *The Doctor of Desire* reads like a novel and the second part like a psychoanalyst's training analysis, we must remember that the entire novel is a work of fiction in which Wheelis deliberately blurs the boundaries between art and autobiography.

Lori enters analysis with Dr. Melville because of a vague depression she can neither understand nor articulate. She is portrayed as a frozen goddess waiting to be thawed. She remains mute during her therapy sessions, forcing her analyst to find a way to break her silence. To his question—"What are you thinking?"—she responds, "Nothing"; to his question—"What do you feel?"—she responds with the same word. Minutes pass in silence, and when he asks her at the end of the hour "What have you been aware of during this absence?" she once again replies, "Nothing" (*The Doctor of Desire* 31–32). Session after session passes in the same way, but it is clear from the analyst's erotically charged questions that he is irresistibly attracted to her and she to him. We suspect that, as in *King Lear*, something will come of her nothing.

Dr. Melville encourages Lori to examine her repressed fantasies toward him, but it is not until she hears him give a lecture at his psychoanalytic institute that she shatters her silence and is transformed from an object of desire into a desiring object. Dr. Melville argues in his lecture that the concept of responsibility, too often ignored by analysts and moralists alike, at their peril, has profound implications for therapy and behavior. "The larger the realm of experience for which one can claim and establish responsibility, the larger the realm of one's freedom" (49). Dr. Melville's thesis suggests that both analyst and patient must accept responsibility for the success or failure of therapy. His professorial voice resembles Wheelis's, particularly in his meditative books such as *The Desert* (1970).

Ironically, the lecture has the effect of igniting Lori's explosive passion for Dr. Melville. Inflamed by his words, she begins to act seductively toward him. The more he resists her advances, the more aggressive she becomes. When he finally insists that she must control her sexual acting out, lest she sabotage her therapy and destroy his reputation, she grows distraught, swallows a bottle of pills, and vows never to forgive him for leading her on. Wheelis's doctor of desire has indeed aroused his patient's sexual feelings for him, and while he doesn't go to bed with her, he is—to take seriously his lecture—partly responsible for her wildly seductive behavior toward him. Although Lori later reenters analysis with Dr. Melville, they cannot restore the therapeutic relationship. She remains unimpressed with his interpretation that she has been "acting out in the transference" (75). Her interpretation of his refusal to go to bed with him is distinctly non-psychoanalytic: he is a "coward" (75). They reach a therapeutic impasse, and she leaves after a few more months of therapy.

Lori's departure devastates Dr. Melville: Self-analysis cannot assuage his tormented desire for her. The knowledge that he has tried to act honorably toward her brings no comfort. Nor does his interpretation of his own desperate predicament bring him relief. Lori represents, he later theorizes, that image of himself associated with weakness, fear, and femininity; she is no simple "other" but a part of himself that he cannot renounce. The interpretation may be correct, but it does nothing to dispel the pain of loss. Wheelis ends the first part of the novel with an image of his protagonist being consumed by an insatiable desire that will torment him to the end of his days.

Wheelis precedes part II, "Meditation," with a quotation from Isaac Bashevis Singer—"hell is made up of yearnings"—and we must inquire into the novel's cheerless vision of desire. And what is Wheelis's precise relationship with his doomed protagonist? "No one becomes a psychoanalyst without worms gnawing at his soul" (127), Dr. Melville exclaims sardonically, a statement that could be the epigraph for all of Wheelis's novels. That so many of Dr. Melville's pronouncements about psychoanalysis reflect those found in his creator's fictional and nonfictional books establishes a kinship between character and author. Many of Dr. Melville's assertions are authorial, as when he criticizes psychoanalysis for claiming scientific status to a non-verifiable theory. He also sounds like his creator when he observes that psychoanalysts are remarkably unaware of the most fundamental assumption behind their profession:

That assumption is simply that it is possible for a human being to be well adjusted, to have a good life, that however rare it may be in fact it is in principle possible. There are a few psychoanalytic asides, always jocose, which stand as disclaimers. "Analysis enables you to cope with the misery of real life," or "to adjust to the poverty in which it leaves you." But this is window-dressing, a specious cynicism to ward off the embarrassment of a real utopianism. The assumption is basic and ubiquitous. Without it we'd have to pack up our couch and ottoman and fade away. Our so-called science is married to a genuine faith: that serious and sustained misery is not inherent to human life, that it is imposed by neurotic conflict or by reality hardship; that, therefore, if neurotic conflict is analyzed and resolved and if reality hardship is absent one will love and will work, will live out one's life span with contentment, with real gratifications, and when the end comes will pronounce it all to have been worth while. (129–130)

And yet despite the authorial insight Dr. Melville reaches in this key passage, he remains blind to one central truth: the importance of genuine faith. Rather than knowing too much, as he claims, he knows too little. He knows too little about his own arrogance, which elevates the intellectual side of life over the spiritual. He knows too little about the joy of marriage and children, a side of life with which Wheelis's fictional analysts seem surprisingly unfamiliar. Dr. Melville knows the difference between lust and love but nevertheless spends too much time pursuing the former and not enough time cultivating the latter. He realizes that his mad pursuit of desire has brought him to the abyss of nihilism, in which nothing matters but carnality, but he cannot bring himself to seek forgiveness and redemption. Even at the end of the novel, when he concedes helplessly that "I know nothing. Know only that I live in desperate ignorance, not knowing how to live" (192), he wallows in pity.

It's hard to know the extent to which Wheelis's fictional portraits of marriage are based on his own marriage. He admits in his conversation with Glass a fundamental difference between himself and his wife, known professionally as Ilse Jawetz, who was herself a prominent psychiatrist, psychoanalyst, and teacher of psychoanalysis. "My wife is constantly saying that I am not present, that I am lost in ideas" (115). She is, by contrast, always in the here-and-now. "She draws me back in and complains how difficult it is to do that. I am aware that her being in the midst of life and totally involved is life-saving for me and prevents me from drifting off into a kind of terminal despair" (116).

In writing a novel about a psychoanalyst who, superficially, at least, voices so many of his life themes, Wheelis runs the risk of being identified with his unsympathetic protagonist, as is evident in the question Dr. Melville raises in *The Doctor of Desire*: "How to live? Who knows the question knows not how. Who knows not the question cannot tell" (150). The question, a paraphrase of the pre-Socratic philosopher Xenophanes, appears word for word in two of Wheelis's other books, *On Not Knowing How to Live* (4) and *The Life and Death of My Mother* (24). Wheelis uses a longer form of the quote as the epigraph to his 1971 book *The End of the Modern Age*. In effect, this is the question that animates all Wheelis's writings. If he knows the answer, he will not tell.

"All writers repeat themselves," Dr. Melville asserts. "Is it not true that any writer, even the greatest—perhaps especially the greatest—has but one message? Is this not true of all artists? Can we not hear the same statement about the world and human life through all nine of Beethoven's symphonies or Mahler's?" (150). Dr. Melville's belief that each artist has a characteristic "fingerprint" recalls psychoanalyst Heinz Lichtenstein's concept of an identity theme. "Identity, in man, requires a 'repetitive doing' in order to safeguard the 'sameness within change' which I believe to be a fundamental aspect of identity in man" (103). The concept of an identity theme would be met with little favor by postmodernist critics, who emphasize disconnection and discontinuity. Nevertheless, Wheelis's writings have been remarkably consistent over half a century. The metatheme infusing all of his books is that while psychoanalysis can help us with remediable pain, we must muddle through life as best we can with or without therapy, hoping we have the strength and courage to endure irremediable pain. Another meta-theme is what Wheelis calls in his conversation with Glass the "intractable yearning for closeness and the disappointment that always ensues" (85). There is no escape from the paradox that as much as we desire intimacy with another person, we fear fusion, which obliterates our identity and autonomy. "This wish for fusion is a beckoning goal, and many of the characters in my novels stumble on the passion and the pitfalls it creates" (85).

The Life and Death of My Mother: "Daylight Says Life Is Knowable, Night Tells the Truth"

Nowhere are these meta-themes better seen than in Wheelis's profoundly moving 1992 memoir *The Life and Death of My Mother*. It is his only book without significant disguise (apart from the invention of a pigeon whose feet were cut off, a metaphor of cruelty and helplessness). He honors the memory of his mother by describing, with almost brutal honesty, her long and troubled life: her childhood in the pine woods of Louisiana; her marriage to a country doctor who died prematurely from tuberculosis; her devotion to her two children and loneliness when they departed to college; her growing dependence upon her son, whom she idealizes; her retirement from teaching and growing isolation; and her gradual loss of memory and selfhood as she succumbs to Alzheimer's disease in a nursing home.

From the opening sentence of *The Life and Death of My Mother*, which evokes the fecal smell in her room as she slowly bleeds to death from her bowels, we realize this will be no sentimentalized biography. Mrs. Wheelis is one hundred years old and has been dying for a long time—dying not from remediable illness but from irremediable old age. The darkness that envelops her life extends to her son's as well and foretells the limits of reason. "Daylight says life is knowable, night tells the truth, says we know not what lies hidden, neither in the darkness out there nor the darkness within" (15). Though he himself would be considered old—he is seventy-four when she dies—he denies having achieved knowledge or maturity.

Wheelis quotes an interview Erik Erikson gave on television in which, asked whether he has achieved wisdom, the elderly analyst replied, "I'm afraid I have." Wheelis's sarcastic response, despite being a good friend of Erikson, who was Ilse Jawetz's training analyst, is characteristic of the tone of the memoir. "Mazeltov. I have not. I'm as old as he, almost. Anyway, like him, slogging along through the last phase, if it is a phase, anyway the last years of life. But not with wisdom. Rather with the vanity, awkwardness, longing, and shame that have characterized my passage through all the other phases" (21). The allusion to Erikson's influential theory of the life cycle, which posits that all people pass through eight stages, contrasts with Wheelis's own belief that life cannot be viewed neatly or schematically. And whereas Erikson's writings are imbued with optimism, Wheelis's vision is gloomier, edgier, more tragic. "I distrust the wisdom of old men," he says immediately after referring to Erikson. "I listen to them and am not convinced. I suspect a cover-up. They don't have things really straight either. They're headed, mapless, into the same dark that awaits us all" (21). Wheelis's vision of old age conjures up Yeats's "Sailing to Byzantium" but without the lyrical affirmation: "An aged man is but a paltry thing, / A tattered coat upon a stick, unless / Soul clap its hands and sing" (204).

No one can accuse Wheelis of a cover-up in his relationship to his mother, for he goes out of his way to portray himself in the least flattering way as he uncovers his Oedipal attraction to his mother's body. This was not a subject that psychoanalysts dared to disclose publicly. Only recently have novelists and memoirists written about incestuous relationships with their parents. In her 1994 memoir *Searching for Mercy Street*, Linda Sexton admits being sexually abused as a child by her mother, the poet Anne Sexton, who would masturbate next to her sleeping daughter or thrust her tongue deep into her daughter's mouth while she was sleeping—or pretending to sleep. As I discuss in *Mad Muse: The Mental Illness Memoir in a Writer's Life and Work*, Linda Sexton first wrote about these experiences in her 1985 novel *Mirror Images*, but admitting this experience in a memoir required more courage. In *The Incest Diary*, the narrator writes about being raped by her father throughout her childhood—but the author of the 2017 memoir remains anonymous.

As difficult as it is to write about being a sexual victim, it is more difficult to confess to being a potential victimizer. There is one moment in Wheelis's memoir when he describes, not long after his father's death, lying next to his sleeping mother and exploring her uncovered body. As he feels his mother's genitals he discovers, to his horror, that she lacks his own anatomical equipment. But rather than offering us a theoretical discussion of the castration complex, as one might expect a psychoanalyst to do—assuming that one would expect an analyst to make such a disturbing revelation in public—Wheelis concentrates on the unruly emotions he experienced at the time, when he was about nine years old: the terror, confusion, and guilt as he reluctantly withdrew his hand from her mysterious orifice. The next morning, the boy wonders whether his mother will be disapproving of him, indicating that she was not asleep during his erotic advances. "As it turns out, she is unusually tender and loving with me throughout the day. But I am surly" (52).

Wheelis's dominant feeling toward his mother, however, is not surliness but love, tinged with remorse, resentment, and guilt. She had enslaved herself to her husband for the six years of his illness, but after his death, she began a different kind of servitude to her children, who would soon leave her to begin their own adult lives. Wheelis's dying father extracted a promise from his wife shortly before his death not to marry, but after his death she became overly attached to her son. "My father was a despot who rendered me powerless. But with his death I assumed absolute power over my mother" (50). He later expands upon this theme, stating that his mother's apotheosis of him resulted in a lifelong dependence that neither father nor son could have anticipated. "So perhaps my dying father was right to fear that she would fall for the first man to lay hand on her flank, but he could hardly have known that that man would be I, that therefore the promise not to remarry which he extracted from her could not protect her" (86). Yet it is misleading for Wheelis to suggest that he "unintentionally had designed for her a barren life, and that she was obediently following my blueprint, unable to break away from my spell, and I powerless to free her" (86). He casts himself repeatedly in the harshest light, emphasizing his vain and duplicitous actions while ignoring his efforts to strengthen his mother's independence and well-being. If she wishes to play Jocasta to his Oedipus, he never encourages the role. Nor does he encourage her other fantasies, such as the desire to be her famous son's best patient.

One of Wheelis's most awkward moments occurs when his mother asks him to examine her breast after learning she has cancer. The eroticized question embarrasses him, but he reluctantly accedes to her request and assures her that a mastectomy is essential. An even more troubling incident occurs shortly before her death when, suffering from vaginal discomfort, she suddenly pulls up her nightgown while lying in bed, opens her legs, and demands that he look at her exposed genitals. The sight of his mother's sexual organs is as horrifying as the view of her shriveled body. But he is responsible neither for her sexual behavior nor for her deteriorating body and mind. The anguish of mother and son arises from the indignity of old age, about which nothing can be done.

Some of the incidents Wheelis relates in *The Life and Death of My Mother* are almost too heartrending to read, especially for those who cling to the illusion that one can die with dignity. Perhaps the most wrenching moment occurs when he describes his mother and sister in the same nursing home, each suffering from Alzheimer's disease, each unable to recognize the other. "What is that woman doing here?" the mother angrily cries to her son. "What does she want? Why is she staring at me? I don't like that! Something ought to be done about a situation like this! Where is the management? I'm going to report her!" (111). Once again, the writer shows that nothing can be done to remediate this sorrow.

Wheelis ends his memoir with a stark description of the burial service for his mother. The cold wintry day sets the mood for the final elegiac pages. Words fail the writer as he begins to eulogize his mother in the presence of his wife and children. It's not that he remains mute, choked with emotion; rather, he is struck by the half-truths of his brief reconstruction of her life. Only when he speaks about her unusual loyalty, devotion, and self-sacrifice does he believe in the truth of his language. The final sentences describe each member of the family casting a shovelful of earth onto the descending coffin. He is attentive to every detail, a writer at the height of his observational powers. Confronted by grave truths, the artist faithfully records experience and empathizes with the living and the dead. Wheelis bears witness to his mother's ordinary life and death and, in the process, transmutes suffering into extraordinary art.

The Listener and *The Way We Are*: "I Have Lost What Now Becomes a Magic Wand"

The Listener (1999) might be more accurately called *The Doctor of Desire* had Wheelis not already used that title for his 1987 novel about a psychoanalyst tormented by insatiable lust. Indeed, many of Wheelis's books are about psychoanalysts of desire for whom a beautiful woman is a deadly attraction. "Great beauty inflicts a wound," he writes at the beginning of *The Listener*. "Private and somehow shameful. It can neither be acknowledged nor complained about. A deep, burning pain. It will not go away. The pain is the longing; the wound is the knowing that the longing can never be fulfilled, that, like hell, it will go on forever, always there, always inside" (16). We might assume that these are the words of a young and perhaps callow man. Not so. Wheelis was eighty-four when the novel was published, and his response to great beauty seemed undiminished—and unmitigated—by age.

Reading *The Listener*, one suspects that as he approached the end of his distinguished career as a psychoanalyst and writer, Wheelis portrayed his life as darker than it was. Honesty compels him to present his life in the most self-accusatory terms, as if acknowledging the truth of his father's denunciation. Wheelis sees himself alternately as a psychoanalytic protector and sexual predator, and while there is no hint that he violated professional boundaries, the reader wonders how he avoids entangling alliances with his patients. There are times in *The Listener* when he wants the reader to dislike him, particularly when he describes the tensions in his marriage and his wife's disappointment in him. Readers who are passionately married may find themselves disagreeing with his assertion that a faithful marriage entails the loss of something magical and mysterious in the life of the flesh. With its lyrical prose style, psychological penetration, and unflinching candor, *The Listener* is a courageous book, challenging the conventional wisdom that self-knowledge and self-acceptance increase with age. Avoiding psychoanalytic correctness, Wheelis has always been interested in the way people are rather than the way they ought to be. It's unlikely that *The Listener* will become required reading in psychoanalytic institutes, but its unvarnished insights into the life of a remarkable psychoanalytic writer deserve wide recognition.

Wheelis's final book, *The Way We Are*, was published in 2006, one year before his death. The nonagenarian sums up his life in this slender volume, reprising familiar themes. A paradoxicalist, he remains suspicious of capturing the truth of his life. "Revealing myself, I remain hidden. As the real self is exposed, it becomes false, the now-real self retreating in shadow behind the newly false. Honesty cannot know itself; aware of telling the truth, I lie" (17). These are the paradoxes usually seen in philosophy, not psychoanalysis—although we shall see different paradoxes in Adam Phillips's writings. Desire is no less treacherous than truth. Like Wheelis's first book, *The Quest for Identity*, his last book contains a beguiling thread of personal narrative interwoven with abstractions. Seeing a young woman on a beach holding her infant, he cannot stop looking at her. "She glances at me, smiles. I think she knows she is torturing me, making me want to do with her what she is doing with the baby" (96). He knows he is trapped in a frenzied fantasy but cannot free himself. "This is the cruelty of great beauty, that it inflicts this wound, that the pain is forever" (99). The wound, he concludes, is life, from which he doesn't wish to recover.

How does an author bid farewell to his readers after a writing career that spanned nearly half a century? Wheelis finds the perfect way in *The Way We Are*. While accompanying his wife to a psychoanalytic conference where she will be attending meetings, he loses his beloved fountain pen, given to him by his daughter. "She knows my fetishistic addiction to elegant writing instruments" (138). But it is more than a fetish or addiction. "By my carelessness I have lost what now becomes a magic wand that could have lifted me up out of dung and death" (139–140). The pen serves not only as an emblem of creativity but also as a talisman to ward off death. Indeed, at the beginning of the book he reveals what may be the central motivation of his late writings. "I am obsessed with death; and this obsession, I am convinced, is not a private terror but the unchanging backdrop to the stage of our existence" (18). Wheelis's fixation with death, along with his recognition of death anxiety as the deepest human fear, links him to the celebrated existential psychiatrist and novelist Irvin Yalom, with whom he has much in common both as a clinician and as an author of psychotherapy tales. Wheelis's loss of his pen conjures up the image of Prospero breaking his magical staff at the end of *The Tempest*, Shakespeare's final play, where he bids farewell to his audience. *The Way We Are* ends with the frantic Wheelis finding his pen, allowing him to complete the book—and his writing life.

One senses that, knowing the hazards of psychoanalysis, Wheelis practiced his craft with consummate skill and care, striving to help his patients with the vicissitudes of life. At least one of his patients has written about him, albeit anonymously. In volume 2 of *Off the Tracks: Cautionary Tales About the Derailing of Mental Health Care*, Paul Mosher and I discuss Harvey Weinstein's gripping 1988 book *A Father, a Son, and the CIA* (later published in the United States as *Psychiatry and the CIA: Victims of Mind Control*), a harrowing account of his father's mistreatment by the psychiatrist D. Ewen Cameron at the Allen Memorial Institute of Psychiatry in Montreal, Canada, in the 1950s. Feeling burdened by his inadvertent role in his father's psychiatric nightmare, as well as by other problems, Weinstein refers to a psychoanalyst who helped him regain control over his life. For two years, Weinstein railed against his "gentle analyst," as he discloses in his book:

> I wept; I thundered; I felt the need to be close; I saw my fear of the closeness. Within the confines of that lovely room, the world of my adolescence became alive once more as I struggled to become a man. Never did he let me feel sorry for myself. "You must live in the present. How are you going to deal with the politics at work?" "If you feel isolated, what are you going to do about it?" His patience and gentle manner enabled me to let go of my preoccupation with the past. My anger at psychiatry could focus on one institution and one

man. From my therapist I gained the freedom to follow my profession; unencumbered, I could use my life experience in ways that would assist others. (70)

As soon as I read Weinstein's description of his "silver-haired" San Francisco analyst, "tall and stately thin, almost cadaverous in appearance," married to a psychiatrist and with an office overlooking San Francisco Bay and the Golden Gate Bridge, I knew the analyst was Wheelis, whom I had interviewed in his office at his castle-like home on Jackson Street in the late 1990s, when I first began writing about him. It's not clear why Weinstein never names his analyst, but in the acknowledgments he pays tribute to Wheelis, "who helped me find my way."

A Splendid Failure

As we have seen, Allen Wheelis's self-accusations appear in his earliest and latest writings and constitute a life theme. Irvin Yalom also wrote about being human, all too human, in his fiction and nonfiction, as I discuss in *Writing the Talking Cure*, but Yalom's self-portraits are far more warmhearted than Wheelis's. The autobiographical *The Path Not Taken* contains a passage that reveals the vanity and duplicity of Wheelis's fictional psychoanalysts:

> Several people love me. Many people think highly of me. Were you to ask, they would tell you of my kindness, intelligence, generosity, empathy. And offer little by way of qualification— other than that I am difficult to know.
>
> Viewing myself, I see a different person, find no ground for love. Anxious, petty, self-centered, tormented, mean spirited, weak. Too bad. I would have it otherwise, would wish for the noble features others ascribe to me. But I know myself better than they, make reference to a range of thought and feeling, of motivation and behavior, unavailable to them. Even those closest to me can know but a fraction of what I know. I've really got the dirt on me.
>
> And beyond what I know lies what I have not permitted myself to know, wherein things even more damaging are hidden.

> Since I intend in this work the utmost honesty, the reader,
> if I am successful, cannot in the end think well of me. If he
> does, I will have failed. (71)

Wheelis's "failure," here and elsewhere, is a noble one. His wife attributes his self-lacerating personality to a "terrible analysis," one that "didn't even touch your superego" (*The Path Not Taken* 119). Paradoxically, Wheelis's failure to understand himself as a psychoanalyst betokens his success as a creative writer, for he knows that conflict is more interesting than resolution. Character remains mysterious in the final analysis, incapable of being known fully.

Wheelis's belief in his own failure is reminiscent of William Faulkner's comment that *The Sound and the Fury* was a "most splendid failure" despite being one of the greatest novels in the English language. "All of us failed to match our dream of perfection. So I rate us on the basis of our splendid failure to do the impossible. In my opinion, If I could write all my work again, I am convinced I would do it better, which is the healthiest condition for an artist." That's why the writer keeps working, Faulkner continues: "he believes each time that this time he will do it, bring it off. Of course he won't, which is why this condition is healthy" (quoted in Stein).

Of all psychoanalysts, Wheelis has confessed most often to his own failures and those of his profession, transforming defeats into highly wrought art. Few of Wheelis's colleagues dared to acknowledge in public the hazards of being a psychoanalyst. "Given that words are the bread and butter of psychoanalytic work," Daphne Merkin wrote in her laudatory obituary of Allen Wheelis published in the *New York Times Magazine* on December 30, 2007, "it would seem strange on the face of it that very few practitioners have written elegant or even lucid prose." Merkin cited only a handful of other psychiatrists who stand out in this "fallow field," including Irvin Yalom.

Wheelis would be the first to point out that both the writer and the psychoanalyst are engaged in parallel quests for self-knowledge and self-healing. "Writer and psychoanalyst are but two faces of the same vocation," Dr. Melville suggests in *The Doctor of Desire*, "the attempt to work out one's own problems by working on the problems of others. Real others for the psychoanalyst; for the writer, imaginary others—or so he would have his family and friends believe. The psychoanalyst conducts his vicarious self-therapy in private; the writer invites the whole world to sit in on his sessions" (151–152). Wheelis is part of a small but vital tradition of psychoanalytic novelists who work out their own problems by working on those of both real and imaginary characters. He takes us on dark journeys to unknown destinations, recalling Henry James's comment that Wheelis uses as the epigraph to *The Quest for Identity*: "We work in the dark—we do what we can—we give what we have. Our doubt is our passion and our passion is our task. The rest is the madness of art."

Wheelis's fiction and nonfiction represent a unique synthesis of art and psychoanalysis. One is reminded of the fictional Sigmund Freud's observation in D.M. Thomas's 1981 novel *The White Hotel*: "Long may poetry and psychoanalysis continue to highlight, from their different perspectives, the human face in all its nobility and sorrow" (143). Wheelis's writings affirm his lifelong pursuit of love, compassion, responsibility, and dignity, values that must silence the most relentless self-criticism. We believe as we complete his books that however much he may mistrust the wisdom of old men, he has achieved it in his art.

The Known, the Secret, the Forgotten

How would a daughter feel growing up with a father like Allen Wheelis? Would she, like the reader, wonder about the differences between autobiography and art? Between outer and inner reality? Would she believe, as Wheelis admitted to James Glass, that her father was not fully present to his wife, lost in ideas, silent and brooding? Our questions increase if we discover that the daughter has become a psychoanalyst herself, like both her parents. Would she regard herself, as her father did about himself, as a technician of loneliness, a clinician of despair? Would she share her father's critique of the mystique of psychoanalysis, experiencing, perhaps, the same disillusionment with the talking cure, the same awareness of the vocational hazards of psychoanalysis? Would she agree with her father that no one becomes a psychoanalyst without worms gnawing at one's soul? Readers of Joan Wheelis's 2019 memoir, *The Known, the Secret, the Forgotten*, do not learn the answers to any of these questions; but they are nevertheless gifted with a deeply moving story of growing up with two analyst-parents whose lives hold many secrets.

"*All* Marriages Are Unhappy"

There are relatively few memoirs by psychoanalysts—mainly because, as the psychoanalyst Muriel Gardiner observes in her 1982 memoir, *Code Name "Mary,"* most analysts are "inhibited by feelings of privacy" and by their training (xvi). This inhibition did not preclude memoiristic writing for Allen Wheelis—nor for his daughter. *The Known, the Secret, The Forgotten* is hardly a tell-all memoir—indeed, Joan Wheelis remains singularly discreet in her revelations about her parents' lives—but she casts further light on their marriage, including her father's categorical statement in *The Listener* that "*all* marriages are unhappy" (164). After her parents' deaths, she found a letter her father had written to her mother in 2000, when he was eighty-five. Allen Wheelis traces his lifelong obsession with unattainable yearning to his father's grim prohibition of all desire. "If I am not allowed to *ask* for anything," Wheelis explains to his wife, "then I will seize the right secretly to *want* everything, including the unattainable ideal" (93). He ends the letter by acknowledging that "what began as an accounting, a balance sheet of profit and loss and intimacy, has become a love letter. So be it. I admit it. I affirm it. I declare it. I love you" (*The Known, the Secret, The Forgotten* 95). Joan Wheelis never doubts that her parents loved each other or that they loved her, "the much-wanted daughter of two physicians who trained in psychiatry and practiced psychoanalysis," as she states on the first page of her memoir.

Nevertheless, Joan Wheelis intimates her parents' marital troubles. Each had been married before, unhappily. Leaving their spouses and, in Allen Wheelis's case, two young children, was predictably difficult. The new marriage endured for more than half a century, but it was not without its own disappointments, particularly because of her father's consuming passion for art, a jealous and demanding muse. After dinner he would return to his office to write, and his wife felt abandoned, retreating to her own office. "With both my parents sequestered in their respective offices, I felt alone and unsettled by the palpable tension" (55).

Joan Wheelis knows her father well, and she underscores the lasting impact of her paternal grandfather's oppressive single-edged razor lesson. "By linking love with his brutally harsh expectations, my grandfather left my father longing for approval, and redemption, which he did not receive." She adds that her father was "never really freed of the criticism he internalized, yet my mother, with her proclivity for playfulness and spontaneity, helped soften the grip" (44).

Joan Wheelis's portrait of her father resembles that which we infer from his nonfiction—and even some of his fiction. "His message," she writes near the opening of her memoir, describing how she felt as a twelve-year-old about the painfully uncomfortable two-day journey in their blue Buick Skylark every summer from San Francisco to their summer home on Puget Sound, "was that all good things in life require sacrifice. Anything short of stoic tolerance was regarded as weakness of character and failure of will" (14). Staring out the back window of their car, she innocently waved to the driver of an 18-wheeler and received her father's immediate rebuke. "I don't want you to do that anymore," he scolded her, and when she asked why, he replied, "You are ignoring the context of your behavior. You are in a car and protected by glass and your parents from a real engagement. It creates an illusion of power and intimacy. You are acting in an overly familiar way with a stranger" (16). Whatever pleasure she had felt was now gone as a result of his unwelcome lecture. She describes her father as disciplined, orderly, exacting, a man whose life lessons were always well thought out and whose logic was ironclad, making disagreement difficult if not impossible. Her mother, by contrast, was easier to be with, more down to earth. Allen Wheelis's statement that one identifies with the stricter, more forbidding parent seems to be true of his daughter.

Loving her mother was easy, her father, more complicated. "Typically my father was so silent and his presence so formidable that I often felt fearful that I might upset or, worse, alienate him. I always worried that I had to be careful around him, that any misstep might incur his wrath or his retreat" (113). And yet Allen Wheelis does not come across as another version of his punitive father. Despite being distant, self-preoccupied, and undemonstrative, he had a special bond with his daughter, though, curiously, he never directly expressed his love to her until she was twenty, a Harvard undergraduate recovering from abdominal surgery and a "brush with cancer." He spent several days caring for her in Cambridge when she was convalescing from multiple postoperative complications, and as he was leaving to return to San Francisco, he whispered, "I love you very much," a "tender moment," she observes, adding, "almost too intimate" (113).

Joan Wheelis conveys this love partly through dialogue, as when he calls her repeatedly "sweetie," a word that he never uses in any of his books. She comes across as a model child, perhaps as a way to gain and maintain her parents' love, as Alfred Adler would say, and also because defiance does not temperamentally suit her. She depicts the unspoken intimacy with her father in many ways. She always sat next to him during her parents' elegant dinner parties, and he takes great pleasure teaching her how to cut Napoleon puff pastry on a plate (by turning it on its side). She appeared to be closer to her father than to her mother. Father and daughter go on long walks together, just the two of them. Her father is the storyteller, not her mother. The daughter counts mainly on her father, not her mother, for protection. Both father and daughter delight in selecting postage stamps to send letters to each other. For years she cut her father's hair; oddly enough, when she was not home, he took to cutting his hair himself, resulting in what was affectionately called his "mouse-eaten" appearance. After his death and cremation, she felt the need to accompany him "all the way to ash" (89). She remembers her conflicted feelings sitting for the first time in his office, which she had visited only in his presence. "I felt guilty yet entitled to be there" (80).

Joan Wheelis captures the childlike wonder she felt when she saw patients entering her home to visit her parents, in separate offices, behind closed door. Feeling like a spy, witnessing something forbidden, she recollects how she felt when she was six seeing patients who came to their appointments "in some form like a ghost and my parents made them visible" (28)—a felicitous description of psychotherapy. Her father often saw "young attractive women who wore perfume" (30). She never reveals whether she felt jealous of these women who spent time with her beloved father. She leaves much to our imagination. When she tells her son about the time in her childhood when she asked her father to kill the mosquitoes buzzing in her room, she mentions that her mother thought this was an "Oedipal bid for my father's attention" (135), an interpretation with which she neither agrees nor disagrees. Like a consummate pianist, she knows how to play silences.

In the chapter "Economy of Motion," Joan Wheelis describes her father's characteristic way of lighting a fire in the living room hearth. There was a right way to do it, she informs us, characterizing the method as aggressively precise without being obsessional. "He liked the power of precision. He wrote that way—spare yet rich. And he spoke that way—with his love of clarity, finding just the right words parsed with powerful eloquence" (138). Economy of motion is also economy of emotion. Joan Wheelis is her father's daughter, and they share a similar aesthetic vision, using muted, understated language that conceals as much as it reveals. "Outside of his writing," she tells us, "my father was a very private man" (111)—a comment equally true of herself.

Indeed, she is so private that, except for one paragraph, she never mentions being a psychoanalyst. Nor could one infer this from her memoir. We learn only from the book jacket that she is an assistant professor at Harvard Medical School and a graduate of the Boston Psychoanalytic Society and Institute, where she is a training and supervising psychoanalyst. She is on the clinical faculty at McLean Hospital and teaches at the joint Massachusetts General Hospital/McLean Hospital Psychiatric Residency Program.

The Talking Cure and the Writing Cure

In an interview with Joan Wheelis at the 2020 American Psychoanalytic Association Conference, Fred Griffin observes that writing (and perhaps reading) a memoir is not unlike what happens during psychoanalysis. Both bring order to one's life, play with memory and time, seek to capture subjective experience, and lead to a discovery of meanings. And both, Griffin adds, depend upon language.

Despite these commonalities, throughout *The Known, the Secret, The Forgotten* Joan Wheelis prefers to evoke emotions and memories rather than analyze them. She uses none of the psychoanalytic diction that appears in theoretical or clinical writings—and never psychobabble or pharmababble. Each vignette, four or five pages long, strives for a "revelation," as Roy Hoffman notes in his positive review in *The New York Times*. The only time she writes about her professional life is in the chapter "The Dove." While dictating a clinical case, she received a telephone call from her mother announcing her father's unexpected death following back surgery. After the call, she returned to dictation and then saw a patient. She wasn't particularly distressed that she could not say goodbye to him. "It wasn't necessary. Enough had been said. And what wasn't said was already known" (72). In other words, economy of emotion. She could have stopped here, but then, in the next paragraph, comes a passage that must have been the hardest one in the memoir to write:

> Six months after my father died, my husband left. My son, in the throes of an adolescent bid for freedom, was rarely home

and, when he was, he had little interest in my company. With
all the men in my life gone, I felt bereft without my familiar
bearings and daily routines. Letting myself fall asleep was a
challenge every night. I crawled into bed reluctantly, as late
as possible, settling into a narrow channel on one side of the
bed I had shared for twenty years with my husband. I slept
up against a life-size stuffed dog. It offered some comfort to
be held in place in the big bed. Books and magazines piled
up on the other side like a dam. (72–73)

This moment is remarkable for many reasons. In exposing her vulnerability,
she summons not only our readerly sympathy but also our protectiveness.
She makes no effort to assign blame to anyone or cast characters into
victims or victimizers. She writes, to borrow one of her father's book
titles, about the way things are. In the words of another title, she conveys not knowing how to live. And she remains, to evoke a third title,
a seeker. Without symbol-mongering, we can say that the little comfort
she experiences during this wrenching moment comes from the books
and magazines piled on her bed, the consolation of art, to which her
father had devoted his life.

"The Dove" is the most memorable chapter in the memoir, not
merely for its evocation of loss but also for what follows. In the spring
following her father's death, Joan Wheelis awoke in the middle of the
night to hear birds singing. "Spontaneously I called out, 'Daddy?'" (74).
Wondering about her sanity, she never could figure out whether the
birds were real or not. They stopped singing on June 4, 2008, exactly
one year after her father's death. There are other unforgettable moments,
including lying next to her deceased mother. "I decided her spirit might
leave her body while I was there and I could have a farewell with her
as she wanted" (147).

Joan Wheelis does not reveal in her memoir the burden of having
a father who was a gifted writer, but she intimates this to Fred Griffin.
Comparing her father's writing discipline with her own was daunting:

Rather than writing from nine until noon each morning like
my father, I had no routine. Sometimes I wrote early in the
morning before I started seeing patients, in the breaks between
patients, in bed late at night or on the weekends. My father
always wrote on bond paper on a clipboard with a fountain

pen. Sometimes I wrote on my computer, sometimes I jotted things down on a scrap piece of paper or in a notebook with a pencil or a ballpoint pen. These comparisons with my father's habits were invidious and often made me feel fraudulent. It took a long time and much encouragement to feel I had a worthy voice of my own.

In her memoir Joan Wheelis does not refer to the magical pen she gave to her father, but she is no less gifted a writer. She has a lyrical, evocative prose style in *The Known, the Secret, the Forgotten*, and as her haunting title suggests, she writes poetically about the mystery of love and loss. Children of psychiatrists do not often fare well, as Thomas Maeder showed in his 1989 book. Drawing on hundreds of interviews with therapist-parents, children, and child psychiatrists, Maeder, himself the son of two psychotherapists, concluded that therapists too often over-interpret their children's behavior and thus intrude on their privacy. Children of two psychiatrists sometimes experience a double whammy. But this is not true of Joan Wheelis. She offers an indelible portrait of two analysts who could not be more different in personality and vision, and whose conflicts, as her father wrote to her mother in 2000, generated profound joy—and a grateful daughter.

"Mending the Mind"

Joan Wheelis has not exactly followed in her parents' footsteps. She has worked to integrate psychoanalysis with other psychotherapeutic approaches, in particular, dialectical behavior therapy (DBT), a form of cognitive behavior therapy, pioneered by Marsha Linehan, that is especially effective for the treatment of patients with borderline personality disorder, a disorder characterized by instability in one's interpersonal relationships, self-esteem, and emotions, often leading to impulsivity, fear of abandonment, self-harm, and suicidality. Such patients, among the most intractable to treat, typically do not do well with insight therapy or analysis of resistance. Joan Wheelis's 2010 article "Mending the Mind" aptly begins with a quote from Eugene O'Neill's 1926 play *The Great God Brown*: "Man is broken. He lives by mending. The grace of God is glue."

Unlike psychoanalysis, which explores unconscious meanings and motivations, DBT emphasizes problem-solving, mindfulness (staying in the present), and dialectics (truth as an evolution of opposing views). As a DBT clinician, Joan Wheelis helps her patients develop positive behaviors to replace dysfunctional ones. She displays the same compassion, modesty, and honesty that appear in her father's writings. There are moments when she sounds like her father, as when she expresses dismay over tracing patients' self-destructive behavior to underlying aggressive impulses or narcissistic injury. The certainty of such attributions, she suggests, leads only to clinical self-deception. Like her father, she embraces paradox, as when she tells a patient that while he was "not responsible for being the way he was, he was responsible for what he became."

Classical psychoanalysis remains wary of therapist self-disclosure, but Marsha Linehan has embraced it for dialectical behavior therapy. As Joan Wheelis describes DBT in a chapter published in *Textbook of Psychotherapeutic Treatments* (2009), there are two types of therapist self-disclosure: self-involving self-disclosures, in which the therapist reveals his or her feelings toward the patient (sometimes referred to as countertransference in psychoanalysis), and personal self-disclosures, which enable modeling of normative responses. Both types of therapist self-disclosure are appropriate within limits. Interestingly, the 68-year-old Linehan shocked the clinical world when she revealed in 2011 that she has struggled herself with borderline personality disorder since she was seventeen. "So many people have begged me to come forward," she told *New York Times* reporter Benedict Carey, "and I just thought—well, I have to do this. I owe it to them. I cannot die a coward." It is the kind of self-disclosure that Allen Wheelis might make, narrowing the distance between therapist and patient.

Joan Wheelis's contribution to contemporary psychotherapy is to find a way to integrate psychoanalysis with DBT. Invoking O'Neill's insight, she ends her article with a statement that would bring a smile to her parents. "Our patients come to us 'broken.' We do our best to help with the 'mending,' offering new ways to understand our behavior but we cannot assume that we are gods with all the answers. Humility is necessary whether we practice psychoanalysis or DBT; ultimately our goal is to discover what works to alleviate our patients' suffering when we can" (336). Or to repeat what Stanley Nichols says in *The Seeker*, much of the misery in life is actually or potentially remediable.

As close as Joan Wheelis was to her father, there are differences. Throughout her memoir lurks a nameless sorrow, but the sorrow is loss, not disillusionment. Allen Wheelis wrote to exorcise the demons that would imprison his soul; his daughter, by contrast, wrote to preserve her memories of her parents and share them with readers. The word "memoir" comes from the French, *mémoire*, and the Latin, *memoria*. *The Known, the Secret, the Forgotten* is a paean to memory—and a tribute to three people. Her father, she reminds us—not that we will forget—was always opposed to the falsification of human behavior. She remains true to his spirit. She worries near the end of her memoir that in opening the boxes in her parents' home after their deaths, she will let the genie out of the bottle and that something will be irrevocably lost. The genie turns out to be magical, transmuting perishable life into imperishable art.

Dying in Harness

We have art lest we perish from the truth, Nietzsche warned. Art inspired Allen Wheelis to express his inner doubts about psychoanalysis, reminding his colleagues that their profession was a work in progress. Many of his stories remain cautionary tales about how *not* to conduct verbal therapy. Wheelis practiced psychoanalysis to the end of his life, a few months short of his ninety-second birthday. After his death, his daughter had to telephone his patients to cancel their appointments. Ilse Wheelis died in 2012 at age ninety-six. Only a few months earlier she had reluctantly given up her practice. One can't recall many married couples who practiced psychoanalysis into their nineties. Both worked to live and lived to work, an ethic that also seems to be true of their daughter.

Jeffrey Berman. What was it like reading your father's books? Did you wonder about the differences between autobiography and art, truth and fiction? Were you able to separate your father from his fictional analysts?

Joan Wheelis. Reading my father's works was complicated. The first piece I read was the short story "The Illusionless Man & The Visionary Maid" when I was nine. The story came out in *Commentary* in 1964. I remember reading it without any thought that this was a parable about my parents until I was asked to play Noel, the daughter of the protagonist in John Korty's movie *Crazy-Quilt*. While filming there was a lot of talk about the characters, and I remember David Marquis, a family friend and San Francisco architect who played Dr. Milton Tugwell, saying to me

"So, you get to play yourself!" It felt thrilling and distressing especially as in the story Noel grows up to leave her loving family for an unsavory motorcycle rider named Falbuck Wheeling. It felt prophetic, and I recall writing a sequel to my father's story ensuring that Noel would preserve harmony with her parents.

Many times at a dinner party a guest would ask my father, "So, Allen, how much of your new book is autobiographical?" My father would smile, swing his long arm to the side, saying slowly and deliberately, "literary license, literary license."

At times it was hard to separate what was fact and what was fiction, and at times I didn't want to think about the distinction. His frequent refrain of literary license made that easier. When my father, however, gave me a draft of the novel *The Scheme of Things*, it was impossible to ignore that the character Abby was modeled on myself, and the dog, Barney, was the exact likeness of my beloved childhood dog, Monty. Yet my father was quick to tell me that the character Paul, who easily could have been based on a boyfriend of mine, was none other than Falbuck Wheeling coming back to take me away. So I read my father's work slipping back and forth between knowing and unknowing fact from fiction. As I mentioned in my memoir, half of *The Scheme of Things* was true, and the other half might as well have been.

JB. Why did you decide to write a memoir?

JW. After my mother died in 2012, the process of sorting through the belongings of my parents led me to discover their journals and letters and took me on a journey into their past as well as my own. I started to write about various experiences growing up with my son in mind as my audience. The vignettes that I wrote started to coalesce around themes of love and loss. Ten years after I wrote the first vignette, "The Last Cut," about cutting my father's hair, a memoir took shape as a kaleidoscope of reminiscence and reflection on my relationships with my parents.

JB. The act of writing often elicits insights or revelations that may not occur otherwise. Was this true when you wrote your memoir?

JW. The first piece I wrote, "The Last Cut," was therapeutic as it helped me take stock of my father's death. I wrote it as a tribute for my father and read it at his memorial in 2007. It also initiated a process of self-analysis as I revisited some of the vicissitudes of my relationships with my parents and my son in each vignette I wrote. Even deciding which vignette should follow another was a way of creating a new narrative distinct from the time line of my life. Like a dream where a vivid piece may stand out to send the dreamer into unexpected psychological excursions, writing the memoir seemed to offer me such opportunity to discover and reorganize what mattered. In the end it was reassuring.

Developing another narrative of my life felt liberating. Mortality felt less tethered to existential angst, allowing the telling of the story to create different structure for closure. Like the satisfaction to leave a house after a full and rich summer: fixing a broken step, storing kayaks and picnic tables, picking apples and pears to take back home, sweeping the deck, finding the missing sandal, pulling down the shades, locking the door. Everything satisfyingly in order with expectation, yet without certainty, that one will return again.

JB. How would you characterize dialectical behavior therapy?

JW. You describe DBT as "problem-solving, mindfulness (staying in the present), and dialectics (truth as an evolution of opposing views)." It might be more accurate, however, to describe DBT as an evidence-based, change-oriented treatment emphasizing behavioral contingencies and utilizing both Zen principle (including mindfulness) and a strategic/philosophical emphasis on dialectics (truth as evolving) to tolerate the constant tension of pressures pushing for change and acceptance.

My father often remarked to me that he thought he was more of a behaviorist than he had thought after I began studying DBT. His 1950 paper "The Place of Action in Personality Change" had a big impact on my interest in behaviorism. That paper, as well as *How People Change*, makes a very strong argument that change requires doing things differently and that too much emphasis had been put on insight without sufficient connection with the mechanism of change.

I feel that I have followed in my parents' footsteps becoming a psychiatrist and psychoanalyst, like both my parents, training analyst (like my mother), and now writer (like my father). My departure from them (and probably more so from my mother) occurs after insight in that I utilize DBT tools to effect change.

I think DBT, based on radical behaviorism, puts more emphasis on what is observable. While the psychosocial theory of DBT is still also a theory, it emphasizes affective deficit more than the assumption often made about the unconscious conflictual basis of problematic behavior (especially related to borderline personality disorder). The reductionistic determinism that can be harnessed to such constructs as the dynamic unconscious can create passivity and lack of accountability. As you know, my father made it a point of noting this in his keen interest in self-deception. Owen Renik, an old friend and teacher of mine when I was in Bob Wallerstein's Doctor of Mental Health program, was also very instrumental in speaking up about these issues. I became very interested in the notion of non-treatment treatments, self-disclosure, and irreducible subjectivity long before I became a psychoanalyst.

JB. Have I made other comments about your father that you would like to qualify?

JW. I don't agree with your comment that loving my mother was easy and my father more complicated. They both made it easy to love them, but with each came different burdens and challenges.

JB. Was it hard to write *The Known, the Secret, The Forgotten*? If so, which sections gave you the most difficulty?

JW. I think it was hardest to end the memoir. It was not a thorough journey through my life but rather a collection of bits and pieces. The last line of the memoir, "Or maybe not," refers to my musing as to whether my son might someday look at a photograph of me and see our physical similarity. He told me he found this last line abrupt. Of course it was. And arbitrary. I thought of how I have responded to the question—"when do you know an analysis is over?"—with, "when you understand it can go on forever." To end my book with another inquiry was in recognition of the timelessness of self-analysis and the liberating acceptance of leaving some questions unanswered.

JB. Has the publication of your memoir affected your patients' attitudes toward you? If so, has this been a problem? Is there a place for therapist self-disclosure in your clinical practice?

JW. Curiously, very few patients have made mention of my memoir. I'm always on the lookout for it in their associations, and sometimes I wonder if they are reluctant to bring it up. I have had no regrets in releasing it out into the world. Perhaps because it took so long to write, I had more than ample time to metabolize its content. With the reality of its publication, I asked myself if I would be comfortable with family, friends, colleagues, and patients reading it, and I was. I still am. And those who have read it report feeling reassured, rather than burdened by my self-disclosure.

JB. I think your father would have been intrigued by the title of your memoir, which not only preserves the mystery of character but also shows the ongoing tension between certainty and uncertainty, being and becoming, remembering and forgetting. Would you agree that *The Known, the Secret, The Forgotten* speaks to aspects of analytic discovery?

JW. Yes. I believe the psychoanalytic process of sorting through is both about being and becoming, which is being comfortable with change and not knowing, while searching for coordinates of what can be known and become meaningful. Being too certain takes one down the familiar roads with little discovery. No compass at all can lead one to being in the woods without light. Finding meaning requires enough comfort to explore the questions and enough discomfort to wrestle with ambiguous answers. The stories told and retold, forgotten and remembered, help that process to occur.

JB. You observe that "We create stories to live by" (7), which recalls the title of Joan Didion's 2006 collection of nonfiction: "We tell ourselves stories in order to live." Do you have other stories you're interested in telling?

JW. Yes. I am currently working on a book about my mother's Austrian parents, who perished in the Holocaust. Again I have an unusual treasure chest of letters and diaries dating to World War I as well as many of their belongings and my mother's stories. As I make this journey, I have discovered new family members and acquaintances enlarging the view into the lives of my grandparents. Looks like more to come on time, memory, and continued self-analysis!

Chapter 3

Listening to Nancy J. Chodorow

Nancy J. Chodorow is one of the few scholars and clinicians whose work has transformed both her academic discipline—sociology—and psychoanalysis. She remains at the top of the list of those who are responsible for the fruitful cross-fertilization of academic and clinical study. She has her roots in hybrid psychoanalytic traditions, combining the best of classical and contemporary approaches. Though she regards herself as a contrarian, I have never encountered another psychoanalytic theorist who is less contentious or defensive—which makes her writing a pleasure to read.

Born in New York City in 1944, Chodorow graduated from Radcliffe College in 1966 *summa cum laude*. She majored in social relations/social anthropology and studied with Beatrice and John W.M. Whiting, authors of the psycho-cultural study *Children of Six Cultures*. Reading Erik Erikson's *Childhood and Society* (1950) in college awakened her interest in psychoanalysis. Though she never took Erikson's popular course on identity and the life cycle, she participated as a graduate student in his seminar on "ritualization" that formed the basis of his Harvard Norton lectures. After attending the London School of Economics and Political Science and Harvard, Chodorow received her PhD in sociology from Brandeis University in 1975. Egon Bittner, the author of *The Functions of the Police in Modern Society* (1970), was her dissertation director and adviser. She also worked with Philip Slater, the author of *The Glory of Hera* (1968), a study of the mother-son relationship in Greek mythology and the Greek family, and the bestselling 1970 book *The Pursuit of Loneliness*. Slater told her, after reading her pro-seminar paper written during her first semester at Brandeis, that she would never understand personality if she devoted herself exclusively to conscious phenomena. Chodorow took the criticism to heart and used the pro-seminar paper as the basis for her first publication, "Being and Doing: A Cross-Cultural Examination of the Socialization of Males and Females" (1971).

Chodorow began her teaching career at Wellesley College in 1973 with a half-time instructorship while she was completing graduate school. Her post-PhD academic career began in 1974 at UC Santa Cruz, where she taught until 1986, when she left to teach at UC Berkeley. In the mid-1980s she began training at the San Francisco Psychoanalytic Institute, thus beginning a second career as an analyst. Chodorow retired in 2005 after thirty years of teaching. But "retired" is misleading, for she gave up her fulfilling life and work on the west coast to return to the east coast, where she continued her life's passion, combining psychoanalysis, sociology, and feminism. Chodorow is currently a part-time Lecturer in Psychiatry, Cambridge Health Alliance, Harvard Medical School, and Training and Supervising Analyst at the Boston Psychoanalytic Society and Institute.

Empirical proof is not a disciplinary requirement in the humanities, but it is in the social sciences, where psychoanalysis continues to be viewed with widespread skepticism. Throughout her long career, Chodorow has confronted her colleagues' intellectual wariness. Despite widespread recognition of her work, she remains, by her own admission, an outsider, like some of the analysts who have most influenced her, such as Erik Erikson.

Chodorow defined herself early on as a psychoanalytic sociologist and psychoanalytic feminist. An interdisciplinary approach enriches her scholarship, but it also left her exposed to criticism, partly because of the inherent tensions among psychoanalysis, feminism, and sociology; partly because she was a trail-blazer, confronting vexing questions that are still unresolved; and partly because the ideological middle is often the most dangerous place in fierce intellectual battles.

The Reproduction of Mothering

Few scholarly books, particularly an author's first book, begin with a two-word sentence. But Chodorow's 1978 book, *The Reproduction of Mothering: Psychoanalysis and the Sociology of Gender*, based closely on her 1974 doctoral dissertation, does. "Women mother." It is both a truism and a scholarly battle cry to which she has devoted her entire career.

What's striking about the book is that it is a bold yet nuanced study that changes our thinking of the ways in which mothering is reproduced across generations. Others have studied mothering; Chodorow explores its profound gender implications. It's no accident that the last word of the book is "mother," conveying the tight thematic unity of the work.

Trained as a sociologist, Chodorow was taught to question assumptions that invoke biology to explain social forces. Though she had not yet started her psychoanalytic training when she was in graduate school, nor had yet become a mother herself, she used Freudian theory to analyze family structure. She carefully balances a commitment to psychoanalysis with the need for reform. "Psychoanalytic theory remains the most coherent, convincing theory of personality development available for an understanding of fundamental aspects of the psychology of women in our society, in spite of its biases" (142). Patriarchal biases, she persuasively shows in *The Reproduction of Mothering*, suffuse Freud's—and his followers'—theorizing on female psychology. She offers example after example of how psychoanalytic theorists have implied that the pre-Oedipal development of girls is somehow inferior to that of boys. Implicit throughout this early book is the belief that we do Freud a disservice if we accept his claims unquestioningly, invoking the creator's name as if he were the source of all psychological truth: "As Freud himself said." She now uses the expression "Freud *ipse*" to describe these unsubstantiated assertions.

An indefatigable researcher, Chodorow appears to have read nearly everything published on the subject. She ranges effortlessly through the entirety of Freud's voluminous writings, citing him either in agreement or in disagreement. She is also aware of the vast commentary on Freud. She has read carefully the writings of "orthodox" Freudians such as Ruth Mack Brunswick, Helene Deutsch, Anna Freud, Phyllis Greenacre, and Jeanne Lampl-de Groot; past "dissidents" such as Erich Fromm, Karen Horney, Melanie Klein, Clara Thompson, and John Bowlby; and more recent dissidents including Robert Stoller and Janine Chasseguet-Smirgel. She is equally conversant with the academic world, including the Frankfurt Institute theorists such as Jürgen Habermas and Max Horkheimer. She quotes the writings of her mentor George Goethals, whose Harvard course on British object relations theory she sat in on while she was a Brandeis graduate student. Additionally, she refers to canonical feminist writers such as Adrienne Rich and Anne Sexton, quoting apposite lines from Sexton's 1962 poem "Housewife": "A woman is her mother / That's the main thing" (*The Reproduction of Mothering* 191). Chodorow engages in scholarly dialogue with all of these authors; her synthetic and inclusionary imagination is always evident.

Tellingly, although Chodorow evolved into what she calls an "intersubjective ego psychology" theorist, this was not her psychoanalytic orientation at the beginning of her career. Ego psychology was the dominant form of mid-twentieth-century American psychoanalysis. Regarded as the second historical stage of psychoanalysis, after "id psychology," ego psychology reveals the ways in which inborn sexual and aggressive drives adapt to or are mediated by the social and physical world. She doesn't deny in *The Reproduction of Mothering* that ego psychology has deepened our understanding of conscious and unconscious behavior, but she agrees with Roy Schafer's conclusion that ego psychology cannot explain conflicting and ambivalent motivations. Some analysts later felt that classical ego psychology was a "straitjacket." Schafer (1922–2018) began his psychoanalytic career as an ego psychologist, authoring books such as *Aspects of Internalization* (1968), but he later became known for his use of storytelling in analysis, emphasizing the role of multiple perspectives.

Chodorow's initial psychoanalytic approach was object relations theory, the formation of internal relationships through identification and introjection of the external world. Aware of the disturbingly impersonal connotations of the term, she reminds readers that "objects" are people or real or symbolic aspects of people. Psychoanalysis at the time did not have an adequate understanding of the social and relational nature of object relations. How does a child form internal representations? How are these internal representations gendered? These questions have catalyzed Chodorow's scholarship.

Chodorow's training as a social scientist shaped her commitment to those aspects of psychoanalysis that remain close to clinical and empirical experience. She must have felt like she was walking on a tightrope, poised precariously between fellow academic scholars, particularly feminists, on the one hand, who were skeptical of if not hostile to Freud's claims of universalizing essentialist theories of human development, and psychoanalytic theorists and clinicians, on the other hand, most of whom were largely unaware of the social sciences. But even doing Freudian scholarship, independent of the academic community, can feel like entering a battle. The tempestuous history of psychoanalysis is a chronicle of internal purges and excommunications; ideological purity has demanded unquestioning loyalty to Freud. This has complicated a researcher's struggle to capture elusive truths. Chodorow notes that Stoller's work has not been received kindly by the psychoanalytic community. "Stoller explicitly rejects some of Freud's basic claims, whereas analysts generally tend to search diligently to show that whatever reformulation they are engaged in is really based in some passage, article, or footnote of Freud's. This forthrightness may have hurt Stoller's cause" (154). And Chodorow's too. Early in her career, her articles were rejected by the dominant journals in the field as "not psychoanalysis," an accusation that was even made of Erikson, considered by many orthodox analysts as iconoclastic. Stoller, I should point out, promoted a stigmatizing model of transgender sexuality that was repudiated by later gender theorists.

Chodorow's own forthrightness is always apparent. She never shrinks from controversy, but she doesn't revel in it for its own sake. Nor does she imprison herself in either/or positions. She values, for example, Juliet Mitchell's efforts to convince feminists to take psychoanalysis seriously, but she laments Mitchell's zealous defense of all of Freud's claims: "she often seems another apologist for Freud's misogyny and patriarchal distortions" (141). Throughout *The Reproduction of Mothering* Chodorow elaborates on Freud's androcentric assumptions, criticizing him for his belief that women have less fully developed superegos than men and reminding us that, contrary to what Freud thought, passivity, masochism, and narcissism appear in both sexes.

Chodorow announces her thesis early in *The Reproduction of Mothering*. "Women, as mothers, produce daughters with mothering capacities and the desire to mother. These capacities and needs are built into and grow out of the mother-daughter relationship itself. By contrast, women as mothers (and men as not-mothers) produce sons whose nurturant capacities and needs have been systematically curtailed and repressed" (7). As with any beguilingly simple thesis, the devil lies in the details. Few doubt that social and psychological (as well as political and economic) forces contribute to the reproduction of mothering, but Chodorow emphasizes pre-Oedipal influences neglected by the early Freudians. Until Chodorow, psychoanalysis lacked an adequate theory of mothering. Her research attempts to fill in that gap. Central to her thinking is that the most salient feature of development is the child's *relation* to others. This has been a lifelong theme in Chodorow's work, no doubt influenced by her own gender, though she doesn't comment on that directly in her book.

Chodorow maintains that there is a fundamental asymmetry in reproduction. "Men are socially and psychologically reproduced by women, but women are reproduced (or not) largely by themselves" (36). Because they are of the same gender, mothers do not experience infant daughters as separate as they experience infant sons. Mothers are thus more likely to experience oneness and continuity with their daughters than with their sons. Early pre-Oedipal attachment differences produce marked differences in childhood. The feminine sense of self is "connected to the world," while the masculine sense is "separate" (169). Chodorow remains attuned to the ambiguities and ambivalences of gender. A daughter is closer to her mother than her father, yet her father "provides a last ditch escape from maternal omnipotence," so she cannot drive him away (195). The father's distance from his daughter and his authority complicate their relationship.

Countless scholars have critiqued Freud's flawed pronouncements on female psychology, but Chodorow makes an astute observation I have never seen before. In one of his most misogynistic remarks, Freud claims in his 1914 essay "On Narcissism" that "Complete object-love of the attachment type is, properly speaking, characteristic of the male" (*SE* 14: 88). By contrast, Freud believed that women love narcissistically; the only time they attain true object love is in relation to their children. "Freud's stance here," Chodorow observes shrewdly, "seems to be that of the excluded man viewing women's potential psychological self-sufficiency vis-à-vis *men*" (202).

Chodorow has much to say about penis envy, Freud's most notorious concept. After discussing the vexed history of debate on the subject, including where individual analysts, male and female, have staked their ideological positions, Chodorow, to her fellow sociologists' and feminists' consternation, appears to endorse the concept, at least on a metaphorical level. "The penis, or phallus, is a symbol of power or omnipotence, whether you have one as a sexual organ (as a male) or as a sexual object (as her mother 'possesses' her father's)" (123). She concludes that girls develop penis envy "for many overdetermined reasons" and then elaborates:

> because they cannot otherwise win their heterosexual mother; because of exhibitionistic desires; because the penis symbolizes independence from the (internalized) powerful mother; as a defense against fantasies of acting on sexual desires for their father and anxiety at the possible consequence of this; because they have received either conscious or unconscious communication from their parents that penises (or being male) are better, or sensed maternal conflict about the mother's own genitals;

and because the penis symbolizes the social privileges of their father and men. (164–165)

As Chodorow implies in an asterisked comment in *The Reproduction of Mothering*, she was not pleased defending a psychoanalytic concept that has horrified fellow feminists. After noting Phyllis Greenacre's assertion that the fantasy of the phallic woman serves to deny, unconsciously, the lack of a penis, Chodorow admits, "I realize that this kind of claim verges on the incredible to those unpersuaded by psychoanalytic theory. It is certainly the area in psychoanalytic theory in which I feel least comfortable, but in this case Greenacre's account is persuasive and illuminating" (107).

One of Chodorow's scholarly strengths is her open-mindedness, often most apparent in her scholarly footnotes, fascinating treasure troves. The footnotes reveal her personal side, often wry, ironic, and mildly mocking, as when she is not sure about the validity of a particular truth claim. Sympathetic to theorists like John Bowlby and Rene Spitz who argue for the importance of mothers, she points out in an asterisk that they were "probably also riding the tide of the feminine mystique and the attempt to return Rosie the Riveter to her home" (75). She admits in another asterisk to "fudging" about the contributory effect of a mother's sexual orientation to parenting (110).

Other times Chodorow's footnotes reveal her incredulity in the face of dubious academic claims. Commenting on two researchers, Eleanor Maccoby and Carol Jacklin, who, looking at the "hard scientific facts," report no consistent gender differences in the first four or five years of children's interactions with their parents, Chodorow responds dryly to the prestidigitatorial act: "I was left feeling a little as if a magic disappearing trick had been performed. All the experiences of being manipulated, channeled, and restricted which women and men have been commenting on, and which they have felt deeply and continuously, were suddenly figments of our imagination" (98).

A Firestorm of Controversy

The Reproduction of Mothering was immediately recognized as a classic, providing a new feminist-psychoanalytic theory of child development. In a retrospective review published in 1996 in *Contemporary Sociology*, which had favorably reviewed the book in 1979, Barbara Laslett hailed *The Repro-*

duction of Mothering as a "major intellectual event in the emerging field of feminist scholarship and in social theory. Its original success reflected, in part, the desires of feminists to find a grand theory that could address the normative questions with which they were so concerned—women's subjectivity, sexuality, and constructions of self in the contexts of gender inequalities" (305–306). Laslett praised the book for providing a way to show the links between individual agents and larger social structures, not by relying on impersonal forces, but by calling attention to the power of feelings and family relationships. Laslett observed, however, that sociologists and feminists immediately pilloried Chodorow's study: it was a book that "sociologists loved to hate" (307).

And feminists too. It is difficult to fathom the firestorm of controversy surrounding the publication of *The Reproduction of Mothering*, as Chodorow admits in her next book, *Feminism and Psychoanalytic Theory*. "I have been criticized by sociologists for being ungrounded empirically and individualistic theoretically, for not understanding societal determinism, and for underestimating the force of social reality. At the same time, I have been criticized by Lacanian psychoanalytic feminists for the opposite, for being empiricist and socially determinist and for seeing the unconscious as a sociological phenomenon rather than an analytically irreducible and unique register of being and level of analysis" (18).

The most acrimonious review was by the sociologist Pauline Bart, who poured contempt on every aspect of the book, accusing Chodorow of mother-blaming, heterosexual bias, flawed scientific methodology, and the oppression of women. Bart appears to be an early conspiracy theorist, discrediting the feminist award Chodorow's book received from the American Sociological Association. "The patriarchy has additionally rewarded Chodorow with a coveted fellowship to the Institute for Advanced Study in the Behavioral Sciences in Palo Alto" (148). All of these accusations and innuendos are untrue, but they must have nevertheless stung Chodorow. Bart ends her review with a chilling sentence. "The rehabilitation of psychoanalytic theories in the women's movement here and in Britain and France makes my blood run cold" (152).

Other feminist critics were less vituperative. In the same edited volume, *Mothering*, in which Pauline Bart's essay appeared, Iris Marion Young argued that Chodorow's effort to explain male domination as arising from gender differentiation is "to overpsychologize the social phenomena of male domination" (135). By contrast, the feminist-psychoanalytic literary critic Coppélia Kahn praised Chodorow's discussion for recasting a Freudian "bugaboo which has justifiably angered many feminists and regrettably alienated them from psychoanalysis" (75).

Chodorow had anticipated some of these criticisms in the afterword to *The Reproduction of Mothering*, in which she makes an unusual statement that is not a disclaimer but rather a qualification:

> Some friends and colleagues have said that my account is too unqualified. In fact, *all* women *do not* mother or want to mother, and *all* women are not "maternal" or nurturant. *Some* women are far more nurturant than others, and want children far more. Some *men* are more nurturant than some women. I agree that all claims about gender differences gloss over important differences within genders and similarities between genders. I hope that this book leads people to raise questions about such variations, and to engage in the research that will begin to answer them. (215)

As a rhetorical strategy, it's always effective to anticipate and thus weaken your opponents' criticisms. But beyond this, Chodorow strikes her readers as unusually thoughtful and conscientious throughout the book, capable of seeing a subject from multiple points of view. She confesses in her extensive acknowledgments that "I did not always learn well" (viii) from the colleagues and friends who read the book before its publication, one of the few statements with which present readers will disagree.

The best a "controversial" author can do is to acknowledge anticipated (or subsequent) criticisms and persist, avoiding the temptations of becoming either ideologically rigid or thin-skinned—or giving up scholarship altogether. Recall Wheelis's observation in *The Quest for Identity* that the analyst's disillusionment can lead to antithetical responses, escape into orthodoxy or retreat into cynical counter-dogma. All of Chodorow's writings herald the call for increased dialogue and understanding. Either/ or gives way to both/and, finding nuggets of truth in otherwise competing ideologies and methodologies.

Along with her other books, *The Reproduction of Mothering* has had a strong influence on academics in other disciplines, including literary studies. Chodorow's book is one of the most cited psychoanalytic texts in the humanities. I quote the book in several of my own writings. In *Narcissism and the Novel* (1990), I refer to one of Chodorow's central observations about motherhood: "[it] may be a (fantasied) attempt to make reparation to a mother's own mother for the injuries she did (also in fantasy) to her mother's children (her siblings). Alternatively, it may be a way to get back at her mother for (fantasied) injuries done by her mother to her" (90). The insight illuminates Dickens's *Great Expectations*, where both motives, reparation and revenge, characterize Estella's ambivalent relationship to her cruel adoptive mother, Miss Havisham. In *Diaries to an English Professor* (1994), I refer to Chodorow's coauthored essay with Susan Contratto, "The Fantasy of the Perfect Mother," in which they discuss how idealization and blaming the mother are twin sides of the same belief in the perfect, all-powerful mother. I've often seen a variation of this belief in my students' writings: the wish to be a "perfect child" results in inevitable guilt when perfection becomes impossible. And in *Risky Writing* (2001), I agree with Chodorow's criticism that Clifford Geertz's rejection of empathy as "ethnographic sentimentalism" forces him to the conclusion that, in her own words, the "native's inner life does not exist, for the anthropologist or perhaps for the natives either" (*The Power of Feelings* 148).

Groundbreaking, *The Reproduction of Mothering* represented a new direction in psychoanalytic thinking. In 1996, the journal *Contemporary Sociology* chose *The Reproduction of Mothering* as one of the "Ten Most Influential Books of the Past Twenty-five Years." She has received many honors and awards from both psychoanalytic and non-psychoanalytic organizations.

Feminism and Psychoanalytic Theory

Authors seldom offer extended critiques of their earlier writings, but Chodorow is the exception. She acknowledges in *Feminism and Psycho-analytic Theory* (1989) two global shifts in her general view of feminist theory. First, although she implied in *The Reproduction of Mothering* that women's mothering is *the* cause of male dominance, she now recognizes the existence of other causes, the "polyvocality we find in women's accounts of their lives and situations" (6). Second, she is now interested in psychoanalysis for its own sake rather than as an adjunct to understanding social or cultural organization. "I am more convinced even than I was during an earlier period that psychoanalysis describes a significant level of reality that is not reducible to, or in the last instance caused by, social or cultural organization" (7).

Despite the fact that eight of the ten chapters in *Feminism and Psychoanalytic Theory* were published earlier, a strategy Chodorow uses in all of her subsequent books, the work has a tight thematic focus, with little repetition. Chodorow reveals that she would have likely become a Marxist feminist had she believed gender inequality was mainly caused by a capitalist-patriarchal society. She also admits that she has become passionately "hooked on" psychoanalytic theory (8), an intellectual love she knows fellow academics and feminists will neither understand nor appreciate. Like any lifelong love affair, it has not been a conflict-free union. Moreover, over time she has loved psychoanalysis for different reasons.

Chodorow implicitly accepts in *The Reproduction of Mothering* Freud's drive (or libido) theory, the belief in psychic charges of energy, or cathexis; but she is now skeptical of drive theory in *Feminism and Psychoanalytic Theory*, critiquing its use by two influential neo-Freudian mavericks, Herbert Marcuse and Norman O. Brown. "They assume not only that drive theory is the revolutionary truth of psychoanalysis, but also that drives are needs, and that these needs are authentic and legitimate, and deserve to be fully satisfied" (117). Chodorow's critique proved prescient. As Paul Mosher noted in the 1998 article "Frequency of Word Use as Indicator of Evolution of Psychoanalytic Thought," the word "libido" has declined steadily in the major psychoanalytic journals. In volume 1 of *Off the Tracks: Cautionary Tales about the Derailing of Mental Health Care*, Mosher and I cite Joseph Schachter's wry observation about the stormy history of psychoanalysis: "discarded theories—like old generals—didn't die, they just faded away" (417).

Chodorow doesn't mention intersubjectivity in *The Reproduction of Mothering*—the word doesn't even appear in the index—but it does appear in *Feminism and Psychoanalytic Theory*, where she implies that it is central to any social or political vision. Intersubjectivity, which is related to but not identical with relational psychoanalysis, becomes increasingly important to her—and another reason for her criticisms of Marcuse and Brown, both of whom have an arelational vision. Chodorow widens her critique in *Feminism and Psychoanalytic Theory* to include fellow feminists who believe that the central arena of gender oppression has moved from the family to the public and social realms. She is convinced that the crucial aspects of gender politics—abortion, marriage, divorce, and parenting—remain the personal and familial, a belief that helps explain the decision to give up academic teaching for clinical practice.

Feminism and Psychoanalytic Theory offers a trenchant early critique of Lacanian feminism at a time when the French analyst's theories were hegemonic in the academy. Referring to the Lacanian belief that there is no subjectivity outside the phallus, Chodorow observes, "Such a theory locates every action firmly in an unequal sexual world and never loses sight of our developmentally inevitable placement in a phallocentric culture" (189). Chodorow takes issue with Lacan's antihumanistic account of a fragmented, alienated subject, a view she rightly points out goes against most of the assumptions of American psychoanalysts. Chodorow's commitment to experiential evidence can be seen in all her writings, and for that reason she is suspicious of any ideological system that denies the empirical world or human agency. Chodorow's relational and intersubjective model of psychoanalysis offers a more persuasive model than the antihumanistic, posthuman one in my own field of psychoanalytic literary criticism, where for decades, as Lisa Ruddick points out in an illuminating chapter of *The Cambridge Companion to Literature and Psychoanalysis* (2022), the preferred bias has been that of a fragmented, discontinuous subjectivity.

"Seventies Questions for Thirties Women"

The most intriguing chapter in *Feminism and Psychoanalytic Theory* is the last one, "Seventies Questions for Thirties Women: Gender and Generation in a Study of Early Psychoanalysts"—Chodorow's chapters often have catchy titles. Central to the chapter is the paradoxical observation that although Freudian theory devalues females, psychoanalysis reveals, from the beginning of its history, many prominent women who have made noteworthy theoretical and clinical contributions. Other writers, such as Paul Roazen in *Freud and His Followers*, have remarked on this paradox, but Chodorow's own contribution to understanding this phenomenon was her interviews with eighty women, forty-four of whom were psychoanalysts trained in the 1920s through the mid-1940s, in the United States, Great Britain, and the Netherlands. The interviewed psychoanalysts represented a wide variety of theoretical positions.

"Lurking in my unconscious," Chodorow admits in a footnote, "was probably a romanticized image of the reproduction of professional mothers" (268 n. 4). The chapter is fascinating partly because of, as she self-mockingly declares, her unresolved positive transference to her research subjects. Chodorow doesn't usually write as a participant-observer, but in this chapter she sustains a lively contrast between interviewer, the hyper-gender-sensitive 1970s feminist, and interviewees, the relatively gender-blind 1930s women. As a second-wave feminist, Chodorow wanted her research subjects, most of whom were her mother's generation, to hold the same views of gender that she did, but to her surprise and dismay, they did not think gender was salient in their lives. Another researcher, one who was listening *for* confirmation of her own views, might have recast her findings to support her anticipated conclusion; but Chodorow, listening *to* her subjects, acknowledged her astonishment, thus demonstrating her receptiveness to new ideas.

The contrast between listening for and listening to appears in several of Chodorow's writings. In a 2005 interview conducted by Paul H. Elovitz and Bob Lentz and published in the psychohistorical journal *Clio's Psyche*, she divides analysts into two groups. "Those who 'listen for' are more theory-driven—I'm thinking of the Kleinians, the Kohutians, the Lacanians, the close-process ego psychologists. As you read them or hear them present, there's often the sense that they know, are even looking for, what they're going to find. Their theory guides what they hear." By contrast, those who listen to "seem to range more freely across theories and to focus with a more open ear and mind on the particularity of the particular patient, and perhaps that the patient at different times can be best understood by different theories" (142). Chodorow, though always a theorist, clearly belongs to the latter group, a listening-to analyst who is not afraid to hear the unexpected. Always acknowledging her sources, Chodorow points out in her interview with Elovitz and Lentz that the French analyst Haydée Faimberg invented the term "listening to listening."

There were many reasons for the female analysts' lack of gender-consciousness, beginning with the fact that most of them did not view their professional success in terms of being women. Critical of contemporary feminists who disparaged women's maternality, they were not predisposed to think much about the positive implications of gender. Many of the interviewees engaged in the (ego psychology) strategy of splitting, separating their private lives as women from their public careers as analysts. They viewed the psychoanalytic theory of female development as relevant to their patients' lives, not their own. Nor did they perceive much discrimination in their professional lives apart from the anti-women bias in most medical schools at that time. Nor is it clear, Chodorow adds, whether her interviewees gave their female patients patriarchal advice.

"One told about a miserable woman painter with a two-year-old who was staying home full-time with her child: 'I said why don't you paint *and* be a mother?' And I never saw her again after I made that suggestion" (214).

Chodorow's counterintuitive conclusion in the chapter is that gender simply did not resonate in her interviewees' lives as it did in her own. "Only with this recognition, that the salience and meaning of gender were products of one's time and place, could I come to understand gender within the fabric of my interviewees' lives" (217). Chodorow succeeds in the chapter, indeed, throughout the book, in allowing female voices to be heard and appreciated. She also succeeds in showing the productive tensions that arise in all scholarship.

"Ms. Chodorow is an exceptionally intelligent and serious writer, and her contribution to the debate on gender and sexual identity is substantial," Stuart Schneiderman enthused in his *New York Times* review of *Feminism and Psychoanalytic Theory*. Schneiderman's only criticism is that Chodorow never addresses the issue of the Oedipus complex and its relationship to sexual identity, particularly the father's prohibition against incest with the mother. Oddly, Schneiderman doesn't mention in the review that he is a Lacanian analyst, which explains why he is miffed by Chodorow's pene-trating criticisms of Lacanian theory. A curious aside: Schneiderman, who studied psychoanalysis with Lacan in Paris, practiced for three decades in New York City, but he has now become, according to his website, a life coach. Why the change? "He did it because many of his clients did not want to get into their minds. They wanted to engage more productively in their lives." They wanted, in short, not interpretation but guidance.

Femininities, Masculinities, Sexualities

Chodorow's next book, *Femininities, Masculinities, Sexualities: Freud and Beyond* (1994), grew out of the 1990 Blazer Lectures at the University of Kentucky. The slender volume challenged the prevailing homophobia that existed within the American Psychoanalytic Association at the time. Confronted with an anti-discrimination lawsuit in 1991, the American Psychoanalytic Association reluctantly allowed for the training of gay and lesbian analysts. (By contrast, the American Psychiatric Association decided in 1973 to eliminate the homosexuality diagnosis from its handbook, the *Diagnostic and Statistical Manual of Mental Disorders*.) Throughout the book Chodorow urges an openness and tolerance of gender and sexual differences, cautioning us to beware of essentializing generalizations.

Chodorow makes several notable observations. In chapter 1, "Rethinking Freud on Women," she states that many daughters do not completely give up their attachment to their mothers, often carrying it over to their attachment to their fathers and husbands. She then likens the female Oedipus complex to the mythic character Persephone, ripped from but always maintaining a connection to her mother, Demeter. Implying that Freud's theory of mourning is inadequate—many choose not to forget about the lost love object, as Freud recommends in "Mourning and Melancholia"—Chodorow remarks that nowhere in his writings do we see mention of Demeter, the mother who loves the daughter for whom she continues to grieve.

In chapter 2, "Heterosexuality as a Compromise Formation," Chodorow questions why psychoanalysts "normalize" heterosexuality but not homosexuality. Demonstrating her love for literature, she has an effective literary answer to the psychoanalytic tendency to assume that heterosexuality is less intense and more diffuse than other sexualities. "Many heterosexuals would not agree, nor does what we learn from clinical experience, literature, or our own and our acquaintances' lives. What would we make, in this view, of such compelled lovers from literature as Tristan and Isolde, Antony and Cleopatra, Anna and Vronsky, Heathcliff and Cathy, Othello, Gabriel Garcia Marquez's Florentino Ariza?" (63).

The final chapter, "Individuality and Difference in How Women and Men Love," affirms that "men and women love in as many ways as there are men and women" (71), a statement that runs counter to the universal claims of most psychoanalysts. Chodorow calls for increased sensitivity to psychological variety and complexity as well as greater cross-cultural knowledge. She ends hopefully: "Psychoanalysts have nearly unique access to many people's sexual fantasies, identities, and practices. We should use this access to help us fully understand gender and sexuality in all their forms" (92).

The Power of Feelings

The Power of Feelings: Personal Meaning in Psychoanalysis, Gender, and Culture (1999) is an ambitious book. Chodorow has two major concerns, as she announces in the introduction. First, meaning is always a combination of the "sociocultural and historically contextualized on the one hand and the personally psychodynamic and psychobiographically contextualized on the other" (2). Second, she seeks to show how the uniqueness of each person is part of a larger story that demonstrates how the psyche functions in all people.

Chodorow's longest book, at 328 pages, *The Power of Feelings* champions the work of the mid-twentieth-century analysts Erik Erikson and Hans Loewald, both of whom have influenced her own psychoanalytic thinking. Chodorow also lauds contemporary analysts: Jessica Benjamin, Christopher Bollas, Stephen Mitchell, and Thomas Ogden. She continues her critique of Lacanian theory; modifies her view of penis envy, which "may or may not be central" to women's sense of gender (107); formulates a provocative concept of "weeping for the mother" (121) that helps to account for women's intense guilt growing up in patriarchal families; and highlights the commonalities between anthropological ethnography and psychoanalysis.

The Power of Feelings abounds in insights, but I want to focus on two moments in the study: how a patient acknowledges or fails to acknowledge the help he receives in writing a book, and how Chodorow expresses gratitude toward others in her *own* books, including indebtedness to a deceased colleague with whom she often disagreed.

Chodorow's case history in *The Power of Feelings* of an academic researcher who could not convey his beholdenness to others piqued my interest:

> Writing the acknowledgments for his now completed book is extremely time-consuming and difficult, because it forces him to make clear what he has previously obscured from himself, especially how many people he has made demands on and what fundamental needs friends have fulfilled for him: they have provided him with meals for days and weeks at a time, and when he does not have an invitation, he subsists on fast food and take-out meals. When he gets an advance copy of his book, he has a small gathering to thank all his friends for their help, and he displays the book. It contains no acknowledgments, and he realizes that he never submitted them to his publisher. He has somehow stashed them away in a lower desk drawer. (28)

I don't know whether Chodorow was thinking about the differences between her patient and herself when she wrote about this case study, but she goes out of her way in every book to thank those who have helped her. Indeed, it would be hard to find another scholar whose acknowledgments in book after book are richer or fuller than Chodorow's. Her expressions of gratitude are always extensive, generous, and heartfelt. "Personal gratitude warrants a volume in itself," she writes in her most recent book, *The Psychoanalytic Ear and the Sociological Eye* (xxiv), and she gives us a four-page account of her personal and professional beholdenness.

Gratitude remains an undertheorized subject in psychoanalysis, but it is a relational issue, a relationship between a benefactor and beneficiary. Both Nietzsche and Freud believed that the benefactor-beneficiary relationship betrays an unconscious battle for power and control, a struggle fraught with resentment and aggression. "The powerful man feels gratitude for the following reason," Nietzsche opines in *Human, All Too Human*: "through his good deed, his benefactor has, as it were, violated the powerful man's sphere and penetrated it. Now through his act of gratitude the powerful man requites himself by violating the sphere of the benefactor. It is a milder form of revenge" (46). Freud publicly expressed his gratitude toward his older colleague, Josef Breuer, with whom he coauthored *Studies on Hysteria* (1895); but privately Freud admitted his ambivalence toward Breuer, who loaned him money and then generously forgave the debt. "Recently Breuer pulled another brilliant stunt," Freud complained to Wilhelm Fliess on January 16, 1898. "It is enough to make one extremely ungrateful for good deeds" (*Complete Letters of Sigmund Freud to Wilhelm Fliess* 294). One need not agree with Nietzsche and Freud's cynical view of gratitude to realize that it is sometimes challenging to express beholdenness toward others, especially those with whom one has disagreed and who are no longer alive. The ancient taboo, speak no ill of the dead, persists, perhaps because of the fear that the spoken words will come back to haunt the speaker.

The most revelatory chapter in *The Power of Feelings* is "Selves and Emotions as Personal and Cultural Constructions." Chodorow speaks about her colleague and friend Michelle Z. Rosaldo, who died in 1981 at age thirty-seven from an accidental fall while engaged in research on the Ilongot people in the Philippines. Along with her husband, the anthropologist Renato Rosaldo, Michelle Rosaldo was one of the brilliant young stars in her field, as Chodorow was, but for different reasons. Rosaldo, who attended Radcliffe with Chodorow, cofounded the Program in Feminist Studies at Stanford and authored the 1980 book *Knowledge and Passion: Ilongot Notions of Self and Social Life*. Viewed as the scholar who created (and named) the anthropology of self and feeling, as well as established the ethnographic linguistics pragmatics approach, Rosaldo maintained, contrary to Chodorow, that affects were cultural expressions rather than subjective emotions or feelings. Rosaldo's approach, explicitly culturally determinant and anti-psychological, could not have been more different from Chodorow's.

Because the two feminist scholars had sharply different views of subjectivity, writing about her deceased colleague and friend awakens conflicted feelings in Chodorow. "Shelly was one of my closest friends and certainly my most clear-eyed critic" (151). Until she began writing *The Power of Feelings*, Chodorow had admired Rosaldo's book but had not fully appreciated its importance. "I was (and am) ambivalent about putting forth a critique of Shelly's work, but her own relentless honesty about intellectual matters would make my avoiding disagreement specious and inauthentic" (151). Chodorow's own intellectual honesty is no less relentless. Writing about Rosaldo involves for Chodorow an "ongoing work of mourning, perhaps—as I continue a conversation and debate that began in our undergraduate days and took specific form in a study group in which we read many of the works . . . that furthered each of our understandings of selves, feelings, and culture but led us in very different directions before her death" (151).

Complicating Chodorow's situation of writing about Michelle Rosaldo was that her husband was still alive. Feelings are feelings, as the old adage goes, but how does one comment in print on the feelings of a widower who, denying the subjective experience of emotions, nonetheless expresses devastation over his wife's death? Chodorow offers a sensitive critique of Renato Rosaldo's article "Grief and a Headhunter's Rage," originally published in 1984 and reprinted in his 1989 book *Culture and Truth: The Remaking of Social Analysis*. Renato Rosaldo compares the grief he experienced arising from his wife's death to the rage of Ilongot men who discharge their anger through headhunting. Because of what she evocatively refers to as the "leakiness of case studies," Chodorow calls attention to the power of Renato Rosaldo's emotions as he conveys heartbreak following his wife's death. "Emotion is a question of personal force as well as cultural meaning," Chodorow reminds us. "By experiencing his own grief, Rosaldo finds that he can understand Ilongot grief" (170). Chodorow takes no satisfaction in showing how Renato Rosaldo betrays intense emotion, which ironically demonstrates the limitations of his and his wife's emotion-as-discourse anthropological approach. She quietly indicates in a footnote that "after his powerful account, Rosaldo himself returned to a more exclusive cultural determinism in the rest of his book" (289 n. 15).

Chodorow's ongoing work of mourning demonstrates the power of feelings, the apt title of her book. *The Power of Feelings* underscores Chodorow's inclination to acknowledge as fully as possible her indebtedness to the many colleagues and friends, living and dead, who helped her—unlike her narcissistic patient, who can only display his book without thanking the people who played a role in its birth. Chodorow ends *The Power of Feelings* by disagreeing with postmodern and poststructural claims that selfhood and identity are merely illusions and that psyches are always split. She argues, by contrast, for psychic health and wholeness, a conclusion that she shows, through her insight and empathy, remains within the realm of possibility.

Individualizing Gender and Sexuality

Published in 2012, *Individualizing Gender and Sexuality: Theory and Practice* consists of eleven chapters that were originally presented at conferences or published in edited volumes between 1999 and 2005. Chodorow addresses old topics, such as commenting on earlier books, and new topics, such as celebrating the work of the pioneering intersubjective analyst Stephen Mitchell, whose sudden death in 2000 at age fifty-four saddened the psychoanalytic community. As with her preceding books, *Individualizing Gender and Sexuality* highlights the evolution of her thinking, including her movement toward intersubjective ego psychology.

The opening chapter, "Psychoanalysis and Women from Margin to Center: A Retrospect," is the most self-disclosing. Chodorow concedes that, until the 1990s, she did not write from a female experiential voice. She describes in a footnote her essay "Born into a World at War: Listening for Affect and Personal Meaning," first published in *American Imago* in 2002, in which she discusses her Jewish family's move when she was three from New York City to a "still traditionally Western, semirural pre-Silicon Valley, emphatically not Jewish," near San Francisco (4 n. 4). Presenting a paper to a group of feminist English faculty in the Boston area in 1972, she was accused of being too confident, "writing like a man" (5), an accusation that shocked her at the time. "My voice echoes, perhaps, those no-nonsense, speak-your-mind, mid-western and western pioneer lineage women with whom I grew up, or my Jewish New Yorker mother and aunts, all of whom had been professionals" (5). She then explains how, like others of her generation, she evaluated psychoanalytic theories of feminism against her own personal experience.

Chodorow refers briefly to her parents and upbringing in a number of her writings, including in the interview with Elovitz and Lentz. She always speaks positively about her childhood and adolescence, which spared her from the Sturm und Drang that can be seen in those who have rejected their past. Her mother, Leah (Turitz) Chodorow, was a social worker before she had children and later founded a school for autistic children. Her father, Marvin Chodorow, was a professor of physics and electrical engineering at Stanford. She proudly admits a strong paternal identification in her voice. "I believe what I call my clear-eyed thinking—my capacity to see the logic of an argument and put all the parts together—comes from my father, who, as he told me, could see widely disparate theories in physics as having particular relationships in terms of designing particular instruments or tubes" (Elovitz and Lentz 135). In *The Reproduction of Mothering*, Chodorow has much less to say about fathers than mothers, an observation that may be explained in part because she was of the generation of war babies who were the subjects of father-absence studies: "fathers were off at war or doing war work, and, after the war, working hard in the beginning of a boom economy, while women were 'returning' to the home" (136).

Chodorow admits in *Individualizing Gender and Sexuality* to being a dutiful if challenging daughter or granddaughter. There is "little processed rage or feminist outrage" in *The Reproduction of Mothering*. Displaying these dark emotions would have prevented readers from reaching thoughtful conclusions about the study. The theory behind her first book was radical, Chodorow suggests, but the writer was not. The only subject about which she is uncompromising, she adds, is the reproductive body: "it would be no surprise to a psychoanalyst that I seem to have been from the beginning more intemperate in regard to theories about the body than about anything else that contributes to psychic life" (13).

One never senses in any of Chodorow's books (as one can see in my own) that she writes counterphobically, that is, to come to terms with traumatic experiences. There are no obvious demons she seeks to exorcise. Nor does one sense, as I have suggested about the writers in *Mad Muse: The Mental Illness Memoir in a Writer's Life and Work*, that psychological instability or illness has been a catalyst behind Chodorow's work. Her books reveal no abrupt shifts in thinking or repudiations of earlier works. Rather, her writings accentuate continued evolutionary growth.

There's little that is personal in the chapter "Glass Ceilings, Sticky Floors, and Concrete Walls," but Chodorow cannot resist mulling over what appears to be a Freudian slip regarding a brochure for the "Women and Power" conference, sponsored by several international, national, and local psychoanalytic associations, for which she had written the present chapter. "With the best of intentions," she remarks, she was listed as a professor of sociology rather than, additionally, as a psychoanalyst or as a faculty member of a psychoanalytic institute. "My own (we could call it) overdetermined professional/personal countertransference reaction was to feel that I could not, finally, ever be accepted as a psychoanalyst" (98).

The Psychoanalytic Ear and the Sociological Eye

The feeling of being an outsider, on the margins, informs Chodorow's most recent book, *The Psychoanalytic Ear and the Sociological Eye: Toward an American Independent Tradition* (2020). In a chapter felicitously called "Why Is It Easy to Be a Psychoanalyst and a Feminist but Not a Psychoanalyst and a Sociologist?"—which began as her presentation upon being honored by the American Psychoanalytic Association Committee on Research and Special Training (CORST) in 2004—she offers vivid examples of being an outlander. She described herself in one of her early talks as a "Jewish New Yorker who grew up in California and who as a preschooler wanted to be a cowgirl (or cowboy)" (227). She gives other examples of being an outsider, including telling us, as she wryly admits, that she described herself as being an "Eastern European rather than German Jew" in the self-reflective section of her application to the San Francisco Psychoanalytic Institute (227). All of Chodorow's self-disclosures, particularly about her religion, are measured and deliberate, generated from within. Writers, particularly psychoanalysts, must be ready to self-disclose, and they sometimes resist self-disclosure in interviews. When, for example, Elovitz and Lentz asked Chodorow in their interview the meaning of Jewishness in her life, she refused to answer the question, stating that an answer would require "500 pages of psychobiography or autobiography" (136). Now, however, she begins to answer the question.

Sander Gilman has written extensively about the complex role Freud's Eastern European Jewishness played in the construction of psychoanalytic theory. Living in Vienna, the most virulently anti-Semitic European city at the turn of the twentieth century, Freud struggled to be acculturated, to be accepted by the "high" culture of German science. American children or grandchildren of Eastern European Jews did not confront the same violent anti-Semitism as Freud did, but Chodorow's move to California in 1947, when she was three, must have involved culture shock.

To what extent did being an outsider affect not only Chodorow's identity but also the construction of her own psychoanalytic theory of gender? One can feel an outsider, as Chodorow did, while at the same time achieving great success in a new community. For many years Chodorow was the book review editor for North America of the *International Journal of Psychoanalysis*, which placed her at the center of psychoanalytic scholarship. Being an outsider was an obstacle for Chodorow to overcome, but it may have also helped her create a psychoanalytic community that would welcome analysts of all theoretical orientations and backgrounds. Within circumscribed limits, Chodorow has little problem in admitting in *The Psychoanalytic Ear and the Sociological Eye* the contradictions in her life. She cites her former student's amused and bemused observation about her at a professional conference: "Nancy, have you noticed? All of the feminists at this meeting are in the humanities, except you, and all the social scientists except you are men" (227). Rarely are psychoanalysts or academics as candid or self-questioning as she is. Moreover, it is rare to come across a distinguished scholar, teacher, and clinician who is so down-to-earth and authentically human.

The Psychoanalytic Ear and the Sociological Eye is a collection of essays, originally appearing as journal articles or invited talks spanning a quarter of a century, with a single thematic focus: the articulation, as the book's subtitle suggests, of a new American independent tradition that she names "intersubjective ego psychology." Essay collections sometimes make for difficult reading because of inconsistencies in tone or audience or because the essays were written for different audiences, but Chodorow deftly integrates the chapters. Part I, "From Freud to Erikson," explores the missing link between psychoanalysis and the social sciences, emphasizing the sociocultural side of ego psychology. Part II, "The Psychoanalytic Vision of Hans Loewald," celebrates a long-neglected theorist whose work has in recent decades been embraced by analysts across the theoretical spectrum. Part III, "American Independence: Theory and Practice," considers other authors central to the intersubjective ego tradition, including James McLaughlin and Warren Poland. Part IV, "Individuality as Bedrock in the Consulting Room and Beyond," examines the strained relationship between psychoanalysis and the social sciences. In the book's afterword, Chodorow boldly proposes a new academic discipline or department, "Individuology," where the main focus is on the complexity of the individual.

Chodorow's vision of intersubjective ego psychology combines two major antagonistic schools, ego psychology, as formulated by Heinz Hartmann, and interpersonal psychology, as defined by Harry Stack Sullivan. She shows in part I how Erikson and Loewald each contributed to a distinctly American independent tradition, the former through his eight stages of development, the latter through his writings on life history. Interested in both the intrapsychic and the relational-interpersonal, Chodorow uses the expression "relational individualism" (5), which she had coined in a 1979 essay, later reprinted in a chapter of *Feminism and Psychoanalytic Theory*, to describe her integrative approach. Her early insight that separateness is defined relationally and that differentiation occurs in relationship has proven prescient. She respects the European origins of psychoanalysis but does not share American psychoanalytic institutes' overly deferential dependence on the old world. "Like the characters in a Henry James novel, these institutes seem convinced that what is European must be better and that European critiques and dismissals of naive, provincial American thought and practice were right all along" (7).

The reference to James is significant, for like the novelist, Chodorow sees with an ironic eye the clash between the old and new worlds, past and present. The original ego psychologists were apprehensive of writing about countertransference. Instead, they advocated Freud's neutral, scientifically objective stance—a position he theorized in a series of influential articles but never put into practice. "I cannot advise my colleagues too urgently," Freud wrote in "Recommendations to Physicians Practicing Psycho-Analysis" in 1912, "to model themselves during psycho-analytic treatment on the surgeon, who puts aside all his feelings, even his human sympathy, and concentrates his mental forces on the single aim of performing the operation as skilfully as possible" (*SE* 12: 115). Contemporary American analysts, unlike the early ego psychologists, are much more attentive to countertransference, which they define in a larger, more positive way. American analysts now see countertransference, their own subjectivity, as potentially more of a help than a hindrance to their understanding of a patient. One of the distinctively American characteristics of psychoanalysis is an emphasis not on hierarchy but on equality.

Thanks in part to her sociological training, Chodorow recognizes the significance of Erikson's work on ethnicity, which is central to his identity theory. "Long before American culture and politics became focused on it, Erikson was obsessed with identity, especially with the particulars of racial-ethnic-cultural identities, spoiled and outcast identities, and identity fragments that must, somehow, be cemented into a psychologically working whole" (13). Few people realize, she points out, that Erikson left UC Berkeley early in his career rather than take a loyalty oath. The war babies' psychosocial theorist, "Erikson shows us that listening with a psychoanalytic ear gives depth and richness to what we see with a sociological eye, and that looking through a sociological eye gives depth and richness to what we hear" (87). Chodorow observes that Erikson's personal conflicts—he changed his name several times in search of his biological parents—contributed to the formation of his identity theory.

Unlike Erikson, arguably the most famous twentieth-century American psychoanalyst, Hans Loewald has only recently begun receiving the recognition he deserves, apart from his classic 1960 essay "On the Therapeutic Action of Psychoanalysis." That recognition will grow, as Chodorow argues throughout part II. She cites a comment she made about Loewald in 1989 that is no less true of herself: He is an "insistent synthesizer rather than polarizer within psychoanalytic discourse, committed to and able to maintain himself as a drive theorist, ego psychologist, and object-relations theorist who respects self psychology, while also remaining fully enmeshed in the clinical situation that ultimately provides psychoanalysis its truths" (94).

Noting that some of Loewald's assumptions on primary oneness and symbiosis are no longer clinically valid, Chodorow favors using the insights of related fields, such as neuroscience and cognitive and developmental psychology, to confirm or disconfirm psychoanalytic theory. "It can only harm and marginalize our field to dismiss such evidence" (97). Providing close readings of Loewald's writings, Chodorow argues that no psychoanalyst since Freud has had a more developed theory of how the mind works. Loewald "integrates, in noncontradictory ways, many positions that we have historically polarized" (142). Humility compels Chodorow to use "we" here, but it would be more accurate to say that she follows Loewald's tradition as an integrator of historically (and sometimes hysterically) polarized theory.

In an article titled "Writing Under the Influence: The Scholarly Writer at Work," published in *American Imago* in 2019, Elise Miller makes an intriguing observation about an early version of chapter 5, "The Psychoanalytic Vision of Hans Loewald," originally published in the *International Journal of Psychoanalysis* in 2003. Referring to Harold Bloom's influential book *The Anxiety of Influence*, Miller remarks that, despite Chodorow's admission that she uses extensive quotes in the essay to capture Loewald's vision, she relies on paraphrasing for Loewald's most challenging passages. What's the difference between quoting or paraphrasing an author's words? "A quotation privileges the precursor's words, as I was trained to do as a literary critic, while a paraphrase might be read as a sign that she has subordinated Loewald's ideas to her own" (635). Chodorow thus "reverses the order of progenitor and offspring by mingling her words with Loewald's in a way that sets in motion a re-birth of Loewald's theories." This suggests to Miller a sign that Chodorow has "subordinated Loewald's ideas to her own," a "reminder of her own position in the larger conversations of psychoanalytic theory."

Chodorow affirms in part III of *The Psychoanalytic Ear and the Sociological Eye* the foundational paradox of psychoanalysis: self-knowledge is based on the assumption of not-knowing, mainly because the mind is divided within itself. She expresses other paradoxes, including one articulated by Warren Poland in his 1996 book *Melting the Darkness*: "How can it be that no man is an island and that at the same time every man is an island?" (Chodorow 153; Poland 33). Lest we fail to recognize the allusion, it's from John Donne's *Meditation XVII*, written in 1623 and published in 1624, leading to the words "for whom the bell tolls," used by Hemingway as the title of his acclaimed 1940 war novel. This example of intertextuality shows how literature shapes psychoanalysis, first through Poland's influential book and then through Chodorow's.

As always, Chodorow seeks common ground when discussing the fierce debates that have roiled the psychoanalytic community. Her unifying imagination is strikingly evident throughout part III. Even as Chodorow historicizes psychoanalytic controversies, she drolly admits that her account "threatens to spill over into caricature" (157), a statement few theorists concede. She affirms pluralistic theory, choosing the best elements of disparate hypotheses in a way characteristic of American pragmatism. One of Chodorow's favorite expressions is "rueful recognition" (as well as "rueful regret"), suggesting the pain in acknowledging blind spots in ourselves and others.

Chodorow calls both Hans Loewald and James McLaughlin quiet revolutionaries, another statement that can be made about Chodorow herself. McLaughlin (1918–2006) was a training analyst associated with the Pittsburgh Psychoanalytic Institute for over half a century. In the chapter "Listening to James McLaughlin," she quotes a passage from his 2005 book *The Healer's Bent* that contains the most poetic description I have read of the insights acquired through self-analysis: "They have been as fireflies: elusive on the wing and enigmatic in the grasp; illuminating in the moment seen, rather dull and diminished when closely scrutinized" (172). Chodorow also pays tribute to Warren Poland, who, in his 1997 plenary address to the American Psychoanalytic Association, coined the expression "two-person separate" to describe how the analyst witnesses a patient's suffering (185). Chodorow's descriptions of deceased or forgotten analysts often have an elegiacal tone, as if she is mourning their loss.

In part IV, Chodorow identifies other contemporary analysts whom she considers American independents, including Dale Boesky, Judith Chused, Theodore Jacobs, Owen Renik, and Glen O. Gabbard. Summarizing the characteristics of the American independent tradition of analysis, she argues for a two-person psychology, a term used in relational psychoanalysis to indicate that both analyst and patient contribute to the therapeutic relationship. Yet after pointing out that relational analysis is based on the co-construction of meaning, Chodorow adds that "it is possible to be co-actor without claiming center stage or being co-star" (205)—moves that may shift the primary attention away from the patient, where it belongs. As a social scientist, she worries that relational theory may lead to what she calls in the Elovitz/Lentz interview "extrapsychic determinism." "I want to take—as is not surprising, given my training, from the great strengths of classical ego psychology and classical Freud— the attention to individuality, to conflict and unconscious fantasy and how it shapes everything. But I also want to see the analytic encounter as created by two equally complex subjectivities, not as an encounter in which an analyst is the objective interpreter and describer of the patient's reality. Intersubjective ego psychology is the best I can do to express this hybrid" (139).

The Individuology Department

As an academic, I found the most intriguing section of *The Psychoanalytic Ear and the Sociological Eye* to be the afterword, provocatively titled "Could You Direct Me to the Individuology Department?" There is no such department, Chodorow bemoans, though there should be one in every major American university. (Psychobiographically, it's revealing that, as an "outsider," Chodorow is searching for an academic home.) The individuology department would be an interdisciplinary field of study combining the humanities, the social sciences, and psychoanalysis. "The absence of individuology in the academy, of a direct way to study individual selves, is a great lacuna, a missing piece, in our conception of what should be studied, learned about and taught in our conception of academic knowledge" (246). I would love to teach in the individuology department, and one of the required texts would be *The Psychoanalytic Ear and the Sociological Eye.*

I would urge my individuology students to read Chodorow's footnotes carefully. She tells us how she felt a decade after teaching her final graduate seminar at UC Berkeley, a course about her own work, "Chodorow on Chodorow: Theorizing and Theory," inspired by her department chair's recommendation. She looks back on the course with fondness—and characteristic rueful irony. "There is nothing like using one's own writing to enable a teacher fully to dig into what may be brilliant or original but is at the same time wrong, misguided, created by sleight-of-pen, and so forth" (240 n. 3). Another footnote is especially noteworthy, when she describes French analysts' hostility toward empiricism:

At the 2000 Delphi psychoanalytic conference, a French analyst assigned to introduce and chair an American infant researcher's presentation announced that she did not believe in empirical research and then walked off the stage and left the room as the American was presenting. In France at a conference two weeks earlier, an American empirical researcher on psychoanalytic process had been booed off the stage as he tried to present. In my own limited experience, I have not seen or read of such dismissal—though of course I have seen and read radical disagreement—going in the other cultural direction. (70 n. 17)

The footnote offers not only a stark contrast between the French and American traditions of psychoanalysis but also an example of Chodorow's even-handedness in describing bias against French psychoanalytic criticism. Indeed, her favorite rhetorical strategy throughout the book is "on the one hand, on the other hand," which she uses (along with the related, "on the one side, on the other side") a dozen times. Her recognition that scholarly objectivity is illusory in the hermeneutic disciplines compels her to be scrupulously fair to all ideological positions and points of view. One cannot ask for more balanced, meticulous scholarship.

I must mention one more footnote that applies more to my discipline than to Chodorow's: "In the academic humanities, we find that psychoanalysis is thought to begin and end (with the exception of Lacan and related theorists) with Freud" (169 n. 2). She can't understand the militant French opposition to ego psychology. Nor can I. No scientist, she adds, perhaps thinking of her father's legacy, believes that the contributions of Einstein, Bohr, Fermi, or Heisenberg are the last word in physics. "So it should be with psychoanalysis and its founder."

JEFFREY BERMAN. Two of your mentors in graduate school were Egon Bittner, who directed your doctoral dissertation, and Philip Slater. What was it like working with them?

NANCY CHODOROW. Egon Bittner didn't write a lot, and his only book was *The Functions of the Police in Modern Society*, but more to the point, he taught me ethnomethodology, the sociology of the taken-for-granted or unnoticed—the preconscious assumptions in everyday life: like, that women mother. He was a student of Harold Garfinkel, who created ethnomethodology. I have a couple of footnotes to this in *The Psychoanalytic Ear and the Sociological Eye*, and throughout my writing. Slater's work—his amazing *The Glory of Hera*—has an absence of mother-daughter relationships, and he told us in a seminar, and wrote something like "mother-daughter relationships are all alike," a statement that became very influential. But it's Bittner who attuned my theoretical eye and ear, from noting the taken-for-grantedness of mother-daughter relationships and that women mother, to, in my recent book, my plenary "Beyond the Dyad," noticing the taken-for-granteds of psychoanalytic treatment: the exclusive dyad, the assumptions about training, and the training analysis.

JB. What was it like "floating between Brandeis and Harvard" when you were in graduate school?

NC. Brandeis was pretty open those days, and so was my connection to Harvard. I was an undergraduate anthropology student, and anthropology was hands on. I did two summers in research settings under professors and their graduate students, so I got to know them and worked directly with them. In 1963 I participated in a Neolithic archaeology project in Northern Greece, and then, as a sophomore, in the Whitings' graduate seminars and lab in preparation for the summer of '64 on the Evon Z. Vogt Chiapas project. My senior thesis research (on children's games in Shiraz, Iran) I did on my own. Plus I spent a year at Harvard in graduate school before I moved to sociology from anthropology and to Brandeis from Harvard (partly a '60s effect: go to a radical sociology department rather than a traditional social relations department!). But I could just go back and sit in on, say, Goethals' undergraduate lectures, or be part of his graduate seminar, or ask him to be a second reader on my dissertation, since Egon was amazing but was completely not expert in psychoanalytic sociology or feminism, and Slater had gone off into the alternate culture sunset of encounter groups and then California early in my graduate career. I sat in on at least one of John Whiting's graduate courses, as well as visiting Bea Whiting in Cambridge after I finished and moved to Berkeley/Santa Cruz, when she was still a professor at the Ed School, up through the senior home in Cambridge to which she finally moved.

JB. It's not often that a first book turns out to be an immediate classic. What was the impact of *The Reproduction of Mothering* on your career?

NC. *The Reproduction of Mothering* had a huge impact on my career: as I've written, "I became famous." But at the beginning, in 1974, when I was finishing my PhD, I couldn't get a tenure track job. The dissertation, which is almost word for word the book, was radical and different, for sociology, or for any field. Remember, women's studies was in its infancy, and psychoanalysis and sociology? At my dissertation defense (in the European tradition, Brandeis had public dissertation defenses), a young woman faculty member commented, "A woman suggests that men share parenting, and a man suggests that this will mean the end of society!"

I received a one-year position at UC Santa Cruz, which became tenure track, and then tenure in my fifth year, a year after the book came out. By then, or shortly thereafter, I was beginning to be well-known, with many translations, awards, invitations and honors. It was especially moving to see how the book was taken up in so many disciplines, how it spoke to literary scholars writing about women characters or women writers, about mothers and daughters in literature, about the fear of women in male writing; to scholars trying to understand widespread features of the political theory and philosophy that had been written by men for hundreds of years; to anthropologists studying family and kinship. I brought a feminist lens to Parsonsian psychoanalytic sociology, psycho-analytic Frankfurt theory, and psychoanalytic Marxism, all important in the legacy of sociology and the New Left. But it took several years after the book, and, I knew privately, several rounds of negotiation, before the UC Berkeley Sociology Department was willing to hire a psychoanalytic feminist sociologist, however famous.

Outside of academia, the book spoke to women who saw themselves as or were becoming feminists, because it was really personal, and what so many women were feeling was how the personal is *personal*, even if the feminist slogan was the personal is political. And those who were psychoanalysts or going into psychoanalysis from other fields were inspired by it and drew from it to think about the psychology of women and of men, to extend my thinking toward women's bodies and motherhood, like Rosemary Balsam and Joan Raphael-Leff, or in the development of relational psychoanalysis, with its attention to the two-person relationship, and its feminist co-founders like Adrienne Harris, Muriel Dimen, Virginia Goldner, and Jessica Benjamin. In 1979, I wrote, "differentiation occurs in relationship," and in 1986 I coined the phrase "relational individualism."

JB. Were you surprised by the success of *The Reproduction of Mothering*? Did the book create pressure on you to write another classic?

NC. Write another classic? Write another *book* at that time?? Like many academic women of my generation, I spent the next years trying to combine mothering with teaching. The book came out in 1978; I got tenure and had my first child the same week, in June 1979. If you look at the vitae of many women of my generation, the post-'60s wave into academia, you'll find that we wrote a book, got tenure, and then wrote an article or maybe two a year during the next ten years or so, while we were raising small children (however much we were all also sharing parenting, as the book had suggested).

One of the wonderful things about feminist scholarship at that time was how it generated academic sisterhood. Even before the book came out, I was part of a network, study groups of feminist scholars from the social sciences and the humanities who taught at UC Santa Cruz, UC Berkeley, Stanford, and UC Davis. We met on a regular basis. That group included Arlie Hochschild, the founder of the sociology of emotions, whose work felt so kindred to my own; my good friend Shelly Rosaldo and other anthropologists; Carol Jacklin, coauthor of the first big book on the psychology of sex differences; literary people like Diane Middlebrook and Marilyn Yalom; Nan Keohane, who went on to be president of various universities. And Brandeis had graduated many founding feminist scholars, who were colleagues or friends—Barrie Thorne, still a good friend, along with Fatima Mernissi, Karen Fields, Judith Rollins, Patricia Hill Collins, many others. I also later had the privilege of becoming close to an extraordinary group of psychoanalytic literary scholars who taught in Bay Area universities or spent time there, Janet Adelman and Elizabeth Abel at UCB, Helene Moglen at UC Santa Cruz, Madelon Sprengnether, Claire Kahane, and others. It's hard to describe in a short space how it felt to be part of that early era of feminist scholarship and women's studies.

JB. You confronted not only early success with the publication of *The Reproduction of Mothering* but also ferocious criticisms from fellow social scientists and feminists. You acknowledge in later books your critics and your own self-criticisms. Has it been difficult to take these criticisms in stride without becoming angry or defensive? What advice do you have for researchers beginning their careers about the criticisms they are likely to receive?

NC. I'm now a psychoanalyst as well as having had a long professorial career: I'd say if ferocious criticism doesn't upset you, there's something wrong. I'm also fortunate, I think, in that I have (somewhere, though it often goes into hiding) an internal sense of peace, or rightness, about my own writing and ideas. I don't know where it comes from, but I'm very fortunate. I have a couple of pieces of advice. First, try, if you possibly can, to have a group, however small, of people with whom you talk about your work, whose work feels akin to yours. If you're fortunate enough that they live in the same town, walk and talk. Second, try to keep in mind that it is not worth doing academic work, or writing, if you don't write about what moves and commits you. Otherwise, you might have saved time, earned more money, and gotten to choose where you live, by going to business school.

JB. You've written in a number of places about being an "outsider, on the margins." To what extent has the experience of being an outsider shaped your life as a teacher, analyst, and scholar? What are the advantages of being an outsider? Are there any disadvantages?

NC. Actually, feeling like an outsider (just to point out, this is probably as much subjective as objective) begins much earlier. In my chapter "Born into a World at War," I write about its beginning at age 3 when we moved to California, leaving our large extended family behind. I note that I was first drawn to psychoanalysis by Erikson's *Childhood and* Society, which I read when I was 19. I immediately identified with his first case, "Sam," the little Jewish boy from New York growing up in California. My "outsiderness" has gone along with (this must be important) an internal sense of writing what I want to write, choosing fields I love, moving academic fields from anthropology to sociology, becoming a psychoanalytic sociologist and then a psychoanalyst. I have an eye for the larger picture and the taken-for-granteds, how theories hang together and what their underlying assumptions are, though I don't know if it's because I stand outside. That sense allowed me, from the beginning, to notice: women mother. And I try to understand, and tried to teach my students, to read or listen from within: what is someone trying to say, even if it's not clear to you or seems wrongheaded? The disadvantages are, who wants always to feel like an outsider?!

JB. I find it ironic that you were accused by fellow feminists of "writing like a man" when you were, in fact, one of the earliest women to write about the mother-daughter relationship.

NC. Yes, there was so much that had been written on fathers and sons, and even on fathers and daughters, because for Freud, it was all about the father (he says somewhere in *Moses and Monotheism*, and I quote him somewhere, that recognizing the father's role in procreation as more important than the mother's is "progress in spirituality"). For the psychological anthropologists and sociologists, it was all about the mother-son relationship. *The Reproduction of Mothering* was a feminist attempt to address that, to fill in the missing parent and missing relationship and to acknowledge the mother.

JB. Was it difficult for you to give up academic teaching?

NC. Yes, I did (alas!) give up academic teaching, but I was sixty-one in 2005, when I "retired." I graduated from the analytic institute in 1993, so it was some time afterwards. The reason was not so much a career choice—I loved being part of the Berkeley Sociology Department and everything else that I could do in Berkeley, with my colleagues in the humanities, in clinical psychology, in women's studies—as personal. After my 2001–2002 year at the Radcliffe Institute, near my huge cousin network and some of my very closest friends, I wanted to move to Cambridge. Which has been a good decision, though our recent December trip to Northern California was full of nostalgia. Here, I married my husband Carl, the widower of a Radcliffe friend (still part of my community when I moved), and here, my son now teaches at Harvard and lives nearby with his wife and two of my grandchildren (whom I can't see for the time because of the coronavirus, so they might as well live in Oregon, with my daughter and her children!).

JB. Would you make the same career decisions if you were beginning your life again?

NC. Your question is the Eriksonian ego integrity (and generativity) question. I could go back and tell you that at each step I would have done something differently, or that every step had both good and bad aspects. I could say that I was overwhelmed with the astonishing recognition, and even tears, from so many younger colleagues, that I got at a 2015 conference on motherhood in Maynooth, Ireland, where I was a keynote speaker, and generations of younger women academics from all over the world told me I'd changed their lives. I am so pleased with *The Psychoanalytic Ear and the Sociological Eye*, and I am thrilled about the amazing honor that the sociologist-psychologist Petra Bueskens is paying me. She has edited the forthcoming book, *Nancy Chodorow and The Reproduction of Mothering: Forty Years On*. It's got chapters by academics and analysts of my generation, my "sisters," by "daughters," mainly my students, and by "granddaughters," younger mothering scholars whom I don't personally know. My chapter is "Women Mother Daughters: *The Reproduction of Mothering* after Forty Years."

JB. You acknowledge in *The Power of Feelings* that writing about Michelle Rosaldo involves perhaps an "ongoing work of mourning." Did writing about deceased analysts in *The Psychoanalytic Ear and the Sociological Eye* also represent an act of ongoing mourning?

NC. It must have, though not in the same active way as with Shelly/Michelle, who was a close friend and died young and suddenly. I'm not sure that "ongoing mourning" best describes it, but there is something very active throughout about bringing together, sort of elegiacally and in retrospect, my two professional identities, psychoanalysis and sociology. I close with a return to the university and advocacy for an "Individuology Department," even as I left the university 15 years ago. I talk about my students and my teaching. I revisit my earliest intellectual identity, already psychoanalysis and the social, beginning with Freud's *Civilization and Its Discontents* and Erikson's *Childhood and Society*, the first psychoanalytic books I read, as an undergraduate. Erikson's writings also introduce us to ego integration and ego integrity, which are what he might call a "good" mourning. I then go to Loewald, the analyst whose writing on internalization and mourning swept me away when I was a graduate student, even before I'd begun *The Reproduction of Mothering* dissertation. And who doesn't write about Loewald with, as he'd put it, love and respect, which is what I think you also want to bring to an active, loving and alive mourning? Loewald also evoked and elided with some of my professors at Brandeis, who were also German-Jewish refugee intellectuals. Then, if I can teach only one Freud paper in a course, it's always "Mourning and Melancholia," where you learn about the intrapsychic meaning of the other and the crucial widening from drives to object relations.

JB. In *The Psychoanalytic Ear and the Sociological Eye* you cite Hans Loewald's often-repeated statement that the analyst's focus requires an "objectivity and neutrality the essence of which is love and respect for the individual and for individual development" (132). What's remarkable is that you *show* us rather than merely tell us about the love you feel for the analysts in your book, including Loewald, James McLaughlin, and Warren Poland. In conveying this love, you affirm, to quote the title of one of your books, the power of feelings. You make a distinction between listening-to and listening-for analysts, but were you aware of the equally important distinction, of which English teachers routinely inform their students, between showing and telling?

NC. Actually, I wasn't. It's always really nice to learn something new.

JB. Whenever I open a book for the first time, I turn to the Acknowledgments page, from which a reader can infer so much about the author. You go out of your way to acknowledge the help of others in *all* your books, particularly in *The Power of Feelings*. I'm *impressed*!

NC. For our mutual cross-disciplinary interest, you'll be interested to know (I say as much in the acknowledgments) that your psychoanalytic literary colleague Elizabeth Abel in fact named *The Power of Feelings*. We were having a conversation, and I was telling her that I couldn't decide what to call the book, and I said, "it's about the power of feelings." And she said, there's your title! or something to that effect.

JB. I am a highly self-disclosing teacher and writer, which is unusual in the academic world, particularly among men. Would you comment on why you're more cautious about self-disclosure?

NC. I guess your larger question is why I only exceptionally write about personal relationships. A mother-daughter theorist and late '70s feminist, I hardly write directly about my own mother or my relationship to her. But that's probably true of feminists of my generation, whatever we wrote about. We'd tell you that you're not allowing us to have the "objectivity" that is accorded to men, that we are still supposed to person-alize everything, that Janet Adelman should have written not only about Lear's painful rage but about her father's! "Born into a World at War" is an exception, in my more personal discussion, but it was semi-private, originally, for my college class, and most contributors wrote a little or a little more about our parents. And I like to think, as I think you think about me as well, that I am very personal in my talk about theorists, and my mind, and how I read and think.

For me, it was from the beginning and still is liberating to get to have my own mind, not to be beholden to explain my personal life. And *The Psychoanalytic Ear and the Sociological Eye* is critical throughout, both in the text and in footnotes, of analysts who make the treatment all about transference, who focus on the analyst's mind, or the countertransference, or even the relationship. It's throughout my "Beyond the Dyad" chapter. I also mention my 2000 American Academy of Psychoanalysis plenary whose subtitle was "Why we still need one-person ego psychologies," or the paper I gave in 2015 called "Focusing on the Patient: Has Our Attention to the Relationship and the Transference Gone Too Far?" I advocate intersubjective ego psychology, two-person separate, focusing on the patient with love and respect.

I'm moved by your discussion of tracing Warren Poland's use of the "no man is an island" quote back to John Donne's "for whom the bell tolls." That brings us right back to my favorite Freud essay, "Mourning and Melancholia," and also to Loewald's "Internalization, Separation, Mourning and the Superego," which, as I wrote, was the first Loewald article that I read.

JB. Your appreciation of literature is evident throughout your writings. If you were teaching in a department of individuology, which literary works would you include on your syllabus? In *The Psychoanalytic Ear and the Sociological Eye* you mention that reading as an undergraduate Erikson's *Childhood and Society* (1950) "affected every part of my career and intellectual trajectory for fifty years or more, right up to the present" (248). Which literary works have most deeply affected your own thinking?

NC. It's so interesting that you ask that, because in a way, the whole point of my advocacy of a field of individuology is because it seems to me that in the university, the fields that are interested in individuals and individuality, the psychoanalytically derived fields, *already* study literary (or philosophical) texts. They are the humanities. What is missing is an epistemological-methodological-theoretical field that tries to understand, theorize, and study *living individuals*, that notices individuality. I couldn't think more highly of the humanities: my closest friends and colleagues were as likely to teach literature as sociology or anthropology, and co-teaching with Janet Adelman was a highlight. But as it now stands, the fields that study people—the social sciences and psychology—do not, with rare exception, have interest in or methods for studying individuals, individual uniqueness, and individuality as something to be described and theorized. It's hard to imagine that some, maybe most, individuology teachers would not want to include a particularly favorite literary work, but, well, just to emphasize the point, that would depend on the individual. I'd say, further, that when I read literature, I just read it, I live within it, I don't think about it, in the sense that you mean. Maybe you could ask students to choose a favorite character in a novel and write about them *as a person*, not as part of a text. But there you have it: isn't that exactly what you're *not* meant to do reading a text!?

I don't know if particular literary works have affected my thinking. I "think," and really like to think, about the theories that I write about, I experience their logic, and their unfolding, and their narrative, and their contradictions. Maybe I absorb theory the way others read novels or poetry. I also experience music in a very immediate way, symphony, chamber music, choral music. I love both the stories and the music in opera, and there are little references in my work to Wagner's *Ring* and to other operas. I'm a late life singer and get totally absorbed in singing or hearing choral music. I once created a panel called "Analytic listening and the five senses," in which I brought together a poet, an artist, and an improvisational pianist, all analysts, to try to explore how these different senses/sensualities affect analytic listening. So, I don't do a lot of "thinking" about literature, though I like what I like. During the early women's movement, I was blown away reading women authors, and I was shocked, maybe 10 years ago, to realize I'd never read John Updike, or anything after early Philip Roth, I think because when they came out, I was only reading women authors. I'm intolerant of most first-person novels, especially ones set in another era, so I would not use those in an individuology course. I feel that the first person is often a false, or cheap, way to bring you into the story, and it doesn't allow you as the reader to think and experience and observe.

The books I've most gotten enmeshed in recently might be Willa Cather's *Collected Stories* and *One of Ours*—I knew *The Song of the Lark* and *Death Comes to the Archbishop*, but who knew that she wrote so much beyond Nebraska, so astutely and gorgeously about Greenwich Village, wannabe arts patrons, about music and musicians, about World War I? That she lived both a western and eastern cultural world resonates with me (it's personal!). An unknown book that everyone to whom I've recommended it has loved is Rachel Kadish's *The Weight of Ink*. It gives you aging academic female (or any aging academic) identity, academic politics, women's being known or not, London history, and much more. I guess the short answer is that it's up to the individual, what literary work to use in an individuology course.

JB. Sander Gilman observed, in his response to one of my questions, that "psychoanalysis, as with all science, is in constant revision and refinement, with new additions, reshaping arguments, and approaches." Can you speculate on some of the changes that might occur in psychoanalysis in the coming decades?

NC. That's a long time! I'd begin by saying I don't know if there's one "psychoanalysis" that will change. When I go to the International Psychoanalytical Association meetings, or even when I compare Boston and San Francisco, where I was trained, psychoanalysis feels so varied. I'll begin with my concerns. As I describe in *The Psychoanalytic Ear and the Sociological Eye*, it troubles me that psychoanalysis since the beginning has traversed adulation of one person after another. First (and it's still there) it was "Freud himself," what I call "Freud *ipse*." Then there were the splits, in the US between ego psychology and interpersonal psychoanalysis, in England between Klein and Anna Freud. And one is usually hegemonic and "right." There's an almost cult-like feel sometimes. In the current period internationally, there's still a reverence for Lacan, especially when people talk or write about sexuality and gender, but first and foremost today, it's Bion—whose name is intoned, preceded by a reverential pause, in so many presentations—and his Italian interpreters.

I worry that psychoanalysis, as already seems to be happening, will become ever more sealed off and self-referential. Not just the theory but the training and organization need to be connected, to the university, to less personalized modes of supervision, teaching, and evaluation, to research, to empirical investigation (of psyche, subjectivity and mental distress) as well as to intersubjective epistemologies and methodologies in other fields. Perhaps for different reasons, some of the major academic psychiatrist-psychoanalysts, like Otto Kernberg, Robert Michels, and the late Robert Wallerstein, agree with me. In *The Psychoanalytic Ear and the Sociological Eye*, I write that I think there are many things wrong with psychoanalytic training, which is, of course, very different depending on which country you happen to be in. Most basic, I think, perhaps as a former professor, that it's ethically problematic to have *anyone* in training negotiating or paying anyone else privately for any part of their training, as candidates do to their training analyst and supervisors.

I'd like to think that psychoanalysts are also learning about the "external" world in which all of our patients live and how to think/feel with them about these externals and their intrapsychic fantasy representations and identities, whether about worldwide pandemic, systematic racial-ethnic inequality, sex-gender complexity, or nation and people. I am always hoping that there will be a return to a focus on the *individual patient's internal life and world*, and away from so much focus on the transference, the relationship, the analyst's fantasy and dreaming. Yet many young people who want to become clinicians are finding it hard, outside of analytic institutes, to learn to listen, to use how they feel with their patients, to think about a patient's feelings and selfhood, so they look to psychoanalytic training.

I very much hope that the core goal and insight of psychoanalysis—to give people their own emotion and minds and fantasies, their own individuality—will return and continue. And I am hopeful about those few contemporary analysts, often child analysts as has been the case since the Anna Freud War Nurseries and Bowlby, who are really working to make a difference in this world, to bring their clinical experience to international work, to work with children—the ones I know personally are Gilbert Kliman, whose Children's Psychological Health Center has been working with the interned children on the Mexican border, and Alexandra Harrison, who's worked training caregivers in an orphanage in Central America and parents and nurses in India. At the same time, I feel so fortunate to have been able to train as a psychoanalyst at the San Francisco Psychoanalytic Institute, and to have been able to practice as an analyst in Berkeley and now in Cambridge. I am so grateful for the colleagues and students, from sociology, anthropology, and psychoanalytic and clinical academia, that I had during my long academic career, and for the supportive mentoring I received early on.

Chapter 4

Christopher Bollas's
Psychoanalytic Literary Education

A student of literature would not be surprised to read that a single play, *Hamlet*, contains more insight into psychological conflict than countless scientific studies. Most clinicians not well versed in the humanities, however, would disagree with this claim, which Christopher Bollas boldly asserts in his 2015 book *When the Sun Bursts: The Enigma of Schizophrenia* (6). Few people know that Bollas, one of the world's most acclaimed psychoanalysts, has a PhD in English literature. Scores of detailed literary references appear in his many books, and while he never explicitly states that a literary background is excellent preparation for a psychotherapist, the truth of this observation becomes apparent through a careful examination of his voluminous writings, which include three novellas and a collection of plays.

Becoming Distressed

Born in Washington, DC, in 1943, Bollas lived in a small rural town south of Los Angeles until he was eight, when his family moved to Laguna Beach, a coastal city known for its beaches and art galleries. His father was French and had moved to the United States in his mid-twenties; his mother was a native Californian. In 1962 Bollas enrolled at the University of Virginia, and two years later, he transferred to UC Berkeley, where he majored in American history.

Most of our knowledge of Bollas's early interest in psychoanalysis comes from *When the Sun Bursts* and from his 1995 "Conversation" with Anthony Molino. Bollas used psychoanalytic theory when he was writing his senior thesis on seventeenth-century New England village life. But as often occurs, there was a personal reason for his fascination with psychoanalysis, an attraction that was not purely intellectual. Finding himself becoming "very distressed," Bollas went to the Berkeley Student Health Service and was serendipitously assigned to see a psychoanalyst. Bollas doesn't explain to Molino why he needed help, but he offers hints in *When the Sun Bursts*. Caught up in the Free Speech Movement, the anti-war movement, and the Black Panther Party in the mid-1960s, he began to be afraid of heights and stairwells. "Although I was not in the least consciously suicidal, I had a thought that I might impulsively leap to my death. Before long I was sitting in the office of a psychoanalyst at the university health center" (*When the Sun Bursts* 1).

Bollas was in weekly psychotherapy for two years. He never offers a diagnosis of his distress, but therapy changed his life. "Through the curious pathways to self-discovery invented by Freud, and especially through free association, the meanings of the symptoms were revealed, and to my surprise they had nothing to do with their manifest content" (*When the Sun Bursts* 1). Around the same time, Bollas took a course with Berkeley's foremost psychoanalytic literary critic, Frederick Crews, the author of the groundbreaking study of Nathaniel Hawthorne, *The Sins of the Fathers* (1966). Crews invited Bollas to visit his graduate seminar on literature and psychoanalysis. Several of Crew's students, including Murray Schwartz, went on to become distinguished psychoanalytic literary critics. This was before Crews aggressively turned against psychoanalysis to become the country's leading Freud-basher: a conversion from a Freudian to a Schadenfreudian.

After graduation in 1967, Bollas began his career by working for two years with autistic and schizophrenic children at the East Bay Activity Center in Oakland, California. This was on-the-job training that involved individual and group supervision. "Working with them I found the mystery of their illnesses so compelling and intellectually challenging that I knew I wanted to continue with that sort of work" (Molino, "Conversation" 192). Uninterested in studying psychology, history, or medicine, he gravitated toward literary studies. He chose the University of Buffalo, specializing in Jacobean drama, the American renaissance, and critical theory. The UB English department, chaired by Norman N. Holland beginning in 1966, had become a leading center for the psychological study of the arts. Bollas doesn't mention any of the specific graduate courses he took, but a turning point in his life occurred when, teaching a course titled "Madness and Contemporary American Literature," he encountered students who were deeply troubled, reminding him of the autistic and schizophrenic children at the East Bay Activity Center. Moved by his UB students' anguish, Bollas had a sudden thought. "You don't want to teach them—you want to work with them" (*When the Sun Bursts* 39).

As a psychoanalyst, Bollas understands the importance of parent-child relationships, but he hasn't written much about his own parents. He offers a few hints in *Being a Character* (1992). Sacha Bollas was present when his son was born, but when Christopher was four or five months old, he left for Europe to serve in World War II, returning home two years later. "Very much in love before the war, my parents found them-selves bewilderingly distanced after their reuniting and a mood of sad vexation pervaded the house for some time. As part of this scene I am sure that I knew something, but I did not have the means of thinking what I knew" (19–20). His parents were politically liberal and educated, "in tune" with their generation. "Toscanini, T.S. Eliot, Rachmaninoff, and Adlai Stevenson were good objects; Nixon, General Motors, the McGuire Sisters, and HUAC [House Un-American Activities Committee, engaged in political witch-hunting] were bad objects" (255). Sacha Bollas must have been sympathetic to feminism; he gave his adolescent son a copy of Simone de Beauvoir's *The Second Sex* to further his education. A hint of a conflicted father-son relationship appears in *Being a Character*. "For years I refused to visit the National Portrait Gallery (always full of one excuse or another), but gradually I became aware of an Oedipally rebellious portion of myself, reluctant to pay homage to these distinguished fathers" (24).

Bollas credits Lloyd Clarke, the psychiatrist who directed the UB university health center, with giving him psychotherapy instruction and the opportunity to work with patients. He received clinical training through the department of psychiatry, which allowed him, as well as Holland, Schwartz, who had recently arrived at UB, and others to create a university program in psychotherapy for people in the humanities. Bollas worked two full days at the university health center while also teaching undergraduate courses and pursuing a doctoral degree in English.

As a graduate student Bollas encountered the writings of the Vien-nese-born psychoanalyst Heinz Lichtenstein, who had moved to Buffalo where he became associated with the UB English department. Lichtenstein's

1961 essay "Identity and Sexuality," reprinted in *The Dilemma of Human Identity* (1977), influenced not only Holland and Schwartz but also Bollas, as he explained to Molino. "Lichtenstein had studied with Heidegger, and really had Heidegger in him. And as his own psychoanalytical vision had been informed by Heidegger, when I taught *Being and Time* it was, in a way, Heidegger taught through Lichtenstein" ("Conversation," 207).

Writing on Melville

Bollas wrote his doctoral dissertation on Herman Melville, whose stories he had enjoyed reading while he was young. Growing up near the ocean in southern California, Bollas recalls an experience as an adolescent that may have influenced his decision to write on Melville:

> As an eleven-year-old I was once swimming off the coast, about one hundred metres off shore, when a very small California grey whale—which didn't seem small to me at the time!—passed right by me. I recall thinking that a reef that had usually been in its place had uprooted itself and was moving toward me. . . . So I therefore had a very particular love of whales from that moment on, because I thought my life had been spared. In an analytical vein, when I was later doing my dissertation on Melville, I was unaware of the link to my own boyhood experiences. (Molino, "Conversation" 206)

In *Being a Character*, Bollas casts new light on his dissertation, which he began writing in 1969. He links the whale to a more traumatic event two years earlier when, riding a wave in the ocean, the nine-year-old boy collided with the bloated body of a woman who must have been dead at sea for some time, "an experience whose memory I repressed, but which 'resurfaced' some years after writing the dissertation when I incorrectly assumed that it was pure fantasy. Although I subsequently discovered its authenticity, it nonetheless collected to it, like a screen memory, many factors in my psyche which had then organized into a repression" (57–58). In *Cracking Up* Bollas observes that the number 9 is traumatic to him because of an event occurring at that age—perhaps his early encounter with death. The number 9 shows up unexpectedly in Bollas's novella *Mayhem*, where the protagonist muses over its significance, not realizing its link to early trauma. Still another reason for Bollas's interest in *Moby Dick* and *Pierre* was Melville's exploration of repressed material from his own life. "The parts of the self have by then shaken him deeply, and writing becomes a means of survival. And to his great credit, mind you, he negotiates and resolves a crisis in such a way that he no longer has to write" (Molino, "Conversation" 206).

Earning a PhD in English—and Becoming a Psychoanalyst

In Buffalo, Bollas studied with Murray Schwartz, a member of the English department from 1970 until 1983, when he left to become the dean of Humanities and Fine Arts at the University of Massachusetts. Both Bollas and Schwartz gratefully acknowledge each other's help in several of their publications. In his 2018 intellectual memoir "Psychoanalysis in My Life," Schwartz notes that he and Bollas helped to set up a program in which humanities graduate students could participate in psychiatric case studies. The two continued to work together, coauthoring the 1976 essay "The Absence at the Center: Sylvia Plath and Suicide," an early psychoanalytic study that shows how Plath imagined only two solutions to the problem of mental illness, suicide or rebirth, neither of which represents a realistic understanding of the therapeutic process.

Bollas earned an MSW at Smith College in Northampton, Massachusetts, studied psychoanalysis at Beth Israel Hospital in Boston, and moved to London in 1973, where he trained at the Institute for Psychoanalysis, eventually becoming a member of the Independent Group of the British Psychoanalytical Society as well as a British citizen. His American analytic training focused on ego psychology, while his English analytic training emphasized object relations theory. In 1975 he began training at the famed Tavistock Clinic, and two years later he began working as a psychoanalyst in full-time private practice, seeing patients at his home in North London.

Bollas told Molino in the 1995 "Conversation," when he was fifty-one, that he had been in psychoanalysis with three different men, all of whom used a language other than English as their mother tongue. The first analyst, at Berkeley, was a Mexican who had a Kleinian training. Bollas's second analyst, during his training period in England, was "Pakistani, from the Independent Group, who was analysed by Winnicott" (Molino, "Conversation" 189). Bollas doesn't name the analyst, whom he saw from 1973 to 1976, but he was Masud Khan, whom Bollas refers to throughout his writings. The third analyst—"one should never say final analysis!"—was with an Italian, Adam Limentani, who was at the time the president of the International Psychoanalytical Association. All three analysts, he remarks, were from different cultures, with different ways of viewing life. Without being specific, he adds that he learned from their insights into his life—and from their mistakes.

In the late 1970s, Bollas and Schwartz traveled together to lecture and offer psychoanalytic seminars in Europe. From 1985 to 1987, Bollas was director of education at the Austen Riggs Center in Stockbridge, Massachusetts, the last residential psychiatric treatment facility in the United States. From 1983 to 1985, Schwartz helped fund Bollas as a half-time visiting lecturer in English at the University of Massachusetts; in 1985, upon his move to Western Massachusetts, his position was upgraded to "Professor of English." Bollas found the members of the English department kind and welcoming. The collaboration with Schwartz was highly productive. "Working together," Schwartz writes in his memoir, "we invited prominent European and American analysts to travel across the state, lecturing and conducting seminars in Amherst, Stockbridge, and Boston" (147), exposing psychoanalysis to a broad interdisciplinary population of faculty, students, and clinicians.

The Shadow of the Object

The title of Bollas's first and most celebrated book, *The Shadow of the Object* (1987), alludes to Freud's 1917 essay "Mourning and Melancholia," where he writes about the ego's identification with the lost object. "Thus the shadow of the object fell upon the ego, and the latter could henceforth be judged by a special agency, as though it were an object, the forsaken object" (*SE* 14: 249). "Mourning and Melancholia" remains the twentieth century's most influential theory of loss and bereavement. In retrospect Bollas may have regretted that he didn't use the book's subtitle as the main of his study: *Psychoanalysis of the Unthought Known*, an evocative expression for which he is best known.

As Sarah Nettleton points out in her 2017 guide, most of Bollas's seminal ideas appear at the beginning of his career, though his meta-psychological model is never spelled out in a single work. Bollas's major contribution to psychoanalysis remains his advocacy of free association, a technique that is often downplayed in relational, intersubjective, and here-and-now clinical approaches. The subject of Bollas's first book, the unthought known, refers to that substantial part of the unconscious that a person has not been able to process mentally.

Another key idea in *The Shadow of the Object*, the transformational object, usually the infant's mother, initiates the lifelong process of seeking other objects. In adult life, Bollas suggests, trying to express what may be ineffable, "the quest is not to possess the object; rather, the object is pursued in order to surrender to it as a medium that alters the self, where the subject-as-supplicant now feels himself to be the recipient of enviro-somatic caring, identified with metamorphoses of the self" (14). Other noteworthy ideas appear in Bollas's first book, including "idiom," sometimes referred to as the "idiom of the ego." The idiom "evolves from the inherited disposition," occurring before birth, which is a "design that distinguishes and differentiates the 'personalities' of neonates" (8). The voiceless pattern-maker of one's self, the idiom may have been inspired by Lichtenstein's theory of the identity theme, which Bollas cites. A paradoxicalist, Bollas speaks about "loving hate," a situation where a person preserves a relationship by maintaining a passionate negative feeling. "Viewed this way, hate is not the opposite of, but a substitute for love" (118). Another intriguing idea is "normatic illness," a condition that occurs when a person feels empty or lacks a sense of self. These people are "abnormally normal" (136). (Bollas later adopted Joyce McDougall's term for the same phenomenon, "normopathic.") A symptom of normatic illness? When a person reads *Hamlet* and responds, "an unhappy young fellah" (137). Recall Allen Wheelis's observation that insight, even when genuine, does not always lead to psychological change and recovery.

To convey abstract theory, Bollas instinctively uses his literary education. It is no surprise that the writer to whom he repeatedly returns is Herman Melville. "Ahab feels compelled to seek the whale, even though he feels alienated from the source of his own internal compulsion" (*The Shadow of the Object* 27). Bollas cites several passages from *Moby Dick* to describe Ahab's monomaniacal pursuit of the whale. Ishmael is also transfixed by Moby Dick, including the pictorial representation of a white whale he sees at the Spouter-Inn, but unlike Ahab, he can put into words his complex feelings, in the process exorcising the demon. "Ishmael therefore reflects the creative alternative to Ahab," Bollas writes, combining a literary and clinical insight, "who scans the seas for a concrete transformational object (Moby Dick), because he occupies Melville's position—that of the artist who is in the unique position to create his own aesthetic moments and find symbolic equivalents to psychohistorical experiences that henceforth (as text or painting) become a new reality" (37).

The Aesthetic Moment

No psychoanalytic theorist or clinician uses the words "aesthetic moment" or "aesthetic experience" more often than Bollas. Sometimes he defines the expression with another literary term. "The aesthetic moment is a caesura in time when the subject feels held in symmetry and solitude by the spirit of the object" (*The Shadow of the Object* 31). Not all of his readers will know that a caesura is a rhythmic pause or break in the middle of a poetic line. Bollas refers to the literary critic Murray Krieger, who describes the aesthetic mode as when we "find ourselves locked within it, freely and yet in a controlled way playing among its surfaces and its depths" (34). One can grasp the meaning of the unconscious, Bollas contends, through a critical activity that resembles literary criticism.

The aesthetic experience involves for Bollas a feeling of rapture, a fusion or oneness with a literary text. This unity, he intimates, recalls the ego state that prevailed during early psychic life. Bollas spiritualizes the aesthetic experience: it evokes in us a "deep conviction that we have been in rapport with a sacred object" (31). Unlike Freud, who admired art but sometimes pathologized the artist, Bollas affirms without qualification art and artists. "Society cannot possibly meet the requirements of the subject, as the mother met the needs of the infant, but in the arts we have a location for such occasional recollections: intense memories of the process of self-transformation" (29). Few joys are greater than the "uncanny pleasure" of being held by a poem, composition, or painting (32). This feeling of rapture perhaps resembles the "oceanic" feeling that Freud wrote about to the French writer Romain Rolland in *Civilization and Its Discontents* (*SE* 21: 64–65), an experience that Freud admitted he never had himself. Bollas never loses faith in the "freedom of metaphor" (*The Shadow of the Object* 15), the power of language to express the deepest feelings and thoughts. Language conveys the unthought known; those who cannot articulate words are speaking a "dead language" (62). Freud referred to dreams as the "royal road to the unconscious," but Bollas uses another propitious expression: dreams contain the "grammar of the ego" (80). Metaphor is a suggestive mode, and the omission of the "as-if" construction provided by simile "erases ordinary ways of expressing truths that have been constituted in relation to reality" (175).

Apart from his favorite author, Herman Melville, Bollas has special affection for William Wordsworth, particularly the idea of "spots of time," a "suspended moment when self and object feel reciprocally embracing and mutually informative" (31). The poetics of the unconscious, Bollas explains, reveals a "Wordsworthian insistence that the ordinary was invested with mystery, that the immediacy of explicit meaning yield to the hermeneutic of the underlying theme; that imagery, syntax and aesthetic of organization be taken as another (repressed) discourse" (67). Bollas cites not only psychoanalytic theorists in *The Shadow of the Object* but also literary and cultural critics, including Krieger and Susan Sontag. He offers extended discussions of literary works, such as Grahame's *Wind in the Willows*. Grahame "invokes the imagery of the infant being held by the mother and places the aesthetic moment in the space between the infant and the caretaker" (38–39).

A Stylish Writer

Adam Phillips observes in *On Flirtation* (1994) that Bollas has been writing "some of the most innovatory psychoanalytic theory of the last few years." Phillips singles out Bollas's stylishness, "immersed in the poetry of romanticism and the nineteenth-century American novel" (154). Phillips was writing about *Being a Character*, but his words apply equally well to *The Shadow of the Object*. In his introduction to *The Christopher Bollas Reader*, Arne Jemstedt points out that Bollas's style is more literary than that of most psychoanalysts, partly because of the musicality of his prose (xxvii).

Bollas has a knack for aphorism, as when he observes that "we learn the grammar of our being before we grasp the rules of our language" (*The Shadow of the Object* 36). A patient who constantly rearranges the cushions on Bollas's analytic couch moves with the "grace of a lumberjack serving tea at a fundraising event" (105). The same patient generates Bollas's paradoxical comment: "To be a failure had been his greatest unconscious ambition" (106), recalling Fitzgerald's admission that he talks with the "authority of failure." Bollas delights in turning a cliché into a new insight. If something is "too good to be true," he reminds us, "it's not true to be so good" (124). Liars who deceive themselves and others engage in a maddening "trauma à deux" (181). A patient who threatened to murder

Bollas if he didn't shut up elicits the droll reply, "Look George, killing me would be redundant, as you spend most of these sessions insisting to yourself that I am not really here anyway" (222). Sometimes Bollas turns a negative into a positive: "We have lost pleasure in being bewildering to ourselves" (238). Other times he'll take a familiar expression and defamiliarize it: "In the beginning there may be the word, but there is also the wordless" (281). Bollas never tells us why he became a psychoanalyst instead of an English professor, but he makes a sardonic reference to the "sheltered industry of literary criticism" (30), hinting that the job might have been too tame for him.

Bollas always seems to know the right words to say to a patient, even when he doesn't. "For example, when in the midst of an interpretation to a patient I may suddenly realize that I am slightly off base, and I will stop myself and say something like, 'nope, that's not it, I can't quite find what I want to say'" (*The Shadow of the Object* 207). He always comes across as human, all too human. Few analysts are more forthcoming about their clinical failures. He uses self-disclosure judiciously to show how he has struggled with the same problems as his patients, as when he reveals his own troubled adolescence to the "normatic" Tom, who recently attempted suicide but denied having any conflicts in his life:

> I said that I had felt dreadfully uncertain at times about how things would turn out in my life. I reminisced about high school sports and recalled how dreadful I felt if I did not do well in competitive games, but how much worse it was if I let the team down, which, I said, I inevitably did. After going on in this vein for a while, I then said that I could not get over how little of the uncertainty and doubt and anger about being an adolescent seemed to be expressed in him. (150)

Recalling these self-disclosures, Bollas admits that he was slouching in his chair, looking more slovenly than usual, at a loss for words, closer to the troubling adolescent experience than Tom, who throughout the session maintained a stiff businesslike appearance that he believed characterized normal behavior. Bollas doesn't tell us the outcome of Tom's treatment apart from expressing the hope that continued psychotherapy will be helpful.

The Shadow of the Object contains several brief vignettes that reveal not only the analysands' conflicts but the analyst's as well. One example will suffice, that of a strikingly beautiful patient, Jane, who was always attacking Bollas. Jane had arranged to meet her boyfriend at an ice-rink, but when they met, he humiliated her and stalked off. As she narrates the story to Bollas, he finds himself becoming angry and distant from her, tersely quipping, "I become the ice-rink" (198). Pages later, Bollas confesses that he tended to look at rather than listen to Jane. He gradually realized that his pleasure looking at her was a defense against her paralyzing emotional life. He soon began to wish she left therapy, even if she had a breakdown and went to the hospital: At least that would get her off his hands. Analyzing his negative countertransference, he concludes that the feelings Jane awakened in him, anger and coldness, were those her mother felt when she tried to dismiss her daughter in childhood. Bollas then makes a statement I've never seen in another case study: "my fortitude in sticking my ground, interpreting the transference, and placing her idiom in a genetic reconstruction began to have some effect, and—to my disappointment, I can now confess—she felt I was helping her" (227). Sensing his coldness toward her, Jane confronted him. His begrudging acknowledgment that he found her maddening led to a therapeutic breakthrough for both of them.

Reading Bollas's early books from the perspective of his later ones, one occasionally encounters contradictions. In *The Shadow of the Object* he writes about Jonathan, who made increasingly real threats to murder someone close to him. "I am not free to provide the details of this planning," Bollas grants, but he was so unnerved by the threats that he consulted a colleague, who advised him, "tell him that if he does kill this person, you most certainly will tell the police." Bollas accepts the recommendation, informing Jonathan that further threats will result in a breach of confidentiality. "Interestingly, it was this action on my part which converted what might been a psychotic action (murder) into a phantasy. For after I said what I did, the truly murderous intent and the planning desisted" (185).

Surprisingly, the clinical vignette contradicts the recommendation that Bollas and his coauthor David Sundelson make in *The New Informants* (1995), where they warn against *any* breach of analytic confidentiality for *any* reason. Allowing patients to verbalize murderous threats, Bollas and Sundelson caution, is always therapeutic. Paul Mosher and I similarly argue against breach of confidentiality in our 2015 book *Confidentiality and Its Discontents: Dilemmas of Privacy in Psychotherapy*. One can only wonder why Bollas changed his mind about confidentiality. Without Bollas's warning that he would contact the police if a murder were committed, would Jonathan have converted a psychotic action into a fantasy? Bollas's discussion of Jonathan may have inspired him years later to write a novella about a psychoanalyst who, opposed to all confidentiality breaches, finds himself in a conundrum when a patient seeks treatment to carry out a suicide bombing.

Forces of Destiny

Bollas's next book, *Forces of Destiny*, published in 1989, only two years after *The Shadow of the Object*, spotlights his fondness for psychoanalytic metapsychology: psychological theory that refers to the structure of theory itself. The destiny drive, we learn, is a "form of the life instinct in which the subject seeks to come into his own true being through experiencing that releases this potential" (211). He introduces a new type of personality disorder, the "ghostline personality," people who have "alter" selves that refuse to acknowledge reality. These people are not multiple personalities; rather, they have internalized objects that are not fully alive or real—"rather like the common notion of a ghost as the spirit of that which has lived" (125). Sometimes Bollas takes established concepts and gives them new theoretical names, as with "dialectics of difference," the productive disagreements between patient and analyst. The liveliest passages in *Forces of Destiny* are Bollas's analytic self-disclosures, yet curiously, he is sometimes wary of these moments. "Of course we all know how embarrassing and irritating it can be when a colleague, in the name of scientific self-scrutiny, or humanist self-knowledge, promotes a 'confessional voice' to bear his disclosure of mind, affect, and self in work with a patient." Bollas admits to having often found himself in that situation, "where we are compelled to listen to a clinician's intercourse with honesty, giving birth to a revelatory issue that none of us believes" (52).

The clinical vignettes in *Forces of Destiny* are brief but nevertheless convey Bollas's willingness to find the best way to overcome clinical stalemates, even if it means becoming a provocateur. One of his patients, Jill, an "ice maiden of rage," resembles Jane in *The Shadow of the Object*. Speaking to Jill, whose "killing silences" awaken his anger, a re-creation, he surmises, of her mother's abandonment of her when she was a child, he says matter-of-factly, "You know, *you* are a monster" (38). During the next tempestuous sessions, they continue to battle over his belief she is a monster seeking to make him suffer, and finally, to his relief, Jill reluctantly agrees with the remark, ending the clinical impasse. "In the months following this session, whenever she would resume a period of killing silences, I would combat her, 'Ah! The deadly silence again!' " (39). Bollas has no trouble enduring prolonged silence from another patient who remained "utterly and eerily silent" during her three-times-a-week therapy sessions. Finally he says to her, as if he's thinking aloud, "You look like a young woman sitting on a park bench" (61). There's nothing particularly funny about the reply, but she unexpectedly begins laughing, and for the first time in *ten months* she resumes talking.

Bollas can be openly confrontational, as with Jane and Jill, but other times he reveals a softer side, one that admits making mistakes. Treating a "furiously intelligent woman" who brought him to an "altogether new low" in his "narcissistic injury spectrum," he sought out the advice of his supervisor, Paula Heimann, who admired his analysand's pluck. Following Heimann's advice, Bollas told his patient, the next time she savaged his clinical skills, "Ah! So you have trounced me once again!" Her rejoinder, "Yes, I did," is followed by silence—the first *good* silence of the analysis (84). He concedes to another patient, without irony or sarcasm, "Ah! So I am an idiot!" (85). Both confessions appear in a chapter aptly called "The Psychoanalyst's Celebration of the Analysand." The chapter abounds in counterintuitive truths, as when he states that a "patient's response to a positive comment is far more complex and conflicting than the response to what they experience as a painful confrontation" (89). The observation recalls Freud's wry statement to Marie Bonaparte: "As a rule when I am attacked I can defend myself; but when I am praised, I am helpless" (*Letters of Sigmund Freud* 368).

As most authors discover, the act of writing generates insights that might not otherwise occur. Bollas calls attention to this in *The Shadow of the Object* when he observes that writing the chapter "Ordinary Regression to Dependence" allowed him to give an example from his own life: sitting quietly as his son fell asleep at night. A parent's or analyst's silence can thus be generative. He observes in *Forces of Destiny* that writing the chapter "The Trauma of Incest" constituted a "working through of a countertransference" he had with a sexually abused woman (179).

Being a Character

Bollas's literary imagination may have shaped his decision to title his third book *Being a Character* instead of the more mundane *Being a Person*. The book elaborates on the innovative ideas he had sketched in his first two books, such as unthought known, idiom, destiny drive, and dialectics of difference. He distinguishes between two types of unconscious, the paternal "repressed unconscious" and the maternal "received unconscious." He cites dozens of nineteenth- and twentieth-century poets, as well as literary critics such as Helen Vendler. He doesn't offer a new theory of creativity, but he writes about "genera," a psychic organization of lived experience that results in creative new envisionings of life. He enumerates the steps in the formation of new genera, including the toleration, indeed, facilitation of chaos, which requires Keatsian negative capability. Throughout the book he rejects the belief that analysts have oracular knowledge of their patients. "I think we fail to 'grasp' them, because anyone—including oneself—is substantially beyond knowing" (131). Bollas also suggests, without elaboration, that he mistrusts his own "ambitions" (131), though anyone who has published a score of books is not unambitious.

In the chapter "Cruising in the Homosexual Arena," Bollas expresses his debt to literary writers such as James Baldwin in *Giovanni's Room*, James Rechy in *Numbers*, and Alan Hollinghurst in *The Swimming Pool Library*. Through their fictional explorations, these novelists have greater insight into their lives that those in other sexual groups, including the "normal heterosexual" (146). Judged from a historical perspective, Bollas's comments about homosexuality are enlightened and nonjudgmental. He observes that homosexuality would not exist without heterosexuality: "heterosexual ambivalence toward the homosexual has, over the centuries, become an intrinsic contribution to homosexual psychic pain" (160).

Another salient chapter in *Being a Character* is "The Psychoanalyst's Use of Free Associations," where Bollas maintains that communication is enhanced if analysts disclose their own free associations to patients. This is especially true when trying to understand a patient's dream. His patient Anton was a Shakespearean scholar who had difficulty finishing a book on *Hamlet*. Anton dreams of walking along a cliff toward a cemetery and a rough boardwalk that extends over the cliff. He wants to reach the graveyard but cannot climb over a barrier or wall. When he finally reaches the graveyard, he wakes up, fraught with anxiety. To understand the dream, Bollas searches for clues from Anton's life, the day residue, beginning with the recent sale of his family home following the death of his father six months earlier. The dream occurred one day after Anton's birthday, suggesting to him that he was struggling to return to the scene of birth and death, a theme that had preoccupied him throughout his life. The family home was adjacent to a graveyard that contained the grave of Anton's sister, who died when she was four months old, one year before Anton's birth. On the day of the dream Anton's brother had called, inquiring about the sale of the family home but neglecting to mention his brother's birthday.

What does this puzzling dream mean? Anyone familiar with *Hamlet* might think of the embattled father-son relationship or possibly an Oedipal theme, the prince's preoccupation with his mother. Bollas, however, himself a Shakespearean, intuits that the dream refers not to *Hamlet* but to *Lear*. "As the patient reported the dream, an image came to my mind of Edgar leading Gloucester to the cliff to create the illusion of death in *King Lear*. I was conscious of this coming to mind because of the cliff image in the dream" (118). For readers unfamiliar with the play, Bollas points out that Edgar, the "good son," unlike the "bad son" Edmund, leads his father, Gloucester, to the cliff to create the illusion of death. The theme of two brothers competing over being the better son to their father resonates in Anton's life. When Bollas suggests this interpretation, Anton suddenly remembers a confirming detail: on the night of the dream he had seen *Ran*, the renowned film by the Japanese director Akira Kurosawa's based on *Lear*. Bollas's ability to use his own free associations to Shakespeare enabled Anton to understand the dream.

Cracking Up

Bollas's 1995 book demonstrates the various ways in which "cracking up" reveals the existence of the unconscious in our everyday lives. "Cracking up" usually implies a mental breakdown, but Bollas uses the expression in novel ways. To begin with, cracking up occurs when the act of condensation, an essential part of dream work, is sundered through free association, an example of creative destruction. Analysts crack up their patients' narratives with counternarratives. Psychoanalysis breaks up the certitudes of knowledge and decenters the listening experience. Questions and musings shatter the illusory unity of inner experience. The memories of analysand and analyst alike are subject to continuous construction, reconstruction, and deconstruction. (One of Bollas's favorite words, "deconstruction" was popularized by the French philosopher and literary critic Jacques Derrida.) Citing Eastern religions, in which the path to self-knowledge occurs only when the ego is dissolved, Bollas reminds us that free association transforms or cracks up ordinary consciousness.

Cracking Up is a paean to the unconscious, yet at the same time Bollas offers prescient criticisms of the trendy and often dangerous therapies that proliferated in the last quarter of the twentieth century, such as regression therapy, the overdiagnosis of multiple personality disorder, and the false memory movement, all of which led to the contemporary "festival of victimology" (201). During the 1980s Bollas had supervised many cases in the United States where clinicians fell into the trap of planting false memories in their patients. He satirizes these movements in his novellas and plays. Other pseudotherapies included the alien abduction craze, promoted by the Harvard psychiatrist John Mack, and satanic ritual abuse, which succeeded in bedeviling the public. Bollas's undergraduate thesis on seventeenth-century New England village life familiarized him with Arthur Miller's 1953 play *The Crucible*, a drama of the Salem witch trials that occurred in Massachusetts Bay Colony from 1692 to 1693. In *Being a Character* Bollas refers to act 3 of the play as the "most harrowing moment in American drama" (166), coining the expression "violent innocence." He uses a darker expression in *Cracking Up*, describing the "malignant innocents" who, professing their own guiltlessness, demonize others.

In Bollas's view, psychoanalysis errs if it rejects reality, "taking refuge either in a theory of narrative or in a misplaced empiricism, where the only facts recognized are those enacted in the transference" (113). He doesn't give an example of narrative theory, but he may have in mind Donald Spence's influential 1982 book *Narrative Truth and Historical Truth*, which advocates the search for historical details while downplaying the value of theory. As a history major, Bollas remains committed to historical truth—he worked as a bibliographer for the history department at Berkeley—but he understands the limits of understanding the past. In one of his most resonant comments, he refers to the past as a "cemeterial concept" that signifies the eradication of the self. "Not only a burial ground of that which was enjoyed and cannot be recovered, of the many prior selves lived that are now lost to their former moments, but a term which eradicates the truth of the lived present" (134). Bollas's cemeterial concept differs from the idea of a "crypt," a concept advanced by Nicholas Abraham and Maria Torok, two Hungarian-born French analysts who formulated a theory of transgenerational haunting that occurs when a loss, inaccessible to the work of mourning, cannot be acknowledged.

As in his preceding books, Bollas instinctively turns to literature to verbalize truths about the self. Referring to what he calls the "aesthetics of nothingness," which involves delusion, denial, repression, and splitting, he invokes Wallace Stevens's poem "The Snow Man," about the "Nothing that is not there and the Nothing that is" (*Cracking Up* 59). Bollas quotes another Stevens poem, "A Primitive Like an Orb," to show how the self comes into existence from several sources. We cannot prove the existence of a poem, Stevens writes, though it is there—like the self, Bollas adds. Bollas writes about a patient named Roger, an unusually intellectual young man suffering from anorexia who found everything and everyone, including Bollas himself, "boring." To convey Roger's obsession over food, the extent to which he subjected every piece of food to a linguistic deconstruction, Bollas uses an image from T.S. Eliot's poem "The Love Song of J. Alfred Prufrock," that of a peach, recalling Eliot's line, "Do I dare to eat a peach?" The image signified to Roger "youth, vulnerability, fuzz but no hair, and it brought to mind 'peachy' as a description of a certain person" (84). Bollas encourages the apathetic Roger to study Camus's theory of the absurd. "*Who* is Camus?" Roger asked. The next months Roger read everything written by Camus, then "devoured" (an ironic word when used to describe an anorexic) Sartre, Heidegger, Kant, and the Greek philosophers. Roger's evolution in analysis "proceeded from an obsession (the anorexia) to a transient preoccupation, to a passion, and eventually to concentration" (86).

Bollas concedes the difficulty of conveying in a case study the immediacy and spontaneity of a therapy session. "The analyst's and analysand's report of his or her history is so often rather deadening, even though it is informative and theoretically enriching to the listener, while a session, even the mundane report of the patient's seemingly far less interesting parochial interests, is more intriguing" (137). Every writer of psychotherapy tales has confronted this challenge. The abridged clinical vignettes in *Cracking Up* do not allow Bollas to create memorable characters or riveting therapy moments, as we see in Freud's case studies, Robert Lindner's *The Fifty-Minute Hour* (1955), or Irvin Yalom's *Love's Executioner* (2000). Part of the difficulty is that Bollas generally uses summary rather than scenic narration, "telling" rather than the more dramatic "showing." Nevertheless, Bollas's vignettes are usually lively and perceptive, and he never comes across as authoritarian, reductive, or omniscient. Indeed, one passage wryly *shows* how analysts must work through their misunderstandings of patients, a process that resembles at times a comedy of errors:

> A patient says, "Last night I went to . . ." and I silently speak
> "the opera" but the patient says "the cinema." A patient says,
> "I am really very . . ." I silently reply "cross," and the patient

says, "pleased with my work on the book." Each analyst engages in thousands of such responses and feels the course of the patient's correction, which gives him an unconscious sense of the patient's way of thinking. It is like learning a new language and may take years. (31)

The insights in the chapter "The Structure of Evil" are singular. Some of Bollas's statements about serial killers, such as Ted Bundy, Jeffrey Dahmer, Henry Lee Lucas, Dennis Nilsen, and Adolfo Constanzo, are jarring, particularly when he takes a favorable word, such as "empathy," and shows its horrifyingly literal meaning. "It is disturbing to see 'positive' sides to the act of murder, when the killer unconsciously seeks to enter the live body of the other by cutting it up in an act of 'examination,' a bizarrely concrete form of empathy, coming to know the other only by cutting it into pieces to look inside it" (195). Bollas compares these serial characters to allegorical figures who usually represent only one characteristic. The serial killer is "squeezed into an identification with one quality, evil, that obliterates other psychic qualities" (218).

Bollas sees Milton's *Paradise Lost* as a trauma text. He's not the first critic to point out Milton's sympathy for Satan—William Blake made a similar comment in the early nineteenth century—but Bollas observes astutely that the prince of darkness is a "traumatized soul" who feels compelled to inflict his trauma upon others. "It is impossible to exclude from our considerations of Milton's Satan the overwhelming power and structural malevolence of God's authority, which seems grotesquely harmonized with the lust for power to which Satan succumbs" (184). Strong words indeed! Bollas is unafraid to poke fun at other fictional or real characters, including Jacques Lacan. He sees Lacan, with his notoriously brief sessions and his "revolving door" that a score of patients passed through an hour, as a jokester. "One never knew quite what he would say. Nor did he. By the end of his life, for better and for worse, he had made a virtue of the ordinary folly of everyday man" (223).

Cracking Up offers us a vision of psychoanalysis that is a pleasure for analysand and analyst alike. "It is blissful to free-associate in the sentient presence of the other who listens without making demands" (47). Bollas revels in cracking up his readers by exposing the humor of his own unflattering dreams, including the "chicken dream," a comic event when he "chickened out" in response to a friend's call to courage. However embarrassing the dream must have been, Bollas knows that everything is grist for the analyst's mill, particularly the analyst's self-disclosures. Similarly, he must have had fun describing the confusion that occurred when, working in the Buffalo Student Mental Health Center, he assumed a silent patient was psychotic because he mistook Bollas for a dentist. "I confirmed every suspicion he had ever held about the lunacy of our profession" (229). Bollas often uses the Lacanian word *jouissance*, but we can use it to describe *Cracking Up*.

The Mystery of Things

The most intriguing chapter in the next book, *The Mystery of Things* (1999), "Occasional Madness of the Psychoanalyst," contains one of Bollas's longest clinical vignettes. Nick was a potentially violent patient who had threatened his mother with a knife and chased her in their home. His bizarre mannerisms appeared to make therapy impossible. He would sit motionless in his chair, staring at Bollas with an unnerving fixed gaze. Every few minutes he would rotate his head in the direction of a window, mindlessly scanning the distance. He would answer Bollas's questions with an automatic "no," leaving the analyst's words hanging in space. As the weeks of therapy in the hospital turned into months, change began to occur—but only in Bollas, who found himself not only loathing the patient but also losing his own identity, regressing, as if he has been seized by a malevolent force. Nick almost succeeded, in short, in driving Bollas crazy—and students of literature will recognize that Bollas has modeled the case study on Melville's iconic "Bartleby, the Scrivener."

One of Bollas's earliest published psychoanalytic essays (1974) was on Melville's short story. Like Bartleby, whose passive-aggressive words, "I would prefer not to," nearly drive the narrator crazy, Nick's monosyllabic replies have a similarly maddening effect on Bollas. The analyst becomes increasingly annoyed and destabilized, like Melville's narrator. "I would greet Nick at the door as he came into the room; he would sit down and then a silence would descend upon us. It is not something I can describe" (143). Bollas paradoxically proceeds to describe the scene in the most powerful paragraph in the book:

> As he rotated his head, I would say, "You are looking at something?," to which he would reply "No," followed by a long silence. One day he said "You hear it?" "What?" I replied. "The

fly." "What fly?" "The fly," he said. "Where?" "Over there, by the window." I could neither see nor hear anything, and hadn't seen a fly since the early autumn. It was winter and there was snow on the ground. Ten minutes of silence ensured. "It's still there." "This fly on the wall?," I queried. No reply.

Suddenly, Bollas has a flash of inspiration, realizing that *he* is the fly on the wall to the patient, who understandably fears that he is being spied on. The vignette is not yet over, however. Furious over the prolonged silence, Bollas shouts, "It's as if you are hiding from a monster! And what is this monster? Where is it? Is it me? Am I a monster: a Bollas monster?" (43). Nick begins laughing, and the next day he cheerfully greets Bollas with the words "Hello there, Monster," leading to a genuine breakthrough in therapy. The vignette ends with a jolting conclusion: "Strictly speaking, psychoanalysts do not know their countertransference" (148).

Hysteria

Of all psychoanalytic diagnoses, hysteria has had the most vexed history. For that reason alone, Bollas's decision to write a book on the subject was audacious. *Hysteria* (2000) is his most theoretical study. He may have rushed into a subject where angels, if not other contemporary psychoanalysts, feared to tread because of the rash of hysterical cases diagnosed at the end of the twentieth century. As he notes in the introduction, his experience with clinical supervisions in the United States in the mid-1980s convinced him to deliver a series of lectures and conduct a number of seminars in this country and abroad in the late 1980s and 1990s.

Arguing that the hysteric is "surely the most complex character in psychoanalytic theory" (162), Bollas suggests that there are as many male hysterics as female hysterics, adding that patients misdiagnosed with borderline personality disorder or multiple personality disorder are sometimes hysterics. He presents us with nothing less than a taxonomy of hysteria: the good-enough hysteric, the death drive hysteric, the ascetic hysteric, the precocious hysteric, the entrenched hysteric, and the malignant hysteric. Sexuality is traumatic to a hysteric, Bollas conjectures, because it destroys the relationship with the mother and leads to repression, theatrical behavior, susceptibility to emotional contagion, and over-identification with the other.

As with *Cracking Up*, *Hysteria* doesn't name transgressive therapists responsible for pseudotherapy, but an infamous example is Flora Rheta Schreiber's *Sybil* (1973), a bestseller that was made into a classic television film starring Joanne Woodward as the maverick psychoanalyst Cornelia Wilbur (1908–1992) and Sally Field as the eponymous patient, Shirley Ardell Mason (1923–1998). There was also a remake of *Sybil* starring Tammy Blanchard and Jessica Lange. The publication of the book provoked immediate clinical skepticism, based on Sybil's admission to her analyst that she was not a multiple personality. "I don't even have a 'double' to help me out. I am all of them" (Schreiber 374). It was not until the investigative journalist Debbie Nathan published *Sybil Exposed* in 2011, eleven years after the appearance of Bollas's *Hysteria*, that readers learned Sybil's sixteen selves were fabrications induced by an analyst who violated nearly every standard of ethical treatment. Nathan's conclusions were based on her meticulous research of the papers that Schreiber left to the John Jay College of Criminal Justice after her death. Clinicians now view Sybil as having suffered from grand hysteria and her relationship with Wilbur as an example of folie à deux.

"Joel" is, for me, the most beguiling patient in *Hysteria*, not because of the depth of his character but because of a dilemma he encounters with his mother, a "phenom" who loved to act out her conflicts in public, to her children's mortification. "When we were in a public place there were times when she would insist upon showing us something instead of just telling us, and by the time we were in our twenties, I remember too often that one of us would say, 'Mom, sit down, and just tell us' or we would see that she was just about to leap to her feet to show us and we would say to her 'Mom, now don't get up . . . just stay put and tell us'" (123). The moment is powerful precisely because Bollas *shows* us his patient's distress.

To demonstrate how the hysteric converts carnal sexuality into spiritual sexuality, thus denying the claims of the body, Bollas offers a literary example, unrequited Petrarchan love. Citing a sonnet by Thomas Wyatt (1503–1542), "Description of the Contrarious Passions in a Lover," Bollas asserts that the hysteric similarly believes that love requires hatred of the body. Bollas uses Iago's reference in *Othello* to the "beast with two backs" to conjure up a child's horror over the primal scene. He describes a patient who "did not go gently into that kind of light" (157), an allusion to Dylan Thomas's canonical poem "Do Not Go Gentle into That Good Night."

Unlike the borderline, the narcissist, or the obsessive-compulsive, the hysteric is often a vivid storyteller. "Some hysterics become intensely interested in telling their story. But the telling is their living, so the repeated telling of the story is needed in order to keep the self and its others alive where they live: in the story" (95). This creates a major dilemma, however, for both the clinician and the psychiatric case study author, as Bollas admits. "I am of course aware of the irony of this moment: in discussing how the hysteric seeks to exist inside the other's story I am creating one of my own, which could become an open house for any travelling hysteric. It could not be otherwise" (57). Bollas is aware of this conundrum, which may have no solution.

Dark at the End of the Tunnel

Bollas's three novellas and collection of plays—*Dark at the End of the Tunnel, I Have Heard the Mermaids Singing, Mayhem*, and *Theraplay & Other Plays*—were all published between 2004 and 2006, a burst of creativity for an analyst who regularly saw patients all day. His clinical writings help us understand the themes of his fictional and dramatic works. All of Bollas's writings reveal an author who is always thinking psychoanalytically, always trying to tap into the unthought known. Bollas's creative writings, like Irvin Yalom's, represent a unique subgenre of literature that has a therapeutic function designed to illuminate aspects of psychotherapy while at the same time entertaining the reader. Bollas's fictional analysts do not lose faith in their profession, as we have seen in Allen Wheelis's novels, but they confront dark existential truths, and they advance theoretical ideas that Bollas was not ready to publish in his nonfiction.

I read *Dark at the End of the Tunnel* (2004) during the onslaught of the COVID-19 pandemic, an apt time to examine a story about a mysterious "Catastrophe" that has ravaged the planet. *Dark at the End of the Tunnel* is not science fiction, but it offers insight into an unnamed psychoanalyst who, appearing in all three novellas, struggles to make sense of an event that he believes will irrevocably alter the course of history. Although the Catastrophe appears to have been caused by terrorists, we learn that humankind has been "infected by a viral spirit that destroys the human soul" (126), an all-too-timely metaphor that conveys the bleakness of the coronavirus pandemic.

The book cover describes *Dark at the End of the Tunnel* as an "irresistibly amusing tale of human frailty." There are amusing moments, but the story's dominant tone alternates between dark comedy and somber meditation. In the preface, Bollas refers to the book as a "mixed genre—a group of essays presented through the conceit of fiction." The story allows Bollas to convey clashing points of view through multiple voices. Alluding to the title of a previous book, Bollas remarks that comedy "cracks up certainties, poses rather than answers questions, and seems truer to life as it is ordinarily lived" (vii–viii).

In an interview with Anthony Molino published in the edited volume *In Freud's Tracks* (2009), Bollas elaborated on his freedom as a creative writer. "I can throw forward quite radical ideas without the burden of proof weighing down the writing." Additionally, writing fiction and drama helped him overcome the writer's block he experienced at the time. His turn, or rather return, to creative writing harked back to the 1960s, when he wrote plays—and when all of his childhood possessions were burned in a fire set by an arsonist. Bollas was dismayed when the editor of the *International Journal of Psychoanalysis* refused to consider reviewing his novellas, declaring that the journal does not review fiction. "Astonishing really," Bollas lamented to Molino. *Dark at the End of the Tunnel* is a novel of ideas, where plot and characterization are subordinated to extended psychological, philosophical, and theological meditations. The story is long on didacticism and short on drama, but it will be fascinating to anyone who seeks to learn about Bollas's evolving view of psychoanalysis.

A Fictional Self-Portrait?

The psychoanalyst in *Dark at the End of the Tunnel* cannot be reduced to Bollas himself; the story is fiction, not disguised autobiography. "While I certainly do borrow from my identity to attach characteristics to the fictional analyst," Bollas told me during our interview, "the pleasure of writing about him is that he is *not* me." Nevertheless, the fictional and real psychoanalysts have much in common. Bollas achieves narrative distance, the degree of separation between author and protagonist, by showing the psychoanalyst in the process of thinking through new ideas that reflect the authorial viewpoint. The other characters in the story, by contrast, serve as sounding boards or foils. Readers familiar with Bollas's clinical writings will have little trouble viewing the psychoanalyst as a reliable authorial spokesman. The fictional psychoanalyst is sixty-four, only three years older than Bollas when *Dark at the End of the Tunnel* appeared. (Bollas's psychoanalyst remains the same age in all three novellas.) A devout Freudian, the psychoanalyst believes in the liberatory power of free association to unlock inner psychic truth. (The "fundamental rule" of psychoanalysis, Freud urged his patients, was to verbalize everything that came into their heads.) Like Bollas, following Freud, the psychoanalyst affirms "evenly suspended attentiveness" (3). Early in his career, the psychoanalyst remained completely silent when he had nothing to say, loath to betray his ignorance, paralleling Bollas's clinical technique as a young analyst. One day, however, the psychoanalyst changes his technique and simply confesses he has not yet understood a patient, a more effective and honest clinical approach.

Like Bollas's, the psychoanalyst's mentors are Melanie Klein, Wilfred Bion (the psychoanalyst's "hero"), Winnicott, and Lacan (whose terminology appears throughout the story). The psychoanalyst is not a fan of C.G. Jung, but another character, a minister, quotes admiringly from Jung's *Paracelsus the Physician*, suggesting the psychoanalyst's willingness to change his mind. Like Bollas, the psychoanalyst loves reading ancient and modern philosophy and literature: Plato, Sophocles, St. Augustine, Shakespeare, Elizabeth Barrett Browning, Matthew Arnold, Marcel Proust, Emile Zola, Albert Camus, William Butler Yeats, Martin Heidegger, T.S. Eliot, and Wallace Stevens. Like Bollas, the psychoanalyst is an etymologist, checking the *Oxford English Dictionary* for the origins and meanings of words, such as "soul," which he then dutifully offers to the reader. Like Bollas, the psychoanalyst appreciates classical music, referring to a new recording of Bach's *Goldberg Variations*. The psychoanalyst reflects Bollas's criticisms of the excesses of his profession, as can be seen in the following passage that contains an unsparing critique of Kleinian analysts' tendency to conflate psychotic states of mind with schizophrenia:

> There was a certain flirtation with the schizophrenic and the notion of the divided self, but for so many analysts this was more like reading science fiction, as few ever came across anyone who was truly psychotic. The Kleinians capitalised on this rather hot topic by claiming that we were all psychotic anyway. This proved to be quite a good selling point (and incidentally returned a sense of Empire to the British, now free once again to colonise the world, not by offering a superior ability to

transform native peoples, but by proposing a transformation of the primitive parts of selves). (31–32)

The funereal tone of *Dark at the End of the Tunnel* at the end, evoking the art of dying, ars moriendi, may have a biographical explanation, the psychoanalyst's ruminations over dying and death reflecting Bollas's own heightened recognition of mortality. As he explained to Molino, shortly before he wrote the novella two of his friends died, and his father had died two years earlier. Bollas also refers, without elaboration, to his "own brush with death" (Molino, "Into Fiction").

Dark at the End of the Tunnel contains signature Bollas concepts, such as idiom, transformational object, and the destiny drive, but there are three major new ideas. The first is "objecthood," a "malignant transformation in which a person's being with the other is destroyed by the other, who replaces one's self-as-other with one's self-only-as-object" (44). Objecthood thus represents the destruction of otherness. The second idea is "descendence," the opposite of "transcendence," a word Bollas dislikes because of its supernatural and religious implications. Descendence, the psychoanalyst explains to another character, is "our participation in the ordinary, in the quotidian" (70), a "spiritual antidote to transcendental ambitions and affiliations" (83). An evocative word, "descendence" expresses the "sacred in the ordinary" (91). The third idea is "projective transcendentalism," Bollas's term for the religious imagination: "our soul is already being projected by our death, into some other place, and it is the task of our imagining, and of many religions, to try to see where that place is, and who we are, or what we are when we get there" (96). *Dark at the End of the Tunnel* enables Bollas to advance innovative ideas that he might not be ready to conceptualize in a clinical book.

Bollas does not give us a full portrait of the psychoanalyst's life. We learn nothing about his relationship to his parents, wife, and children. Nor do we have insight into his sexual life, his training analysis, or his education. The psychoanalyst speaks about childhood as a period of "illness" (76), but we learn nothing about his own childhood. Nor do we know whether he has experienced any personal or professional crises. Other clinician-novelists offer more self-lacerating portraits of psychoanalysts. Has Bollas's psychoanalyst been tempted to transgress sexual boundaries, as Irvin Yalom dramatizes in his masterful novel *Lying on the Couch*? Has Bollas despaired over the failure of self-knowledge to effect analytic cure, as we see in Allen Wheelis's novels, where analysts have lost confidence in the talking cure? Has Bollas struggled with the impact of early parental loss, as Daniel Jacobs explores in *The Distance from Home*?

Despite its limitations, *Dark at the End of the Tunnel* succeeds in conveying Bollas's vision of psychoanalysis. The reader never doubts the psychoanalyst's authenticity or the seriousness of his ideas. By changing a single word in the title, Bollas transforms a platitude into an arresting expression. "Light at the end of the tunnel" would have been a cliché. As the poet Robert Lowell mordantly quipped, "if we see a light at the end of the tunnel, it's the light of an oncoming train" (quoted in Jamison 131).

There are a few differences between the real and fictional psychoanalysts. Sometimes the latter makes statements that prove to be awkward or embarrassing. When asked at a dinner party, "So, what are you doing these days?" he responds, "I'm trying to write about life." Before elaborating with a "litany of recalled quotations," he sensed that "he was about to ruin the meal" (13). In a generally positive review of *Dark at the End of the Tunnel* and *I Heard the Mermaids Singing*, Victoria Hamilton faults the psychoanalyst for "stupidly and unwittingly" disclosing information about his writerly struggles (533), but this strikes me as a harsh response to a situation with which many people, writers and non-writers alike, would identify.

Bollas's psychoanalyst never loses faith in his profession despite the fear that the Catastrophe has produced a moral and existential crisis from which humanity might not recover. The story ends with the psychoanalyst comforting a dying patient, expressing the hope that she needs by affirming the only form of afterlife in which he believes, remaining alive to those who have internalized her goodness. After speaking with his patient for the last time, he muses on the penultimate page, "Being a psychoanalyst was a strange life" (134). A strange but nevertheless good life. As his patient declares at the end, the psychoanalyst "found consolation, because the human mind—or psyche, or soul—could still find in the last moments of an existence a turn of phrase, or a form of ending, which caught the spirit of humanity and blessed existence with it" (135), an insight that helps one survive a catastrophe or pandemic.

I Have Heard the Mermaids Singing

Bollas's next novella, *I Have Heard the Mermaids Singing* (2005), is livelier than *Dark at the End of the Tunnel*, though ironically it is about depression. One effect of the Catastrophe, we learn, is the "departure of the unconscious" (9), an ominous movement that is both the cause and effect of superficial treatments of mental illness. Bollas critiques the siren call of psychopharmacology, big pharma, particularly the use of antidepressants, satirically named "Napalmtrek" made by "Dawn Chemical," an allusion to the incendiary napalm manufactured by Dow Chemical that American soldiers used during the Vietnam War. As he does in *Hysteria* for a different mental illness, Bollas offers a taxonomy of depression and shows, consistent with Freud's theorizing in "Mourning and Melancholia," that the mood disorder is internalized violence directed against another person.

Bollas gives other examples of derailed psychotherapy: here-and-now transference analysis that ignores the underlying causes of mental illness; twelve-step programs that represent secular conversion experiences; the proliferation of attention deficit disorder in children caused by, in Bollas's view, neglectful parents; and corrupt analysts who believe that legitimate ethical complaints are "almost inevitably part of a pathological process" (122). One of the psychoanalyst's colleagues bemoans the fact that psychoanalysis is "now the disease that promotes itself as the cure" (29), recalling Karl Kraus's gibe a century ago that psychoanalysis is the illness it purports to cure.

The psychoanalyst cannot convince all of his patients that depression is treatable through talk therapy. Enid Sullivan maintains that depression is a purely biological event. She has become, as a result of her failed quarter-of-a-century analysis, a "champion of psychotropic intervention, and was violently anti-therapy" (167). Psychoanalysis has helped his other patients, however, who recognize that depression may be a symptom of buried conflicts. To achieve narrative distance, Bollas tells us that the psychoanalyst "hated research, found writing almost impossible and loathed public speaking" (115), the opposite of the prolific Bollas. Nevertheless, the three-page section in the psychoanalyst's notebook, inveighing against the shallows of fundamentalism in psychiatric thinking, resembles Bollas's prose. There are inside jokes, as when the narrator refers to Buffalo as one of the "low smile parts of the world," containing a bar "famous for its poetry readings, where no one had been seen to smile in fifteen years" (71). The psychoanalyst loves the same poems as Bollas does, including Eliot's "The Love Song of J. Alfred Prufrock," from where Bollas has taken the title of his novella.

The main plot of the novella focuses on the psychoanalyst's encounter with a would-be terrorist who seeks treatment to help him carry out his violent mission. The psychoanalyst is stunned when Kalid al Walid displays his suicide bomber's vest. The psychoanalyst, a member of the Association for Confidentiality in Psychoanalysis, finds himself in an impossible situation. The only solution, he fears, is to murder his patient to prevent widespread death. Bollas resolves the dilemma when the psychoanalyst convinces the bomber that his desire to blow himself up, along with countless innocent people, is motivated by rage toward his father-in-law, who had humiliated him. However unlikely that a potential terrorist would seek analytic treatment, the situation allows Bollas to propose a new theory of the "malignant transcendent," an "odious form of transcendence achieved by the serial killer, who offered himself as a kind of helping angel to his victim-to-be: eliciting trust, becoming like a God of sorts, and then transforming himself into evil before the victim's eyes, prior to killing him, and in this moment transcending the terms of life and death" (85).

Like *Dark at the End of the Tunnel*, *I Have Heard the Mermaids Singing* is a meditation on death. Bollas never uses the word "existential" in the story, but the psychoanalyst experiences death anxiety. Six feet four inches tall, he recognizes his own shrinkage: "Now he was less than himself." Worse, looking into a mirror, he is preoccupied with liver spots, "awful signifiers, marring his hands and his face" (62). He's so concerned that he asks his wife to accompany him to a drug store to buy a cream, "Out Spot" (echoing Lady Macbeth's "Out, damned spot" while washing blood from her hands), to conceal the signs of aging. Like his patients, he suffers from bouts of depression, in his own case brought on by the "deepening crisis of age" (159). And yet the psychoanalyst almost seems to welcome these dark moods, believing, with Bollas, that "depressions were in fact inoculative," helping people "cope with the ardours of life" (164).

Mayhem

Mayhem (2006) begins when Mrs. Stottlemeyer, a woman "everyone avoided," barges into the psychoanalyst's office without an appointment and announces that she has recently seen her husband who died six years earlier. Upon learning from the analyst that she is still angry and guilty over her husband's death, Mrs. Stottlemeyer declares war on the unconscious. Attending a new-age health center that offers a series of workshops on the theme of "Out with the unconscious," she signs up for "Becoming empty," a workshop that melds psychotherapy and Eastern spirituality. "The small group of eight participants had to sit on coloured mats and chant the word 'out,' sonically elongated to sound like 'oooooowwwwwwwtttttt.' This was repeated for half an hour and then the group leader uttered the phrase 'I am what I am.'" The members then repeat the chant with the words "I am not what I am not" (19).

Some of the lampooned therapies in *Mayhem* are credible enough to seem true. A new psychological movement advocating the "therapeutics of funeralism" arises when a marital therapist utters the phrase, "This marriage is *dead*," and, with the help of the couple who no longer wish to be married, coauthors the bestselling book *Bury the Living Dead*. The theory behind funeralism is simple. "For decades marital therapists had been in a state of denial and did not know how to say to the many couples they saw that there was no good reason for these two people to stay together. Instead, they should leave one another, bury the past, and get on with a new life" (47). The funeralist therapist conducts a burial service where husband and wife ritualistically return their wedding rings to each other and utter the vow, "This marriage is dead." Bollas has ingeniously worked out all the details of funeralism. "There was subsequently to be no physical encounter, and both parties were to sign release forms prohibiting them from any further contact with one another, or with people on one another's designated 'enemy list'" (48).

As in *Dark at the End of the Tunnel*, *Mayhem* spoofs psychoanalytic theorists. The Lacanians never say anything offensive because no one understands what they are talking about. The Kleinians have the opposite problem, offending everyone because their interpretations "seemed to come from 'some feeling' which they blamed the patient for 'putting into them,' and often what they said seemed to have nothing to do with what the patient was actually talking about" (54). Many of the incidents in *Mayhem* are funny, but Bollas's tone changes when he describes "clone-analysis," a "special form of necromancy in which writers elected dead subjects about whom almost no information existed at all." The novella's psychoanalyst recalls two long-dead members of his own professional society.

Mish Mash's unusual intimacy with his patients had occasioned widespread interest, although it was not so unusual for analysts to have sexual relations with their analysands. There was also a certain curiosity about his other "boundary violations." He and one patient, for example, had bunked off and visited bookshops, rather than engage in an analytical relation. . . . The real fascination with Mish Mash, however, was down to the fact that he had been in analysis with Dr Wool—a treatment of which there existed no clinical records at all—and the clone analysts believed this gave them a golden opportunity, in a series of essays and books, to attribute Mish Mash's violations to failures in the analysis. (64–65)

Masud Khan

Mayhem condemns these clone-analysts' writings as forms of "wild analysis," but there is abundant evidence about the transgressions of the real Mish Mash, Masud Khan, Bollas's own training psychoanalyst. One of the most prominent analysts of the second half of the twentieth century, Khan (1924–1989) was born in the district of British India that later became Pakistan. Bollas may have sought out Khan as his training analyst because Khan's undergraduate and graduate training at the University of Punjab focused on English literature and psychology; he wrote his master's thesis on James Joyce's *Ulysses*. Khan was himself analyzed by Winnicott, whose middle name, "Woods," resembles the name of Mish Mash's analyst, Dr. Wool. A graduate of the British Psychoanalytic Association, Khan authored several highly regarded books, including *The Privacy of the Self* (1974), *Alienation in Perversions* (1979), and *Hidden Selves* (1983). Linda Hopkins observes in her 2006 biography *False Self: The Life of Masud Khan* (2006) that in 1976 Erik Erikson proclaimed, "The future of analysis belongs to Khan!" (xxii). Hopkins documents Khan's self-destructed career as a result of alcoholism, grandiosity, and mental disease, which she speculates was bipolar disorder.

Some of Masud Khan's analysands have written about his startling boundary violations with them. In an article appearing in the *London Review of Books* in 2001, the Cambridge economics professor Wynne Godley recalled going into analysis in his early thirties with Khan, to whom he had been referred by Winnicott. Godley's analysis was a disaster. Khan intruded himself into every aspect of Godley's life, savagely criticizing Godley's English culture, talking about his own social life in London and New York, answering telephone calls during sessions, disclosing confidential information about other patients, and even recommending that the happily married Godley meet another Khan patient, "Marian." Godley,

Khan, and Marian then started "meeting à trois." Khan showered Godley with expensive gifts and invited him to his home, where the analyst's ballerina wife, Svetlana Beriosova, played hostess. On one occasion Khan and his wife had a violent fight and both passed out drunk. Khan began showing up uninvited at Godley's home. Worst of all, Khan attacked Godley's pregnant wife. "The perception that, at the level of reality, Khan had made an attempt on the life of our unborn only child was painful beyond anything I can convey." That was the end of analysis.

Godley told Robert S. Boynton in a 2003 interview in *Boston Review* that Khan discouraged him throughout the seven-year analysis from recounting anything about his childhood or past because everything of *real* significance was taking place between the two men in their sessions. "Of course this gave him a license to interfere actively, judgmentally, and with extraordinary cruelty in every aspect of my daily life." Godley emphasizes at the conclusion of his own article, enigmatically titled "Saving Masud Khan," that his devastating criticisms of Khan should not be interpreted as an attack on psychoanalysis, for which he has great respect. "I could not have gained the insight to write this piece, nor could I have recovered from the experiences I have described, if they had not at last been undone at the hands of a skilful, patient and selfless American analyst."

The psychoanalytic community was stunned by Khan's virulently anti-Semitic slurs in his last book, *The Long Wait* (1988), published in the Great Britain as *When Spring Comes*. The eminent American literary critic Harold Bloom went into analysis with Khan, perhaps because of the analyst's literary background. The analysis lasted for only three sessions. In a letter to Linda Hopkins, Bloom elaborated on the instant antipathy that developed between the two men. "Khan loathed me at first sight and let me know it, and I rapidly reciprocated, though I believe that generally I am amiable enough. All that I truly recall is that he attacked me for being unkempt (I still am), told me innumerable times that he was much more intelligent than I was, and seemed to have read my earlier books. What I remember most vividly is that I walked out half-way through the third session because his abusiveness became overtly anti-Semitic" (Hopkins 129).

In an obituary published in *The Guardian*, Bollas focuses on Khan's paradoxical nature. After directly addressing Khan's anti-Semitism and mental illness, Bollas ends the obituary with a poignant statement: "*When Spring Comes* is a repelling work, but if mental illness can be forgiven, and time's passing often does so, then the literary works of one of the most gifted psychoanalytic writers of this century may yet survive his tragically driven effort to dismantle himself before his death."

The major part of *Mayhem* focuses on a controversial art installation called *A Life*, which turns out to be a hoax created by three art students who seek to demonstrate that art always has political implications. Bollas's psychoanalyst is alarmed by the mass hysteria arising from *A Life*, which, as a result of the sensationalistic media, goes viral—a metaphor that unites *Mayhem* and *Dark at the End of the Tunnel*. We learn on the last page of *Mayhem* that as a youth, Bollas's protagonist had hoped that psychoanalysis was the "beginning of a daring, thoughtful and soon to be widespread investigation of unconscious factors in cultural life." Now, however, he realizes he had underestimated the forces of hatred in the so-called civilized world. The story ends with the psychoanalyst's recognition that he is nearing the end of his life, "an old man, just a small speck on the planet, soon to be gone from it all," a realization that he finds consoling.

Theraplay & Other Plays

Turning from fiction to drama, Bollas penned *Theraplay & Other Plays* (2006), a collection of five dark comedies that satirize humanity's depersonalization. The dramas enable Bollas to criticize contemporary trends in psychotherapy, including regression therapy, resexualization, self-help books like Norman Vincent Peale's *The Power of Positive Thinking*, and the multiple personality craze. The plays demonstrate Bollas's conviction that psychoanalysis is conducive to the theater of the absurd.

Piecemeal, the most engaging of the five plays, opens with Charles Flount, a cognitive therapist, and his wife, Virginia, preparing to host a small dinner party. The marital tension is palpable. Before the arrival of the guests, Virginia places a pin on a chair and later watches her husband sit on it, exploding in pain. One of the guests, Tom Henders, is grieving the loss of his wife, Antonia, who succumbed three weeks earlier to breast cancer. Tom states that he has recently seen his deceased wife. Is he referring to a literal or metaphoric presence? The arrival of a young woman, Clarissa, who had been attacked by a stranger on the street in front of the Flounts' house and rescued by another dinner guest, stuns everyone, for she is the spitting image of Antonia. Tom is convinced that his prayers have been answered. "You could be her double," he cries. Clarissa agrees: "I felt that someone had been dreaming me" (137). Clarissa claims that as a result of being struck by a bus, she has lost her memory of the past. She was hospitalized for ten months, in the same hospital, one room away, from where Antonia was treated. Tom now vaguely recalls the nurses speaking about the patient who could have been Antonia's identical twin. "They knew something sacred was happening, something beyond the ordinary, something out of their grasp, something they dare not interfere with, something . . ." (139). In short, something uncanny.

Intriguing parallels exist between *Piecemeal* and two of Freud's essays: "Delusions and Dreams in Jensen's *Gradiva*" (1907) and "The Uncanny" (1919). In the former essay, a man sees a figure who mysteriously conjures up the presence of a deceased woman. "Is she a hallucination of our hero, led astray by his delusions? Is she a 'real' ghost? or a living person?" (*SE* 9: 17). Freud's questions are precisely those raised by the characters in *Piecemeal*. In the latter essay, Freud defines the uncanny as "that class of the frightening which leads back to what is known of old and long familiar" ("The Uncanny," *SE* 17: 220). Freud links the uncanny to the double, a topic explored by Otto Rank. Adds Freud, "fiction presents more opportunities for creating uncanny feelings than are possible in real life" (251). Pre-Freudian and post-Freudian fiction writers have explored the theme of the double: Edgar Allan Poe in "William Wilson" (1839), Fyodor Dostoevsky in *The Double* (1846), Joseph Conrad in "The Secret Sharer" (1910), Vladimir Nabokov in *Lolita* (1955), and Sylvia Plath in *The Bell Jar* (1963). Apart from Nabokov, who parodies Humbert's relationship to his dark double, Clare Quilty, most writers treat the theme of the double without irony or caricature.

Bollas, however, develops the farcical implications of the double. Clarissa has disguised herself to look like Antonia because she has long been in love with Tom. Clarissa, it turns out, is the Flounts' long-estranged daughter; the stranger who has attacked her is their son, Robert, a member of a terrorist group that may have been responsible for the Catastrophe. Charles fatuously justifies his daughter's deception by claiming that the idea is "transformational" (173), but Robert furiously dismisses the rationalization. "You psychologists don't know what the fuck you're doing, so you come up with some nifty words, a few clichés, and band together in your thousands chanting 'cognitive therapy,' 'cognitive therapy,' 'cognitive therapy,' so that it becomes a kind of bonding litany—a new Song of Songs" (174). If we did not know that Bollas is a distinguished psychoanalyst, we might assume that he agreed with Nabokov's mordant jest in *Lolita* that the difference between "therapist" and "the rapist" is a matter of spacing. *Piecemeal* ends on a Pirandello-esque theme, with the dinner guests, recognizing that they are trapped in their characters, exiting the stage.

The Evocative Object World

After reading his novellas and plays, one misses Bollas's wry humor and flights of imagination in his later clinical books, but they are, like all his writings, thought provoking. It's probably no accident that Bollas returns to his favorite novel in *The Evocative Object World* (2009) to describe a psychoanalytic concept:

> In *Moby Dick*, when Melville puts Ishmael before a painting in the Spouter-Inn, he explores how unexpected encounters are mind-expanding. Ishmael sees a large oil painting that was "besmoked, and every way defaced." It had "unaccountable masses of shades and shadows" and required viewing and reviewing before it began to make some visual sense. But what puzzled Ishmael the most was "a long, limber, portentous, black mass of something hovering in the centre of the picture" which seemed "boggy, soggy, squitchy." After many attempts to define its subject matter Ishmael concludes that it is a whale impaling itself on a ship. (85)

Bollas uses the oil painting in the novel as an example of an evocative object, which refers to the internalized mental representation of an object. When looking at the dark sea-scene, Ishmael cannot decide whether the inscrutable image is a foundering ship or a leviathan—both of which foreshadow the novel's events. Bollas then tells us that the famed psychologist Henry Murray, like himself an avid reader of Melville's fiction, was rumored to have co-created (with Christiana Morgan) the Thematic Apperception Test (TAT) based on this scene from the novel.

The Infinite Question

A companion volume to *The Evocative Object World*, *The Infinite Question* (2009) highlights three analysands, Arlene, Caroline, and Annie, whose analytical insights arise from their unconscious thinking as expressed through free associations. Bollas demonstrates the value of evenly suspended attentiveness first proposed by Freud. Bollas distinguishes between *working within* transference and *interpreting* transference, a distinction that reveals major differences between French and British psychoanalytic approaches. British analysts wonder why their French counterparts don't interpret transference; by contrast, French analysts generally observe and follow transference without interpreting it. The volume concludes with a discussion of the two most psychoanalyzed plays, *Oedipus the King* and *Hamlet*, both of which involve the murder of a father-king and the sexual transgressions of a widowed mother.

Catch Them Before They Fall

In the felicitously titled *Catch Them Before They Fall: The Psychoanalysis of Breakdown* (2013), Bollas argues that a breakdown can become a breakthrough if caught in time. In the late 1980s, he treated a patient whose sessions lasted all day, for three consecutive days, from 9 a.m. till 6 p.m. Convinced of the value of all-day sessions for patients on the verge of breakdown, he began speaking to groups of psychoanalysts, nearly all of whom responded with disapproval. Undeterred, Bollas wrote the present book. Not only does he describe hospitalizing a disturbed but non-psychotic patient as a psychological disaster, he adds that in his thirty-five years of experience working with people on the verge of breakdown, he has never had to hospitalize a patient.

Bollas is characteristically thorough in working out all the details of all-day sessions. Over the years, he has had a handful of patients who benefit from all-day sessions—three days has been the time limit. Paradoxically, patients who *consciously* seek out this form of therapy are unlikely to benefit from it—though he doesn't explain why. All-day sessions involve a change in the analytic frame but not in the process of treatment. Bollas tells his patients that although he is increasing the number and length of sessions per week, there is no increase in analytic fees. "This is not an exception made for you," he reassures them; "it is my usual practice" (32–33).

Bollas's freedom to imagine dialogue in his fiction and drama may have helped him with the sparkling exchanges with the perfectionistic "Anna" in *Catch Them Before They Fall*. Anna cannot conceal her mortification when she confesses that she "shat" herself while in bed the morning of the therapy session. Rather than expressing surprise or concern, Bollas responds counterintuitively: "Anna, I think it was a good thing." The dialogue proceeds as follows:

> "What?"
> "You have been *too* self-controlled, keeping all your shit in. So you had a good rest, you were calm, and you were free enough to let some of the shit out."
> "Are you kidding?"
> "Of course not."
> "But I can't go around shitting myself like that!"
> "Actually, Anna, I think it would be a good thing if you had a little more shit on yourself than you do."
> At this point Anna roared with laughter and continued to chuckle for the next ten minutes. (56–57)

Bollas acknowledges making mistakes with patients. As Margaret Parish observes in an otherwise sympathetic review, one wishes that he had written more about these problems. *Catch Them Before They Fall* ends with an interview between Bollas and his son, Sacha, a clinical psychologist practicing in Los Angeles. Comparing a patient having a breakdown to a drowning person, Bollas likens himself to a lifeguard throwing a lifebelt. When his son exclaims, "You are a saviour!" Bollas modestly disagrees. "No, I am a professional. A lifeguard may save a person's life but they have been trained to do it. It is their job" (116).

When the Sun Bursts

When the Sun Bursts: The Enigma of Schizophrenia (2015) argues that almost all psychotic behavior is understandable, including thought disorders long considered untreatable through psychoanalysis. Bollas's preoccupation with the subject began in the 1960s when he worked with autistic and schizophrenic children at the East Bay Activity Center in Oakland. He treated many schizophrenic patients during the nearly twenty years he worked in private practice at his home in North London. He also taught and supervised at the Institute of Child Neuropsychiatry at the University of Rome, where he treated psychotic children and adolescents.

When the Sun Bursts—the title comes from a patient—demonstrates that Bollas put his literary training to good use. His first deliberate use of free association as an educational tool began when he was a graduate student at the University of Buffalo. Noting that his undergraduate students were "terrified" of English composition, he introduced them to a poem by Sylvia Plath and urged them to write down their free associations. His faith in the unconscious paid off. Around the same time, Norman Holland began interviewing his students about the reading process. Bollas never became a reader-response theorist, but he discovered that readers' awareness of their own free associations can heighten their connection to a poem. As in his other books, Bollas cites poets for clinical support. "The poets may have more to teach us about schizophrenia than do psychiatry and psychopharmacology" (197).

One of Bollas's most suggestive ideas is that schizophrenics defend themselves by transforming lived experience into applied literature:

> Unable to bear the uncertain nature of live company, a schizophrenic may secretly transform others into figures in a narrative. The surrounding world becomes a book that can be controlled by moving it page by page. We might see him scanning the room as if he were reading it, maybe making a particular sound as he mimes turning a page. I recall one patient who would say "ka-ching" and close his eyes emphatically each time he moved his gaze from one sector of the visual field to another. (82)

Turning lived experience into applied literature is not simply an elaborate conceit, for Bollas shows how he has learned to decode his patients' often bewildering speech, sometimes called "word salads." To give only one example, his patient Mark asked him whether he heard a noise, that of a fly. Assuming that Mark meant a fly on the wall, Bollas said "no," but then, sensing that Mark was speaking symbolically, Bollas corrected himself, realizing that he was to the patient a fly on the wall, listening to and spying on him. "When I said this to him it brought a big smile to his face and he indicated that I had understood his previously enigmatic communication" (175). Mark, we realize, is "Nick" in *The Mystery of Things*.

Central to all of Bollas's writings is the conviction that narrating one's life story invariably strengthens one's well-being. Those who struggle with schizophrenia must be allowed to speak—and to be heard. "Part of the cure lies in narrating the quotidian" (170). The quotidian becomes remarkable in *When the Sun Bursts* as Bollas shows through several clinical vignettes how schizophrenics are helped by analysts who know how to "read them, be with them, understand them, and talk to them" (187).

Meaning and Melancholia

Bollas's participation in the politics of protest during the 1960s is evident in his most recent book, *Meaning and Melancholia: Life in the Age of Bewilderment* (2018), where he seeks to explain the disturbing victory of Donald Trump in the United States, the vote for Brexit in the UK, and the rise of right-wing nationalism in Europe. Bollas's title evokes "Mourning and Melancholia," but whereas Freud wrote about grief, Bollas underscores the despair, disorientation, and anger of Western civilization. The book requires, he admits in the preface, the reader's negative capability, the willing suspension of disbelief.

Bollas's most overtly political book, *Meaning and Melancholia* is a work of literary and cultural criticism. The book contains references to dozens of texts, including, as a partial list, Melville's *Billy Budd*, Hawthorne's *The Scarlet Letter*, Strindberg's *Miss Julie*, Hemingway's *The Sun Also Rises*, Eliot's "The Hollow Men," Beckett's *Waiting for Godot*, and Camus's *The Stranger* and *The Myth of Sisyphus*. These literary writers have indelibly shaped Bollas's imagination. He reads literature for its prescient criticisms of human greed and folly, as in this commentary on Conrad's *Heart of Darkness*: "Colonialism was many things, but perhaps above all it was the march of absolute ignorance, invading rather than understanding the human universe. Kurtz's dying words—'The horror! The horror!'—are both an epitaph for the nineteenth century and an uncanny foretelling of the era to follow" (17). Bollas cites E.M. Forster's emblematic line in *Howards End*, "Only connect," to show that we must combine our speech with our feelings. In *Meaning and Melancholia* Bollas has connected literature, psychology, and history to show how we must seek to create a meaningful life and a humane world.

Bollas's instinct for neologisms (terms like interformality, ghostline personality, normatic illness, trisexuality) inspires him to coin a new word, "sightophilia." "A person who is drawn to seeing rather than thinking is a sightophile." He offers the following clinical exchange:

"I think your being indispensable to your friend allows you to covertly attach yourself to her."

"You got it. I am indispensable, and I should probably watch that. That's brilliant—thanks so much."

"You seem to have grasped this thought so quickly that I'm not sure we have had a chance to think it."

"Oh, no, I mean it was great. Am I . . . am I . . . supposed to think about it?" (64)

Bollas ends *Meaning and Melancholia* with a statement that sums up his career. "Psychoanalysis and the depth psychologies may be imperfect but their ambition is not. They are 'works in progress' that point towards a crucial function. We have always known that we need to 'know thyself' and this is as true now as it has been over the millennia" (128). Socratic self-knowledge has always been his goal. Christopher Bollas understands that suffering is part of existence, but he also knows that we can find the meaning and strength for a fulfilling life with the help of his twin passions, literature and psychoanalysis.

JEFFREY BERMAN. In affirming your literary background, I don't mean to imply that it was more influential than your formal training in psychoanalysis. And yet I find it interesting that your psychoanalytic writings abound in literary examples.

CHRISTOPHER BOLLAS. If I publish my *Notebooks* (1973–2016), it will show that all my writings emerge from my *clinical* experience. My patients taught me, not my books. I do use many literal examples in order to illustrate something or to illuminate an issue and so forth. I also did not want to refer readers to the psychoanalytic literature—which most other writers did—because I think that puts a block between the writer and the reader, even if the reader is an analyst. That is not the case when one refers to works of fiction or philosophy which hopefully connect with the reader's unconscious and allow them to make their own way through the text in a more profound way.

JB. If you were beginning your career over again, would you first become an English professor and then a psychoanalyst?

CB. I think I have done both alongside one another. So, for me it is not a matter of beginning with one of these disciplines and then moving to the other. Indeed, at the University of Buffalo I worked two days a week in the University Health Center (doing psychotherapy) and the other days I was taking courses in the English department or teaching. I decided to study literature rather than history because history was too easy for me and literature was difficult. I knew it would stretch me in ways that work in history could not.

JB. I've just written a book about Norman Holland, with whom you worked when you were a doctoral student in English at the University of Buffalo. How do you feel about the identity theory he formulated?

CB. Norm constantly indicated how readers changed texts to suit their identity theme, and this led to many discussions about how it would involve misreading, which he argued was inevitable. I think he went too far in advocating the identity theme. I loved Norm and believe he was a great teacher. But we disagreed—he was great about it—and he was most gracious when I told him I would have to change dissertation director as Norm really did want all of us to agree with his approach. So, I went with Leslie Fiedler. All of this proved moot as I destroyed my finished dissertation (threw it into a dustbin outside my apartment on Exeter street in Boston) because I had gotten Melville all wrong. Took me five years to return to the task and wrote a new dissertation.

JB. Throwing away your doctoral dissertation must have been an act of desperation—and courage. Can you recall how you felt at the time—and whether, since then, you have completely rethought and rewritten other chapters or books?

CB. I certainly did not experience discarding my dissertation as either desperate or courageous. I had been uneasy for months about an increasing realization on my part that I had utterly failed to properly respect Melville's own understanding of his layers of meaning. I gradually knew that I could not send it in as a final edition as it was simply wrong. I do not have a problem discarding essays or even manuscripts if, upon further thought, I think they are inadequate. And, I rethink all my writing. Typically a book takes me at least eight years to complete from start to finish. I lay manuscripts aside for weeks—sometimes months and occasionally years—in order to wait for further understandings of the topic. I believe in the unconscious foundation of writing and I have to set my consciousness aside for periods of time in order to allow for further unconscious thinking.

JB. One of your responsibilities as Director of Education at Riggs was to set up the visiting lecturer program. That must have involved much time, effort, and collaboration to advance psychoanalytic education. Would you describe the visiting lecture program?

CB. I wanted to bring people from Europe but the cost was prohibitive. However, a colleague in New York City, Ed Corrigan, was in a position to set up and manage an opening teaching event in NYC. The guest would arrive on a Thursday or Friday and give a one day event in NYC: a part time conference/an evening lecture. The two institutions who hosted guests were the ICP (Institute for Contemporary Analysis) and the Post Doc program at NYU. On Sunday the guest took Amtrak to Hudson, where I greeted them and drove them to Riggs. They would stay the week at Riggs and give seminars, supervisions, and the all-important Friday Night Guest Lecture, which was attended by many town folk. On Wednesday morning I would drive the guest to the University of Massachusetts, where they would give one or two seminars during the day. Murray Schwartz was the host. I drove the guest back to Riggs, they did their Friday lecture, and on Friday night (after the lecture) we would be driven by limo to Boston, where we would stay two nights. This was the final leg of the trip and the guest would then give a seminar and also an evening lecture to the Boston Psychoanalytic Society. Andrew Morrison was the point person in Boston (sometimes it was Howie Levine). Because Riggs was the host organizer— the invitations came from Riggs with all the details of other events—the person keeping tabs on progress was my secretary Betty Homich and a local travel agent who took care of all bookings.

Over the two years of this program Corrigan, Schwartz, Morrison, and I developed a rhythm and worked as a team. A partial list of who we brought over for this program includes Andre Green, Janine Chasseguet-Smirgel, Hannah Segal, Joyce McDougall, Eric Brenman (UK), Dennis Duncan (UK), and Nina Coltart. Murry organized a remarkable Winnicott conference and Riggs joined him and we brought over for the week Enid Balint, Adam Phillips, Harold Stewart, and others.

JB. Would you describe your two analytical "homes" from 1978 to 1999?

CB. The one in Italy—where I was visiting professor of psychoanalysis—was the place where I presented all my work and received highly creative and non-dogmatic critiques. The other was in Sweden. We met every year from 1983 to 2016 in Arild (a small village near Malmö) for a long weekend conference in the month of May. I also lectured many times in Stockholm. These two groups of colleagues—Italy and Sweden— provided independent critiques of my work and in a way we collaborated.

JB. You also travel back and forth between the United States and the UK. What's that like?

CB. I left England in 2012 and moved to North Dakota and California. I have a late-nineteenth-century farmstead on the prairie, twenty miles from the nearest hamlet and miles from other homesteads. I also live (winter really) in Santa Barbara. I became a UK citizen in 2010 and hope to return to England to live.

JB. You observe that writing became for Melville a "means of survival." Does writing serve the same role for you? Can you imagine life without writing?

CB. I was not a born writer. I was much better at speaking my thoughts about a novel than writing what I thought. I did not really start writing until I was in my mid-thirties. Most of what I wrote went into the *Nouvelle Revue de Psychanalyse* and that suited me. Pontalis actually liked my literary idiom and so I wrote for him and for the French. Once a year or so I would write an essay. It was not so easy as I was working ten clinical hours a day and also from noon to five I was looking after the children while my wife, Suzanne, who is an architect, was working. But I kept notebooks and would jot entries in them and this was helpful. They are now some thirty or more volumes and I reckon it was this writing-with-no-audience that enabled me to find my own idiom. Still, my first book was published when I was forty-four years old. And as you know, that is not precocity! Indeed, I never thought I would write a book and frankly had no wish to. It happened when a colleague told me that he thought that if I collected my essays (written over the previous ten years) I might have a book and sure enough I did. Now, as with any writer, I value this form of thinking.

JB. You've changed your attitude toward confidentiality. In your clinical vignette in *The Shadow of the Object*, you warned your patient Jonathan that if he didn't end his threats to murder someone close to him, you would notify the police. Your actions seemed to convert his actual death threat into a fantasy. Yet you warn against any breach of confidentiality in *The New Informants*. Why did you change your position?

CB. The events are separated by twenty years. My supervisor recommended I say to the patient in 1976 that I should inform him that I would call the police. In time, I changed this position. The genesis of the change was the mandatory reporting hysteria in the United States. I could see then that any compromise of confidentiality was the thin edge of the wedge. I agree I should have footnoted my change, but frankly I had long forgotten the clinical vignette to which you refer. But to his credit, John Forrester also noted this change.

JB. You are probably best known for your expression "unthought known." You make the following statement in *Being a Character*: "'The more original a thought,' says Derrida, quoting Heidegger, 'the richer its Unthought becomes. The unthought is the highest gift (*Geschenk*) that a thought can give'" (64). You quote the same Heidegger passage in *Cracking Up* (176). Did you conceive the term from reading Derrida?

CB. Actually the expression popped into my mind when I was reading a draft of *The Shadow of the Object*. Ironically, the term describes my own process. I knew something but had not yet thought it. What was that? The idea of "the unthought known."

JB. I'm curious about Tom, the "normatic" patient who attempted suicide but denied having any conflicts in his life. Can you recall the outcome of his treatment?

CB. I saw him on a grand round at UC Irvine medical school. So it was just a consultation and I never did know how he fared.

JB. I'm surprised that unlike many analysts, you embrace rather than reject Freud's impersonal and mechanistic analogy of the analyst as a "telephone receiver is adjusted to the transmitting microphone." Would you explain why you are drawn to this analogy?

CB. I have always made it clear that I am a pluralist. Freud's analogy is just another way of looking at things. There is a thread throughout my writing that takes up the intersubjective. I do not think Freud's way of listening is mechanistic although you may be concluding that as he used a mechanical object (phone) as his metaphor. It's not a great metaphor but an intriguing one in my view.

JB. *Hysteria* is, I believe, your most controversial book, at least to American (as opposed to Continental) analysts. Your theorizing incorporates the often disparate lexicons of Freud, Lacan, and the British object relations theorists. You contend that "in the unconscious life of any person—male or female—there is a fantasy of having been molested by the father" (16)—a supposition impossible to confirm or disconfirm. Some readers may believe that you are engaged in mother bashing, as in assertions like "each hysteric feels the tyranny of the mother's over-appropriation of the self" (113). You readily concede that you are walking a "thin line" in characterizing the hysteric's imagined and real mother (57), but the line sometimes becomes blurred.

There are extensive criticisms, as I'm sure you know, by both clinicians and feminists, of Freud's insensitive treatment of "Dora," Ida Bauer, in his 1905 case study *Fragment of an Analysis of a Case of Hysteria*. The case study shows Freud at his most vindictive, as when he declares at the end, "I do not know what kind of help she wanted from me, but I promised to forgive her for having deprived me of the satisfaction of affording her a far more radical cure for her troubles" (*SE* 7: 122).

Still another controversy in *Hysteria* may lie in your lack of sympathy for non-psychoanalytic treatments that provide symptom relief, such as university support groups for students with eating disorders. "Although these programs do save the lives of many anorectics, they do so, ironically, by colluding with the hysterical process, implicitly accepting the reduction of this complex adult into a simplified being" (*Hysteria* 105). This may be true, but isn't relief from suffering welcome no matter how limited? In your efforts to resurrect the concept of hysteria, Glen Gabbard points out in a review, you sometimes cast your net too broadly. Nonetheless, Gabbard praises your book as the "most intelligent and comprehensive survey of the psychoanalytic perspective on hysteria in decades" (689). How do you feel about these criticisms?

CB. I don't agree that I was engaged in "mother bashing" in *Hysteria*. In my opening comments in the book I differentiate the actual mother from "mother." Indeed, I coined the term "maternal order" partly to avoid the pitfalls of discussing the maternal role in early life. *Hysteria* was published in France about two years ago and was widely praised by the French, including Laurence Kahn and Regine Prat. Nor do I agree that I lacked sympathy for non-psychoanalytic treatments of hysteria. My point is that treatment teams—especially in hospitals—actually unwittingly reinforce the regressed infantile state of the hysteric. I offer, I think, a valid, clear, and open critique of the treatment, or mistreatment of hysterics, especially in the United States. Given that even experienced American analysts would be unlikely to know how to analyze the hysteric—including the anorectic—then of course hospitals or group therapists are valued over here because it is the only thing offered.

JB. I've noted many parallels between your play *Piecemeal* and two of Freud's essays, "Dreams and Delusions in Jensen's *Gradiva*" and "The Uncanny." Did you borrow the plot from these two essays?

CB. No. The fact that *you* see a similarity is fine. But to jump from that observation to suggesting that I have borrowed the plot is inaccurate.

JB. As a professor, I always enjoy receiving emails from former students who update me on their lives. Do former patients remain connected to you and, if so, how does that affect your relationship with them?

CB. Yes, many former patients do remain in touch with me. And as some do return for a further period of analysis, I do not have the sort of evolving personal relation to them that would be true of students at a university.

JB. You advance three provocative ideas in your novella *Dark at the End of the Tunnel*: "objecthood," "descendence," and "projective transcendentalism." Would you be comfortable writing about these ideas in your clinical books?

CB. I found a freedom in writing fiction that is simply not to be found in writing essays. So I am sure I would not have hatched ideas and noted how they seemed to link up with one another through an essay when in fact I think fiction gives one much greater freedom. And I should add that "objecthood"—I was to find (or refind)—is a term used by Fanon to describe his status as someone who is "overdetermined from the outside."

JB. In *I Have Heard the Mermaids Singing* the psychoanalyst tells a patient violently opposed to psychotherapy that in his thirty-five years of practice, he has seen only a handful of biologically driven depressions. Does that coincide with your own experience?

CB. Yes. The sad thing about depression—ironically enough—is that we do not have enough time for it and so it becomes a thing that hits us, or slows us down in worrying ways, or whatnot. *If* you get someone in analysis when they are young enough—adolescence or early to mid-twenties—then you can begin to understand this remarkable mood. There are all kinds of depressions, just like there are all kinds of people. And like all "disorders" it is an unconsciously intelligent solution to unthought-out problems.

JB. Your fiction and drama were published at the beginning of the twenty-first century, from 2004 to 2006. Have you been tempted to write new fiction and drama?

CB. I have finished a work of fiction which I term "Conversations." They might look like poems and read a bit like theatre of the absurd. But they are mostly conversations between two people about a wide range of topics. I wrote the work during the Iraq war and then put it aside and forgot about it. I picked it up a few months ago, realized much of what

I wrote then could apply to our times and so I spruced it up a bit and now it will look for a publisher.

JB. Do you often put work aside? You seem quite prolific, as if you are producing works every year or two.

CB. Typically it takes eight to ten years from start to finish. I always put work aside—usually for months but sometimes for years—as I need time for further missing ideas to show up. So I have to be patient. I am finishing up a work on character that will be published in 2021 but which was written up in the late 1990s and left for many years; I am finishing up an odd abstract book on the realms of being in an analysis.

JB. You end your 2009 "Conversation" with Anthony Molino by saying that if you are not optimistic about the future of psychoanalysis in the short term, you are not pessimistic about its long-term future. "Psychoanalytic theory was an important revelation within the history of Western consciousness. If it has been repressed, as looks to be the case, it will certainly return some day." Do you still feel the same way?

CB. I don't know, now, how to answer this question. I fear that the creative movement that was psychoanalysis may have ended with Lacan, Bion, and Winnicott. These three figures (Lacan the wizard; Bion the mystic; Winnicott the clown) are like totems to which we all pray as if in unconscious celebration of how it should all end. Each of these remarkable stand-alone figures has come to embody a whole school of thought. Entire movements have been built up around these three analysts that are completely inconsistent with who they were, how they thought and wrote, and the actions they performed within the psycho-analytical movement. Were they so spellbinding that we are in a trance? How many more Bion conferences do we need before we finally let go of such attachments?

Freud, to his credit in my view, was a dialectical thinker. Good luck trying to find his main themes. He contradicts himself all the time, which for some is unsettling, but his writing enacts his theory of the unconscious. His thinking is overdetermined. His essays at times are deeply evocative condensations that can only be unraveled over time and in differing intellectual contexts. To be sure, many analysts have "their Freud": they get rid of entire swaths of his theory in order to promote the segments of Freud they fancy. I think when we get rid of part of his theory we decline to experience him and indeed to learn something from him we did not know.

Chapter 5

The Paradoxical Adam Phillips

"Phillips is one of the finest prose stylists at work in the language, an Emerson for our time," enthused John Banville in *The Irish Times*. "A new book by Adam Phillips is a literary event worth noting," raved Anthony Storr in *The Times* (London). "Phillips has virtually invented the essay as a suitable form for penetrating psychoanalytic enquiry," rhapsodized Frank Kermode. Banville, Storr, and Kermode, among the world's most distinguished novelists, psychoanalysts, and literary critics, respectively, are not known for effusive praise, yet their opinions—quoted as blurbs for *Promises, Promises* (2000), a collection of essays on literature and psychoanalysis—testify to Britain's "foremost" psychoanalyst, as Joan Acocella described Phillips in a 2013 profile in *The New Yorker*.

There are, of course, dissenting views, though they often appear in generally sympathetic reviews. Witness the opening of Lisan Jutras's review of *Unforbidden Pleasures* (2015) in *The Globe and Mail*. "Undoubtedly, it would please Adam Phillips to no end to hear about the many times I threw his book down in exasperation, scribbled irritable marginalia in it and harangued friends ('Here, you're smarter than me!') to help me decipher his prose." In her review of *Missing Out* (2012) in *The New York Times*, Sheila Heti complained that Phillips "doesn't argue in a linear fashion but nestles ideas within ideas, like Russian dolls. The result feels less like a clean literary feat than the underground rumblings that produce literature." And in her discussion of *Missing Out* in the *Los Angeles Review of Books*, Lisa Levy is not enamored of Phillips's "endless allusiveness as well as his evasiveness," adding that "Over and over he asks the same questions, not always reaching the same conclusions."

169

Despite fame, Phillips is not a household name among contemporary psychoanalysts. His books are reviewed in the most prestigious publications, but he garners surprisingly few citations within contemporary psycho-analytic journals (an exception, as we shall see, is David James Fisher's interview with him in the *Journal of the American Psychoanalytic Association*), perhaps because he hasn't "add[ed] anything to psychoanalytic theory at all," as he cheerfully admits in his 2016 book *In Writing* (259). But this may be disingenuous. From the beginning Phillips has been dismantling psychoanalytic theory, not by colonizing it but by making it his own. The result is a psychoanalysis strikingly unfamiliar to most analysts.

Phillips was born in Cardiff, Wales, in 1954. He went to an English public school, which in the United States would be called a private school, but he is among the least snobbish or elitist analyst-writers. As an adolescent he read only history books, but his passion was literature. He studied English at Oxford in the early 1970s and turned to psychoanalysis in the late 1970s. He was analyzed for four years by Masud Khan, who was also Christopher Bollas's analyst. Phillips told Jill Choder-Goldman in a 2019 interview that Khan was a "wonderful analyst" from whom he learned a great deal. Khan's expulsion from the British Psychoanalytical Society for boundary violations occurred after Phillips's training analysis.

Phillips began psychoanalytic training at the Institute for Child Psychology and then studied at the Hampstead and Tavistock clinics, two rival approaches to child analysis, led by Anna Freud and Melanie Klein, respectively, that could not have been more theoretically different. Trained in a Freudian, Kleinian, and Winnicottian tradition, Phillips identifies himself, as he explained to Choder-Goldman, with the British middle group object relations approach, with a Lacanian influence. (Phillips's first wife, the literary critic Jacqueline Rose, has translated and edited Lacan's writings.) Phillips's approach to psychoanalysis, however, is uniquely his own.

Phillips worked in the 1970s and 1980s in schools, hospitals, and child-guidance clinics, including serving as the Principal Child Psycho-therapist at Charing Cross Hospital in London, part of the National Health Service (NHS), the United Kingdom's publicly funded healthcare system. "When I started seeing children," Phillips disclosed to Susanna Rustin in a 2012 interview in *The Guardian*, "I could see them for as long as the treatment took. By the end people were saying, 'we'll pay for three sessions.' For me the project was not to meet the criteria but to ditch the criteria and do something else." Phillips then left the NHS and went into private practice. He is a visiting professor in the English department at the University of York and, since 2003, the general editor of the *Penguin Modern Classics Freud* translations. He is also a Fellow of the Royal Society of Literature.

To my knowledge, Phillips is the only psychoanalyst (with the possible exception of Christopher Bollas) who believes that literature is "probably a better preparation for the practice of psychoanalysis than the reading of anything else" (*Promises, Promises* xvi). Freud believed, in Harold Bloom's view, that "poetry might be a discipline roughly parallel to psychoanalysis" (*Yeats* 215), but Phillips makes a more radical—and polarizing—claim at the end of *Promises, Promises*: "For me—for all sorts of reasons—there has always been only one category, *literature*, of which psychoanalysis became a part" (364).

Paradoxical

Paradox is central to Phillips's vision as both a psychoanalyst and a literary critic. Paradox is a logically self-contradictory statement that contains unexpected truth. Søren Kierkegaard offers one of the best descriptions of paradox in *Philosophical Fragments*:

> But one must not think ill of the paradox, for the paradox is the passion of thought, and the thinker without the paradox is like the lover without passion: a mediocre fellow. But the ultimate potentiation of every passion is always to will its own downfall, and so it is also the ultimate passion of the understanding to will the collision, although in one way or another the collision must become its downfall. This, then, is the ultimate paradox of thought: to want to discover something that thought itself cannot think. (37)

Phillips delights in paradoxes not only because they encourage imaginative thinking but also because they generate new questions and truths. "In entertaining a paradox," he writes in *Equals* (2002), "we are free of mutually exclusive options" (133). Unlike a contradiction, which leads to a double bind or dead end, a paradox creates new complexities.

Phillips is not a self-disclosing writer, but in *Promises, Promises* he refers to his parents and grandparents:

As second-generation Jews from Poland and Russia, my parents, very determinedly, wanted to protect their children from
struggle; to make the struggle for survival, which had been
the project for them and their parents, seem like a thing of
the past. For my grandparents this survival was not, as it was
to us, heroic; it was itself demeaning that they had had to
suffer such heroism. Their history had been an insult to their
often good-natured natural snobbery. So my parents—fervent
socialists with a passion for the Bloomsbury group—wished
they had been the beneficiaries of long-standing English
wealth and culture. But they instinctively identified with the
people they would never—must never—aspire to be: all those
who were the potential victims of other people's privilege.
(329)

Phillips never writes about being self-conscious as a Jew in England,
with its long history of genteel as opposed to virulent Eastern European
anti-Semitism. His paternal grandparents were given the Welsh name
Phillips because "no one could understand the name Pinkus-Levy." Phillips's parents did not deny being Jewish, but they wished to assimilate, to
become British citizens (*In Writing* 238–239). Reading Freud seemed to
Phillips a version of the Jewish family he knew. Unlike Sander Gilman,
whose parents also came from Eastern Europe, Phillips is not obsessed by
the need to bear witness to injustice, "writing/righting wrong," as Sandra
M. Gilbert observes in her 1995 spousal loss memoir *Wrongful Death*,
but he is certainly one of the "people of the book," having authored or
edited over thirty. A fiercely independent and often iconoclastic thinker,
he affirms provisional and nomadic truths, the opposite of oracular verities.
   No contemporary psychoanalyst is more provocative than Phillips.
The word "provocative" usually means "serving or tending to provoke,
excite, or stimulate" (*Merriam-Webster.com*) or "causing an angry reaction,
usually intentionally" (*Cambridge Dictionary*), but Phillips offers his own
idiosyncratic definition in *The Concise Dictionary of Dress* (2010), coauthored
with his wife, the fashion curator Judith Clarke: "(1) Interested in other
people. (2) The arousal of curiosity, curiosity as arousal; showing off to
discover what can be seen, what can be shown, and what is showing; quest
for a more reflective, a more interested mirror; the research of the shy.
(3) Taking the stage, whatever; a drama out of a crisis. (4) Loss of faith
in the audience; distrust of the evocative. (5) A composed tantrum" (np).

Phillips is certainly provocative in the first three meanings, probably not provocative in the fourth meaning, and it's anyone's guess whether he's provocative in the fifth meaning. Provocations, like evocations, "require an answering response but not an answer" (*In Writing* 100).

Phillips's enthusiasm for Freud and psychoanalysis remains undiminished, but he is not a salesperson selling a product for everyone. Having no illusions about psychoanalysis spares one from disillusionment. One must not put an analyst on a pedestal, he admitted to Rustin; psychoanalysis doesn't work for everyone:

> I would say to people, if you're curious, try it out. There are plenty of other treatments in the culture and something else may work for you, it may be aromatherapy, but this is what psychoanalysis is like, give it a go. But that's all. To make too much of a case for it beforehand is to make a false promise. Some people find it wonderful. Some people find it absolutely pointless. Some people find it exploitative. It's only for the people who are moved by it, amused by it, interested by it, comforted by it. People who find it fraudulent, diminishing and absurd shouldn't do it. That's fine. (Rustin)

Winnicott

What draws one author to another? The question is avowedly speculative, but one suspects that Phillips began his writing career with a book on D.W. Winnicott (1896–1971) because each viewed paradox as central to his vision of life and theory of psychoanalysis. Next to Freud, Winnicott is Phillips's favorite psychoanalytic writer, the one he quotes most often. Phillips opens his 1988 book with Winnicott's brow-furrowing statement "Health is much more difficult to deal with than disease" (1). Winnicott is best known for the expression the "good enough mother," which has a paradoxical ring to it, representing a realistic, non-idealized vision that is the best possible maternal environment for a child's development and emotional well-being. Another Winnicottian idea is the transitional object and transitional space, a bridge between two disparate worlds, self and other, subjectivity and objectivity—worlds that seemed, before Winnicott, mutually exclusive. A transitional object, the child's first not-me possession, such as a teddy bear or doll, has a unique permanence, resilience, and autonomy, though it's fated to be gradually cast aside when the child outgrows it.

Winnicottian theory is paradoxical in other ways. He famously said that there is no such thing as a baby. "If you show me a baby you certainly show me also someone caring for a baby, or at least a pram with someone's eyes and ears glued to it" (5). A central paradox of childhood for Winnicott is that the child's growing confidence will be reflected by the willingness to be difficult, even defiant. Winnicott saw the infant, in Phillips's koanlike words, as an "isolate who needed the object, above all, to protect the privacy of this isolation" (145). The paradox gives rise to another: the object must be found to be created.

In what Phillips wryly calls a "negative theology of the Self" (97), Winnicott distinguished between the True Self and the False Self, but the former could be described only as the opposite of the latter. Winnicott's minimal definition of these terms allowed him to achieve maximum ambiguity. As Phillips declares in the last sentence of *Terrors and Experts* (1996), "Too much definition leaves too much out" (104). Whereas Freud believed that reality creates destructiveness, Winnicott maintained the opposite: destructiveness creates, paradoxically, reality.

Two Good Enough Psychoanalysts

Paradox unites Winnicott and Phillips. Both seek not to close the gap of knowledge but to examine it, even if the ground feels precarious. Both value observation, empathy, and relatedness; both mistrust dogmatism, abstraction, and mystifying language. Both attempt to make psychoanalysis understandable and acceptable to the larger non-psychoanalytic community. Phillips's statement about Winnicott's writings—"there are no comparable echoes of previous psychoanalytic writers" (*Winnicott* 15)—is also true of Phillips himself. He cites Winnicott's remark about brief, economical interpretations: "I never use long sentences unless I am very tired" (142), from which we can infer that Phillips writes only when he is alert. (He requires little sleep, which contributes to his remarkable productivity.) Another statement—"It was often Winnicott's inclination to dispel a contradiction, here between Klein and Anna Freud, with a paradox" (46)—is also true of Phillips, whose synthetic imagination enables him to bridge the gap left by contesting psychoanalytic accounts of childhood development. Phillips's comment about Winnicott's imagination and independence is no less true of himself: "Winnicott had the psychoanalytic virtues of his scientific vices: he did not become systematically coherent at the cost of his own inventiveness" (99). One more similarity: Both became leading psychoanalysts of their generations, but they did not set the academic world on fire as undergraduates. Winnicott was a pre-medical student at Jesus College, Cambridge, and received a third-class degree. Phillips studied English at St John's College, Oxford, and received a third-class degree. Stardom came for both in due time.

There are differences between them. Phillips suggests that Winnicott sometimes sounds like Lewis Carroll. Phillips sounds like Oscar Wilde, perhaps the supreme paradoxicalist in the language. Phillips points out that Winnicott rarely used the word "insight," which never appears in the indexes to Phillips's own his books—though most of his books do not have indexes. Phillips's index in *Winnicott* contains two references to insight, but it is not a conspicuous word in his vocabulary. Like Allen Wheelis, he writes more about unknowability than knowability, but his emphasis on the former expands our understanding of the latter. Both Winnicott and Phillips use interpretation judiciously, never seeking to dazzle patients with their superior knowledge. Both are paradoxicalists, but Phillips is more of an ironist: "irony" is one of his favorite words, along with "ironise" and "ironisation" (usually using the British spelling). The range of Phillips's reading is broader than Winnicott's, almost encyclopedic. Both writers are whimsical and playful, but Phillips is more of a wordsmith, capable of using quirky language like "unbeglamoured," a word likely to trigger one's spellcheck. "If Phillips has a flaw as a writer," Tim Adams observed in a review of *In Writing*, "it is probably that no stray word choice can ever go unanalysed; it's never fatal to his sentences, but there are plenty of near-death experiences."

In a cautionary statement that literary critics and biographers would do well to heed, Phillips warns in *Equals* that "writing about someone turns too easily into writing on their behalf" (228). Phillips admires Winnicott, but he is not blindly in love with him. There's a "certain disingenuousness" in Winnicott's writings, Phillips admits, as Winnicott disguises his radical departures from Freud and Melanie Klein. "With blithe defiance Winnicott recreated, often beyond recognition, the work of everyone who influenced him" (5). Winnicott's terminology can sometimes be confusing, and his use of double negatives calls attention to his doubts about a truth claim, as when he states that a child's communication is "not non-verbal" (147). Phillips, by contrast, seldom uses double negatives, but he comes close in expressions like "less strictly noncollusive" (44). Mistrustful of mawkish language, Winnicott occasionally used words like "natural" that led him into sentimentality, which Oscar Wilde defined as having the luxury of an emotion without paying for it. "Sentimentality," Phillips observes in *Houdini's Box*, "is the prevailing vice of those who have doubts about their own virtue" (120). Phillips knows, in short, that we cannot have emotions for nothing.

Phillips's book on Winnicott was published during a time when Lacanian theory dominated the academy. Lacan conjectured that children saw a unified image of themselves, which resulted in a misleading image of unity and completeness. This dichotomy led to formative misrecognition for Lacan. Winnicott, by contrast, believed that the image children saw in a mirror was determined by their relationship to their mothers. Mirrors, to children with good enough mothers, could be reliable and accurate.

Phillips deftly characterizes the differences among psychoanalytic theorists. "Each psychoanalytic theorist, it could be said, organizes his or her theory around what might be called a core catastrophe; for Freud it was castration, for Klein, the triumph of the Death instinct, and for Winnicott it was the annihilation of the core self by intrusion, a failure of the holding environment" (*Winnicott* 149). Phillips's words convey the catastrophic differences that have riven the psychoanalytic community from its inception, with theorists unable to accept clashing perceptions of psychological reality. Phillips's theorizing cannot be distinguished by a core catastrophe. It's rare to find a psychoanalyst who is skeptical of all psychiatric diagnostic labels—and even rarer to find an analyst who diagnoses why such labels are seductive. "Diagnosis," he writes in *Promises, Promises*, "is the way analysts cure themselves of anxiety, when their anxiety can be the most valuable thing they have" (290). Additionally, he avoids pathologizing language. "All the now infamous psychoanalytic categories"—he remarks in *Promises, Promises*—"hysteria, obsessionality, narcissism—are, among other things, parodies of rule-making." He singles out the diagnostic category called "character disorder," adding, "as though character could be anything else" (60).

The test of any good scholarly book is its ability to bring to life its subject, whether it is a person, a historical age, or a set of ideas. Phillips succeeds admirably in *Winnicott*. He is interested in both Winnicott the theorist and the man. He quotes the first sentence of Winnicott's unpublished autobiography, "I died," written in his seventies, along with his prayer: "May I be alive when I die" (19). The dying writer Anatole Broyard cites this prayer in his book *Intoxicated by My Illness* (19–20).

As I wrote in *Dying in Character*, "For Winnicott and Broyard"—and for Phillips too—the wish to be alive when they die means "enjoying life to the end, using their days to the fullest, feeling fulfilled in love and work, and leaving written records of the stories of their lives" (19). One can see why Phillips was so drawn to Winnicott, a psychoanalyst who, affirming the primacy of creativity, remains among the most vital of all psychoanalytic writers, like Phillips himself.

Phillips's biography of Winnicott is not nearly as comprehensive as F. Robert Rodman's 2003 biography, which is more than twice as long and much more detailed. Rodman, the author of the heartfelt *Not Dying: A Psychoanalyst's Memoir of His Wife's Death* (1977), which I discuss in *Psychoanalytic Memoirs* (2022), praises Phillips's biography as an "incisive port of entry into Winnicott's life and, especially, his work," yet he also faults Phillips for "unnerving" factual inaccuracies, such as suggesting that Winnicott's father had specialized in selling women's corsets, a statement that "carried overtones suggesting certain vague preoccupations of a possibly perverse nature" (Rodman, *Winnicott* 212–213).

On Kissing, Tickling, and Being Bored

Psychoanalysis turns the familiar concept of cure into the "problem rather than the solution," Phillips quips in the introduction to his 1993 book *On Kissing, Tickling, and Being Bored* (3). If this statement isn't paradoxical enough, he intimates one page later that psychoanalysis reveals how life is "always unexamined" albeit simultaneously "endlessly examinable." He revels in head-spinning sentences like "If psychoanalysis can make worrying more interesting, then worrying can make psychoanalysis more interesting" (5). How can this be true, worried readers ask, unsure whether they should be worried or not. Doctors speak about the "worried well," patients who do not need medical treatment but who nevertheless visit their physicians for reassurance. Phillips writes for—indeed, creates—worried readers who turn to him for vertiginous pleasures.

Psychoanalysis is for Phillips a narrative and, therefore, literary art. Many writers have stressed the role of storytelling in the talking cure, but Phillips regards psychoanalysis as "ritualized improvisation" (3). All of Phillips's writings affirm improvisational art—and, like every superb stand-up comic, he conjures up a spell of spontaneity that has carefully been thought out in advance.

It's easy to misread Phillips's unsettling paradoxical truths. How can the aim of psychoanalysis be "not to cure people but to show them that there is nothing wrong with them" (26)? Phillips is not saying what Karl Kraus sneered a century ago: Psychoanalysis is the disease it purports to cure. Rather, Phillips deepens our appreciation of what it means to be human, reminding us, as Hamlet says to Horatio, that there are more things in heaven and earth than are dreamt of in your philosophy—and psychology. Phillips declares on the last page that "the one thing psychoanalysis cannot cure, when it works, is belief in psychoanalysis." And that, he adds, "is a problem" (121)—a problem that sparks, paradoxically, his creative imagination.

Phillips writes about topics that Freud largely ignores, such as solitude, a word that appears only twice in the index to the *Standard Edition*. Phillips casts light on the topic by contrasting Freud's view with Winnicott's: "Freud could not conceive, in his own psychoanalytic terms, of a solitude that was constituted as a full presence rather than as a lack; and psychoanalysis, of course, has an impoverished vocabulary for states of plenitude that are not considered pathological. For Freud, solitude could be described only as an absence, for Winnicott only as a presence. It is a significant measure of difference" (41). Notwithstanding "of course," it was not obvious to me that psychoanalysis rarely focuses on fullness or completeness. Nor was it apparent that "there is no explicit or coercive description in Freud's work of what constitutes a good life" (33).

Long before many writers, myself included, appropriated the words "and its discontents" as a book title, echoing Freud's 1930 *Civilization and Its Discontents*, Phillips used the expression as a chapter heading: "Worry and Its Discontents." The chapter abounds in astute judgments. Offering a definition and brief history of the subject, Phillips observes that "It is now impossible to imagine a life without worry" (52). Few would disagree, but it's curious that the word never appears in the index of the *Standard Edition*. Evoking the title of another Freudian classic, Phillips considers the "worrying of everyday life," referring not to *The Psychopathology of Everyday Life* (1901), but to something more mundane, perhaps like a phobia, which he describes memorably as a "kind of quotidian sublime" (22). We may be surrealists in our dreams, Phillips says, "but in our worries we are incorrigibly bourgeois" (55).

On Kissing, Tickling, and Being Bored contains only a few clinical vignettes, but the take-home lessons are double-edged. A sixteen-year-old girl referred to Phillips for antagonistic behavior engenders this observation: "I began to suggest to her in bits and pieces that being provocative was one of her ways of getting to know people; that in order to find out whether she could like people she had to find the hate in them" (19–20). This is part of a larger truth that only by not caring for an object, by "hating it wholeheartedly," do we get to know it (38). Phillips is himself a provocateur, not by offending his readers but by challenging their preconceptions. A twelve-year-old girl who treated Phillips as part of the problem in her life rather than as a potential solution seemed indifferent to the canceled therapy sessions while he was on vacation. "I found her absolute refusal to take me seriously as someone who went away rather endearing" (80). How does one remain angry at an analyst who makes pronouncements like this, who welcomes a patient's expression of dark emotions without becoming defensive? Love/hate is not a binary, as most people believe, but a singular human truth known by poets and psychoanalysts, natural allies, in Phillips's view.

Phillips enlists literature, past and present, high culture and popular culture, to raise clinical questions. In the captivating chapter on kissing, he references a canonical text that few English PhDs read nowadays, Shakespeare's *Troilus and Cressida*: "In kissing do you render or receive?" (97). Other references need no annotation, including a reference to the 2016 recipient of the Nobel Prize in Literature. "When Bob Dylan sings of a kiss, 'her mouth was watery and wet,' he is referring to the fact that not everything that is wet is watery" (97). Phillips then invokes Freud to express an idea few have considered. "Freud offers by implication the intriguing, grotesque—almost unthinkable—image of a person kissing his own mouth, and suggests that it is a narcissistic blow that he is unable to do so" (99).

Few subjects are off limits to Phillips, including the scatological. Asking a ten-year-old boy, referred to him because of his despondency at school, what he was worried about, Phillips receives a triumphant example of toilet humor, "Farts that don't work." Most authors would probably not report this detail, but Phillips enthusiastically agrees with his patient. "Yes, some farts are worth keeping." Then, like the improvisational artist that he is, Phillips riffs on the subject, quoting with approval Auden's citation of an Icelandic proverb, "Every man loves the smell of his own farts." Phillips then adds his own solemn clinical comment: Not everyone loves the smell of his own thoughts (48).

Writing about boredom, authors must avoid the unpardonable aesthetic sin, being boring. No worries. The eleven-page chapter "On Being

Bored" is riveting. Little has been written, psychoanalytically, on children's ordinary experience of being bored. Phillips coins the arresting oxymoron "attentive boredom," waiting for something without knowing what it might be (78). He might have recalled Freud's confession to Wilhelm Fliess in a letter written at the turn of the twentieth century: "Woe is me when I am bored" (*Complete Letters of Sigmund Freud to Wilhelm Fliess* 415). For Freud and, we suspect, Phillips too, creativity is the antidote to boredom, a way to turn an obstacle into a pleasure.

On Flirtation

On Flirtation (1994) is less a study of the psychology of coquetry than a delightful glimpse into the pleasures of the uncertainty principle. Flirtation is Phillips's metaphor of playing with stimulating ideas to explore anew their singularity without fear of adhering to stultifying orthodoxy or succumbing to overearnestness. "In the terms of this book flirtation is among other things a way of acknowledging the contingency of our lives—the sheer unpredictability, how accident-prone we are—without at the same time turning this unpredictability itself into a new kind of master-plot" (xii).

As in all of his writings, Phillips proves to be an engaging flirt, and readers will find themselves irresistibly attracted to his passionate advances. Lest there be any doubt about the seriousness of its scholarship, *On Flirtation* interrogates some of the most important subjects imaginable, including love, loss, memory, and the self. Phillips is a teaser (of the truth), but he is never a heartbreaker; he toys with ideas but never trifles with them.

On Flirtation consists of a series of lectures, book reviews, and previously published essays appearing in non-psychoanalytic magazines and journals. Avoiding technical and theoretical shoptalk, including psychobabble and lit-crit jargon, Phillips, contrary to Lisan Jutras's complaint, writes to be understood. Part I, "The Uses of the Past," explores the postmodern fascination with contingency, Freud's attitude toward remembering and forgetting, and the relationship between psychoanalysis and autobiography. Part II, "Psychoanalysis Reviewed," focuses on selected figures in the history of psychoanalysis, including Anna Freud, Ernest Jones, and Erich Fromm, as well as key subjects: depression, perversion, cross-dressing, guilt, and the future of psychoanalysis. Part III, "Writing

Outside," discusses Philip Roth's *Patrimony*, the early-twentieth-century English Romantic poet Isaac Rosenberg, the fin-de-siècle Viennese satirist Karl Kraus, and the "mad" English Romantic poet John Clare. There is no particular inner logic connecting these disparate essays; the book does not present an overarching theory embracing Phillips's two great loves, psychoanalysis and literature. Rather, the value of *On Flirtation* lies chiefly in Phillips's disarming insights into familiar subjects and his capacity to enchant us with his rare wit.

Phillips writes about psychoanalysis from an insider's perspective, yet he remains a central outsider. He candidly acknowledges that because psychoanalysis has been historically a closed profession, with its adherents forced to undergo a long education that is, as Erik Erikson pointed out, comparable to monastic training, an outsider's perspective is also valuable. Phillips's irreverent observations will dismay conservative psychoanalysts and charm liberal ones. Scholars from other professions, unburdened by the need for psychoanalytic correctness, will find the book especially rewarding. Outsiders will find much to cheer about in the following assertion: "If a lot of the most interesting psychoanalytic theory and history is now being written by people outside the profession, it is partly because the people inside the profession are more prone to the kinds of fundamentalism that stifle imagination in the name of something often called professional integrity (by 'fundamentalism' I mean here the assumption that something can only be legitimately criticized from within)" (149).

Valuing skepticism over certainty, questions over answers, Phillips practices what Freud could only preach. Freud urged readers of the *Introductory Lectures on Psycho-Analysis* (1915–1917) to be benevolent skeptics of his work, yet he usually demanded strict allegiance from his supporters. Phillips is a psychoanalyst, but he is no one's disciple. He pokes fun at himself, but he is no one's fool. There is never any doubt about where Phillips stands on crucial psychoanalytic issues. "Nothing—apart from the pathologization of homosexuality to which it is related—has been more coercive or misleading in psychoanalysis than its generalizations about women" (116). He is suspicious of any totalizing psychoanalytic or literary system, including, paradoxically, what has been called the hermeneutics of suspicion.

Phillips is equally critical of the numerous schisms that have splintered the psychoanalytic movement, isolating analysts from themselves and the larger community of scholars. Witness this observation about Melanie Klein: "What was revolutionary about Klein was that she succeeded where others had failed in dividing the psychoanalytic community" (120). In the uncorrected page proofs review copy of *On Flirtation* sent to me by the publisher, Phillips was more censorious: "What was revolutionary about Klein was not so much her theory or technique (her views are often a logical and often parodic extension of Freud's), but that she succeeded where others had failed—in dividing the psychoanalytic community." Ironically, Phillips notes that although ambivalence has long been central to psychoanalytic theory, analysts are loath to write about their own ambivalence toward their profession—as can be seen in the softening of his own ambivalence toward Klein in the published edition of the book!

Phillips's psychoanalytic heroes and heroines include those who acknowledge the impossibility of mastery and the value of difference. He singles out Erich Fromm, Jacques Lacan, Julia Kristeva, Christopher Bollas, and Malcolm Bowie. Phillips views psychoanalysis as the treatment of choice for gaining freedom in our personal lives. We may not be able to relive our lives, but we can reconstruct them. Phillips would agree with Faulkner's gnomic observation that the "past is never dead. It's not even past." Phillips urges upon us the broadest shape and meaning possible, one that embraces life's inherent randomness.

Just as psychoanalysis had extended the realm of intention at the expense of contingency, so has it tended to locate a single master-plot governing our lives. The problem, Phillips points out, is that we ignore the multiplicity of the human self. For this reason, he encourages psychoanalysts to pay more attention to creative writers whose stories, poems, and plays reveal the richness and variety of character. As much as Freud loved literature, he sometimes couldn't or wouldn't read certain writers (such as the Austrian physician/playwright Arthur Schnitzler) because he feared the loss of originality. "I do not want to read anything," he complained to Fliess in October, 1895, "because it plunges me into many thoughts and stunts my gratification in discovery" (*Complete Letters to Fliess* 141). One cannot imagine Phillips forgoing the pleasure of reading. Nor does he seem to fear Harold Bloom's anxiety of influence. "If psychoanalysts could think of themselves," Phillips writes in *On Flirtation*, "as the makers of sentences rather than of truths they would feel less at odds with—feel less need to privilege and covertly disparage—what Freud called 'Creative Writers'" (81).

Phillips understands that literary and psychoanalytic truths are complementary. Although he is a provocative rather than abrasive critic, he comes close to accusing his colleagues of being woefully ignorant of literature, thus impoverishing their own profession. "Because psychoanalysts have thought it better to write psychoanalytic papers for each other than to read novels or poems, they seem always to be writing about the same two or three people with the same three or four 'problems'" (132). The art of literature, like the art of psychoanalysis, is "turning what feels like contradictions—incompatibilities—into paradoxes." This does not mean, Phillips quickly notes, resolving conflicts. He always prefers a good question to a banal answer, a lively paradox to a dead-end resolution. Psychoanalysis, he tells us in *The Beast in the Nursery* (1998), is the "art of keeping the contradictions going" (136). He would agree with Fitzgerald's observation in the posthumously published *The Crack-Up*: "The test of a first-rate intelligence is the ability to hold two opposed ideas in the mind at the same time and still retain the ability to function" (69).

Phillips's dual allegiance to literature and psychoanalysis is evident everywhere in *On Flirtation*, not simply in his incisive observations about Roth, Rosenberg, Kraus, and Clare, but in his aphoristic prose style. One rarely associates psychoanalytic theorists and clinicians with sparkling wit, but *On Flirtation* is fun to read. A child psychologist, he speaks with both authority and self-effacing humor when he declares, "Infants, after all, have always been useful in psychoanalysis to attribute things to because they don't answer back" (19). Reviewing *The Complete Correspondence of Sigmund Freud and Ernest Jones 1908–1939*, published in 1993, Phillips remarks that one of the pleasures of reading the volume is Freud's wit, which "thrives on Jones being true to his (first) name" (111). Phillips's words are true to his own first name. According to Jewish tradition, Adam and Eve, and possibly God Himself, used Adamic language in the Garden of Eden.

If Freud is Phillips's psychoanalytic mentor, Oscar Wilde is his literary muse. Phillips admires Wilde's imagination and wit without indulging in his extravagant theatricality. One of Phillips's best aphorisms in *On Flirtation* occurs during a discussion of tangled parent-child relationships in Roth's fiction. "Children first become moralists," Phillips states, "when they realize their parents are children" (174). Was Phillips thinking of Wilde's shrewd insight in *The Picture of Dorian Gray*—"Children begin by loving their parents; as they grow older, they judge them; sometimes they forgive them" (66)? Like Wilde, Phillips delights in pun and paradox, taking a cliché and turning it on its head. Also like Wilde, Phillips searches for the true mask.

The most noteworthy chapter in *On Flirtation* is "The Telling of Selves," where Phillips writes about psychoanalysis and autobiography.

Because of repression and screen memories, the memories least likely to be recorded by an autobiographer are the most significant ones. Phillips reminds us that we must never trust the teller, only the tale, words that come from D.H. Lawrence's *Studies in Classic American Literature*. Autobiography and psychoanalysis are both forms of self-telling in the movement toward elusive truth.

Quoting from Freud's late essay "Constructions in Analysis" (1937), Phillips points out a crucial concession Freud makes regarding the difficulty of determining historical truth: construction in analysis "can be inaccurate but sufficient" (73). I haven't been able to find those words in the Freud essay—Phillips does not footnote his sources—but Freud does acknowledge that "We do not pretend that an individual construction is anything more than a conjecture which awaits examination, confirmation or rejection" (*SE* 23: 265). If it is true that a construction can be inaccurate but sufficient, does that mean, as many clinical and empirical studies suggest, that the most important part of the therapeutic process is not the therapist's theoretical approach or training but rather the strength of the patient-therapist relationship?

Like many people who have devoted their lives to studying the intersections of literature and psychoanalysis, I pay particular attention to how creative writers and analysts portray the talking cure. Phillips is the first analyst to point out that our choice of a particular psychoanalytic theorist determines the life story that we will end up with: "a Kleinian good life-story would not be one inspired and gratified by revenge; a Winnicottian good life-story would not be defined by its states of conviction but by the quality of its transitions" (70–71). A good life story of a Phillipsian analysand would encourage desire, curiosity, openness, and pleasure. He distinguishes between "bizarre" psychoanalysts, like Lacan and Bion, and "common-sense" analysts like Anna Freud, Heinz Kohut, and Erich Fromm. Phillips, I imagine, would embody the best qualities of both, fantastic excitability, like the former, and pragmatic intelligence, like the latter.

On Flirtation will fascinate readers who wish to restore the importance of contingency in human life and who, committed to psychoanalytic inquiry, realize that nothing can be completely understood or mastered. Allen Wheelis also realized this, but whereas he found this insight deeply distressing, Phillips remains untroubled. Celebrating precisely those qualities that Freud sought to dominate and subdue, Phillips reminds us that "we are all beginners at contingency because it is the only thing we can be"

(21). Given Phillips's subtle mind, appreciation of complexity, tolerance of conflicting views, rejection of closure, and epigrammatic style, it is no accident that he has written an enthralling book.

Terrors and Experts

"The test of a book is how much good stuff you can throw away," Hemingway told Lillian Ross (64). My test of a good book is how many sentences I underline. My pen ran out of ink as I was reading *Terrors and Experts* (1996).

Phillips may be an "unregenerate Freudian," as John Banville observes (xiii) in his introduction to Phillips's 2013 book *One Way and Another*, a selection of writings published in his earlier books and periodicals, but in *Terrors and Experts* he presents us with a "post-Freudian Freud," a man who was "always ahead of himself, and who we are beginning to catch up with" (6). A post-Freudian Freud is an ironist of Enlightenment thinking; the unconscious is that which is tantalizingly strange or foreign about ourselves. Psychoanalysis is itself a theory of the "unbearable" (13), more confounding than comforting. Instead of achieving enlightenment, one learns to live with and appreciate unknowability, which is not the same as ignorance. Phillips's post-Freudian Freud anticipates the expression "dark enlightener" Joel Whitebook uses in his 2017 *Freud: An Intellectual Biography*, where he seeks to show that Freud confronted the irrational to integrate it into a fuller conception of reason. Mistrustful of words like "integration," Phillips sees Freud as a disenlightener. George Makari's remark that Kant became the central figure of the German Enlightenment, the thinker who "simultaneously represented its apogee and its end" (409), is no less true of Phillips's Freud, the figure who represents the zenith of psychoanalytic knowability and the decline of therapeutic optimism.

Phillips startles us throughout *Terrors and Experts*, sometimes charmingly, other times maddeningly. One never encounters a dull sentence. Some of his pronouncements are incendiary to the psychoanalytic establishment. "Psychoanalysts take themselves, and their professionalization, too seriously, something their theory should make them a bit suspicious of" (xiv). Wisdom doesn't come with age: "the most cursory contact with any respectable psychoanalytic training institution would quickly disabuse one of this" (31). Indeed, the average age of members of the American Psychoanalytic Association is 70 (Almond 13). Perhaps most inflammatory of all, psychoanalytic theory has become a contemporary version of the etiquette book, "improving our internal manners" or "advising us on our best sexual behaviour" (87). As a writer, Phillips is never well behaved though not quite an *enfant terrible*. Why should people go to psycho-analysts if they can only allow us to be unhappy in new ways? Phillips withholds his answer until the last page, where he tells us that the ana-lyst is an expert on "human possibility, something no one could ever be, despite the posturing of our own favourite authorities" (104). *Terrors and Experts* is Phillips's most paradoxical book, but in what may be a subtle self-criticism, he acknowledges the contemporary psychoanalyst's risk of becoming "merely a curator of paradoxes, a master of the absurdities of mastery, with all the glib Socratic trappings; wisdom as the tyranny of disingenuousness" (8). But Phillips is more than an archivist of paradoxes. In taking a stand against the "enemies of ambiguity" (xvi), he reminds us of the vagaries of desire, which helps explain his appeal as a writer.

Monogamy

Notwithstanding Peter Swales's improbable speculation that Freud had a sexual affair with his sister-in-law, Minna Bernays, Freud led a strictly monogamous life. He was, however, no fan of monogamy, arguing in his 1908 essay " 'Civilized' Sexual Morality and Modern Nervous Illness" that monogamy "cripples the factor of *selection by virility*" and is responsible for "modern nervous illness" (*SE* 9: 182). Freud never wrote about infidelity, a word missing from the index to the *Standard Edition*. Phillips seeks to edify and entertain us in his slender 1996 book *Monogamy*, enlivened by psychoanalytic and philosophical aperçus.

Unlike Camus, who said that the only serious philosophical question is suicide, for Phillips the most urgent question is whether one should be monogamous. Each of the book's 120 axioms, most only a paragraph or two long, is mind-bending. "At its best monogamy may be the wish to find someone to die with; at its worst it is a cure for the terrors of aliveness. They are easily confused" (27). He leaves many questions unan-swered. "Why are we more impressed by the experience of falling in love than by the experience of falling out of love?" (36). A few adages hint at Rochefoucauldian cynicism: "So what would we have to do to make monogamy glamorous? Or rather, what would we have to stop doing?" (53).

Freud had much to say about masturbation; there are scores of ref-erences in the index to the *Standard Edition* about its compulsive nature.

Freud did not, however, write about the pleasures of masturbation, as Phillips informs us in a footnote to *Winnicott*. "The idea of developing a capacity for satisfying masturbatory experience has never, for some reason, found a place in psychoanalytic theory" (167 n. 30). Phillips corrects that omission in *Monogamy*. "Masturbation is traditionally taboo not because it damages your health—it is not only safe sex, it is safe incest—or because it is against the law, but because we fear it may be the truth about sex: that sex is something we do on our own" (101). Monogamy points out the hidden truth of masturbation. "The virtue of monogamy is the ease with which it can turn sex into masturbation; the vice of monogamy is that it gives you nothing else. If two can be one too many, so can one be" (101–102).

The Beast in the Nursery

The title of Phillips's 1998 book *The Beast in the Nursery* evokes Henry James's haunting 1903 novella *The Beast in the Jungle*, a cautionary tale about retreating from life because of a lurking fear that turns out to be, ironically, the fear of life itself. Phillips used the allusion deliberately; elsewhere he refers to other Jamesian masterpieces: "The Art of Fiction," *The Wings of the Dove*, and *What Maisie Knew*. For James, life and art were integral to each other, neither more important than the other. The same is true for Phillips.

Why the beast in the nursery? Many prominent psychoanalysts, including Freud, Klein, Winnicott, and Lacan, theorized the child, each suggesting that something essential is missing, lost, or destroyed in childhood. "Making a fetish of absence," Phillips drolly observes, "is the last move in a worn-out theology" (17). *The Beast in the Nursery* is about not absence but presence: the joy of childhood and children's instinct for pleasure that theorists ignore, perhaps because they are too old or jaded to remember their own childhoods. In an abrupt departure from other psychoanalytic theorists, Phillips values childhood not because it is a prelude to adulthood but because of its own uniqueness: "there is no purpose in the child's life other than living it" (17).

Phillips is typically wary of binaries, but he cannot resist dichotomous thinking about his profession. There are two kinds of psychoanalysis, he opines: one that promotes a "corrective emotional experience," a term coined by Franz Alexander and Thomas M. French in 1946, the other that aims to "restore the artist in the patient, the part of the person that makes interest despite, or whatever, the early environment" (4). There is no question which he prefers. In his view, the analyst's function is to promote not adaptation but innovation. In the chapter titled "A Stab at Hinting," he distinguishes between two kinds of psychoanalytic interpretations, a distinction he conveys epigrammatically. "One kind aims to turn hints into orders; the other kind tries to turn orders into hints. Both are useful, but they make very different kinds of world" (96). Again, there is no doubt which he prefers. He observes a few pages later that Melanie Klein arouses "ferocious hostility" in some people because of her view of the unconscious (105), a criticism he was not prepared to make in *On Flirtation.*

Although Phillips quotes more literary writers than perhaps any other contemporary psychoanalyst, he doesn't usually cite Nabokov, who detested the "Viennese quack." The novelist's statement in the afterword to *Lolita* about art existing only for "aesthetic bliss"—"curiosity, tenderness, kindness, ecstasy" (305)—is no less true of Phillips's vision of psychoanalysis. Aesthetic pleasure also characterizes, as we have seen in the preceding chapter, Christopher Bollas's writings. Phillips conveys aesthetic bliss partly by the litany of creative writers he quotes throughout *The Beast in the Nursery*—a partial list includes Shakespeare, Blake, Wordsworth, Coleridge, Yeats, Heaney, Kafka, Proust, Auden, and Hughes—and partly by his own joyous language. Children take for granted, Phillips never allows us to forget, that "lives are only livable if they give pleasure" (xxii). The rest of us, he implies, should not take this truth for granted; instead, we should do everything possible to keep this pleasure alive until the end of our lives. One of the virtues of Phillips's writings is that they perform what they value: the pleasure principle.

Darwin's Worms

Freud famously referred to three "'impossible' professions" in his 1937 essay "Analysis Terminable and Interminable": education, government, and psychoanalysis. He knew that psychoanalysis, his creation, was a lifelong process, though he reluctantly conceded that the termination of an analysis was a practical affair. A fourth impossible profession, one for which Freud had no use, indeed, poured contempt upon throughout his life, was biography, the art of creating a subject's life. "Anyone turning biographer," he warned in a 1936 letter to Arnold Zweig, who had proposed to write a biography of him, "commits himself to lies, to concealment, to hypocrisy, to flattery, and even to hiding his own lack of understanding, for biographical truth is not to be had, and even if it were it couldn't be used" (*Letters* 430). Freud never considered that autobiography may be the most truthful writing when scrutinized in a certain way, as Mark Twain, one of Freud's favorite authors, quipped in *The Mark Twain-Howells Lectures*: "An autobiography is the truest of all books; for while it inevitably consists of extinctions of the truth, shirkings of the truth, partial revealments of the truth, with hardly an instance of plain straight truth, the remorseless truth is there, between the lines" (2: 782).

How do we explain Freud's lifelong antipathy to biography? Without explicitly referring to biography as an impossible profession, Phillips teases out the paradoxical implications of life stories and death stories in his 1999 book *Darwin's Worms*. Phillips begins by quoting the twenty-nine-year-old Freud's 1885 letter to his fiancée, Martha Bernays, boasting about destroying all of his notes, letters, and scientific manuscripts. "I couldn't have matured or died without worrying about who would get hold of those old papers." Let future biographers worry, Freud gloats; he has no desire to make their task easy. Phillips's response? "Freud clearly wants to be the Sphinx, rather than Oedipus who solved its riddle. By getting rid of the written evidence of the past he has unburied that Sphinx again, recovered the riddle of himself, at least for posterity" (68). Other scholars might have stopped here, but Phillips is just getting started, warming up, like an improvisational artist. Freud destroyed biographical evidence to taunt his future biographers because of the desire to become the kind of person for whom biographers will compete. Freud has it both ways, Phillips continues, receiving two pleasures for the price of one: "the pleasure of reading his biographies (in the plural), and the pleasure of watching, or just secretly knowing that his biographers have gone astray" (69).

Phillips conjures up the image of the Sphinx to suggest that Freud wants to be the one who asks but never answers questions, to protect the idea that a person remains a secret or, as Winston Churchill expressed in a different context, a "riddle, wrapped in a mystery, inside an enigma." The psychoanalyst's sphinxlike character remains deeply paradoxical, Phillips avers, given that Freud believed he had unlocked universal truths about human nature, solving the Sphinx's riddle with the discovery of the Oedipus complex. As further evidence of Freud's "Sphinx complex," the wish to be the "mysterious monster that asks the impossible questions" (70),

Phillips points out that Freud wrote the mistitled *An Autobiographical Study* (1925) without revealing *anything* personal about his life. Phillips then speculates that Freud's mistrust of biography may betray his misgivings about psychoanalysis itself. Freud uncovered the fundamental truth about people, ambivalence, which both biography and psychoanalysis confirm. In Phillips's words, "It is an insufficiently acknowledged—insufficiently enjoyed—paradox that the more Freud elaborated psychoanalytic theory the less impressed he was by the knowability of the human subject" (94), a conclusion that calls into question the perception of Freud as a child of the Enlightenment.

Tellingly, whereas this paradox may disturb other analysts, Phillips revels in it. *Darwin's Worms* confronts us with one paradox after another, many of which involve death, a paradoxical form of loss, "at once ours and not ours" (15). In a different way, death is paradoxical because it is the "object of desire that finally releases us from desire" (110–111). Moreover, death makes life lovable: "It is the passing of things that is the source of our happiness" (26). *Darwin's Worms* offers other paradoxes, including Freud's speculation in *Beyond the Pleasure Principle* (1920) about the existence of a death instinct, which Phillips defines as the "idea that not knowing things will get us the life we want" (74).

Did Phillips realize when he was working on *Darwin's Worms* that fifteen years later he would write his own biography, *Becoming Freud: The Making of a Psychoanalyst*? One can see how a central idea of *Darwin's Worms*—the conviction that human nature will always be puzzling, enigmatic, ultimately unknowable despite our best (and worst) efforts to pluck out the heart of its mystery—prepared him for writing the Freud biography.

Promises, Promises

At 376 pages, Phillips's next book, *Promises, Promises*, one of his longest, is a compilation of essays on literature and psychoanalysis originally published in leading British and American newspapers and journals, including the *London Review of Books*, *The Observer*, *The Guardian*, *The New York Times*, *Contemporary Psychoanalysis*, *Raritan*, *Salmagundi*, *Threepenny Review*, and *Slate*. "As an essayist," David James Fisher observes in a 2018 interview, "Phillips writes like a *flaneur*, leisurely strolling through his themes with no definitive goal or destination" (915). Yet at the same time, each essay is well wrought, suggesting a tightly-knit argument.

Promises, Promises contains only one footnote, but it is startling, an undogmatic polemic: "I think it is more illuminating to read psychoanalysts as poets—mostly, of course, poor ones—rather than failed or aspiring scientists; if we do this we need not worry about whether they are right or wrong, we can just argue instead about whether their words are persuasive, eloquent, evocative or beautiful. Whether they have made something haunting rather than true" (38).

Why does Phillips consign this battle-cry to a mere footnote? Footnotes, he tells us nearly three hundred pages later, "are often for the people who don't quite make it into the text; people just this side of being left out" (332). For people who *do* make it into a text, and who read every word *especially* footnotes, Phillips's statement is provocative because he is writing as both a literary critic and a psychoanalyst, suggesting that his two professions may be not only complementary but also identical.

Few American psychoanalysts, however, particularly if they are psychiatrists, trained in medical school, would agree that their writings should be read as poetry. It's true, nevertheless, that if one wishes to study psychoanalysis in an American college or university, one must turn not to the psychology but the English department—though as Phillips ruefully admits, the status of literature as a definable discipline is "up for grabs." If psychoanalysis is mainly an art, a form of literature, how can we tell whether it is persuasive? What does "persuasive" mean?

A signature idea in *Promises, Promises* is unknowability. It's easy to write about the unknowability of character, either real or fictional, but to have credibility, one must point out something new about unknowability. Phillips understands the conundrum. "What could be more omniscient than knowing that I do not know myself? But I don't think we should get out of this dilemma, or find ways around it, so much as be in it in better ways" (224). Unknowability for Phillips means that there are no universal psychological truths, no master theories, as Freud believed. Phillips never regards himself as a *conquistador*, the disturber of the world's sleep, as the creator of psychoanalysis did. Nor is Phillips in quest for the *Key to All Mythologies*, the provisional title of the book that the pedantic scholar in George Eliot's *Middlemarch*, Edward Casaubon, fails to complete. Rather, unknowability affirms a not-knowing that is in the service of better knowing, as Phillips reminds us was always true of Wilfred Bion and usually true for Winnicott.

Of the twenty-eight chapters in *Promises, Promises*, "On Translating a Person" is the most singular. Phillips uses the metaphor of translation to argue by analogy that just as an interpreter translates texts, so do psychoanalysts translate people. But a problem immediately arises. How can an analyst translate a person if there is no original text, no essential self, no true self? Phillips's paradoxical solution is that there are an "unknowable series of translations of translations; preferred versions of ourselves, but not true ones" (143). If so, we don't need to worry about unlocking the deepest self. "In other words, at least in psychoanalysis—and perhaps not only there—the *only good translation is the one that invites retranslation; the one that doesn't want to be verified so much as altered*" (146). Lest this sound facile, Phillips concedes that the idea of the analyst as collaborative translator is always a "cover story" (one of his favorite expressions) because the analyst's preferred version of patients may differ from their own preferred versions of themselves. Psychoanalysis always involves competing accounts of life stories, generating inevitable conflict. The aim of psychoanalysis, then, is to help people make their own translations.

Phillips's case studies are true to this principle, for neither he nor his patients experience life-transforming epiphanies or dramatic turning points. He is wise enough not to be a "deep reader," as so many psychoanalysts (and literary critics) are. He prefers small gains to larger ones that may fail to withstand the test of time. Some of his clinical vignettes simply show a patient gaining trust in him. A fourteen-year-old Jamaican boy, referred to psychotherapy because of aggressive school behavior, confessed during his first session that he hated school, an admission that made him instantly likable to Phillips. He never gave up on the patient despite the fact that the teenager missed several sessions. At one point the boy exclaimed, "Man, you're just translating my words. I don't need this every week" (142). But he said this with a grin on his face—and he continued to see Phillips every week. Another patient, the fifteen-year-old anorexic Chloe, abruptly left therapy because her parents felt it wasn't working. Comparing Chloe to Melville's "Bartleby, the Scrivener," Phillips observes from experience that trying to reason with people who would prefer not to has an ironic effect: "nothing exposes our fantasies of reasonableness more than the refusal to eat" (288).

Wary of theory throughout *Promises, Promises*, Phillips's preferred vision of psychoanalysis is that "it should be more about living day-to-day as oneself than about being initiated into a sophisticated or prestigious theoretical system" (xiv). One can never accuse Phillips of being ignorant about theory. The opposite is true. Sometimes he admires a theory but not the theorist. He regards Lacan as the "greatest analyst since Freud" while also admitting that "Lacan's writings are the 'confessions of a self-justifying megalomaniac'" (108).

Phillips's writings are highly performative. He often reserves his best sentences for chapter endings. "Perhaps good stories about our ignorance should not be too informative" (173), he muses at the conclusion of a chapter on open-mindedness. He ends the chapter on Hart Crane's poetry with the words, "It is perhaps a sign of the times that he has become more and more our contemporary as he is read less and less" (237). (Phillips's statement reminds me of the American novelist and essayist Harold Brodkey, known as much for his chronic writer's block as for his massive ego, who was said to grow more famous with each book he failed to publish.) The last chapter, which bears the title of the volume, ends with a sentence that may—or may not—be rhetorical: "Why have an analysis when you can read?" (375).

Houdini's Box

Phillips's next book, *Houdini's Box* (2001), is a meditation on escape artists. The central focus is on Erik Weisz (1874–1926), a Hungarian-born Jew who came to the United States when he was four and later renamed himself Harry Houdini, arguably the supreme magician and illusionist of all time, the "Greatest Necromancer of the Age." The chapters in the book juxtapose Houdini's life with two of Phillips's patients' lives, a young girl who loved to play hide-and-seek, and an academic in flight from a woman devoted to him. There's also a brief discussion of Emily Dickinson, who spent the last twenty years of her life in self-imposed isolation in her home in Amherst, Massachusetts. Phillips raises questions about the nature of psychological escape, but there's one question he doesn't explore: How is a psychoanalyst an escape artist?

There are dozens of biographies of Houdini, a performer whose astounding escapes from what appeared to be certain death continue to mystify readers. Phillips relies on Kenneth Silverman's 1996 study for factual details. Curiously, Phillips omits any mention of Bernard C. Meyer's 1976 psychobiography *Houdini: A Mind in Chains*. (Both biographies have the same cover, a photograph of Houdini in chains.) One can see why Phillips was drawn to the inscrutable Houdini, as I suggested in a 1979 review of Meyer's book:

Both his life and death were surrounded by paradoxes: an illusionist who died on Halloween; a fanatical foe of Spiritualism who nevertheless engaged in countless seances in a desperate effort to be reconciled with his dead mother; and a man who even as he obeyed one of the Ten Commandments, to honor his parents by erecting a moment to their memory, simultaneously violated another Commandment by crowning the entire exedra with his own graven image—which someone smashed in 1975, nearly fifty years after his death. But above all, Houdini was a man whose obsession with death repeatedly compelled him to defy it and thus preserve the illusion of his own immortality. (307)

Meyer, a classically trained psychoanalyst in the tradition of American ego psychology, invokes Freud's repetition compulsion principle, outlined in *Beyond the Pleasure Principle*, to explain Houdini's death-defying exploits. The impulse behind Houdini's efforts to master intolerable anxiety, Meyer conjectures, derives from the active repetition of a frightening experience to which he had been subjected as a helpless and passive onlooker. Lack of biographical information prevents Meyer from knowing what this early traumatic event might have been. Houdini's performances of binding and escape were, psychoanalytically, desexualized forms of sadomasochistic practices. Meyer contends that the latent claustrophobia enveloping Houdini's life reveals a more deeply buried claustrophilia. Houdini's motivation to become the world's most legendary jailbreaker appeared to be an unconscious identification with the criminal imagination. Meyer points out the striking parallels between Houdini's self-burials and the identical themes of death, burial, and resurrection found in Edgar Allan Poe's fiction. Phillips would agree with many of these observations, though he downplays the repetition compulsion principle. Words like "mastery" are not part of his theoretical vocabulary. Nor does he affirm adaptation, which smacks of conformity to him. Phillips views Houdini as a performer who, without necessarily feeling depressed, staged repeatedly a "grotesque parody of a suicidal act" (83).

Phillips's thesis is that psychoanalytic patients resemble Houdini because they, too, are risk takers, torn between two forms of escapism. "One can escape into doubt about what one wants, or one can escape *from* doubt about what one wants" (159). Doubt besets all of us, Phillips adds, resulting in two types of people: those who flee from confusion and uncertainty into conviction, and those who become faultfinders, ironists, and skeptics. The academic patient fleeing from romantic commitment, betraying a lifelong pattern of failed relationships, produced a counter-transferential "stridency" in Phillips. The analyst began to feel that he was being recruited to help the patient become a better escape artist, escaping from all relationships. Phillips, on the other hand, wanted the patient to become a better risk taker. "You're so busy making choices that you never take any risks" (158). This is not what the patient wanted to hear, however, and he abruptly terminated therapy.

Phillips doesn't see himself as an escape artist, but isn't that what psychoanalysis is, a process in which the analyst helps patients free themselves from self-imprisoning doubts and fears? Psychoanalysis is a game of hide-and-seek, an effort to plumb the unconscious that always resists discovery. Houdini and Phillips are both conjurers who have their own magical bags of tricks, both committed to the art of the inexplicable. Disenchainers both, they narrate stories of safety and danger with uncertain outcomes. Both are meticulous in their craft: Houdini spent hours researching and rehearsing his performances; Phillips read the unreadable *Finnegans Wake*, where Joyce writes about the "escape-master-in-chief from all sorts of houdingplaces" (164). There are differences, of course. Houdini called himself not a magician but a mystifier, whereas a psychoanalyst is a demystifier (except to critics, who see the talking cure as nothing but black magic, mumbo jumbo, mystification). Despite these differences, Houdini and Phillips have much in common. Phillips's statement about Houdini—"Without saying so, he could show people just how close, just how muddled up, our virtues and vices could become" (120)—describes the psychoanalyst himself. Another observation about Houdini is a prophetic self-characterization: "it was part of Houdini's magic to make his contradictions seem quite untroubling" (119). The analyst, in other words, helps the patient transform troubling contradictions into life-saving paradoxes.

Equals

"Treating someone as an equal, as psychoanalysis shows so well, is not as simple or easy or uncostly as it might seem" (29). No one would dispute this statement from Phillips's next book, *Equals* (2002), but ironically, psychoanalysis has difficulty learning this truth, as he sardonically remarks in the book's most self-disclosing passage:

When I was training to be a child psychotherapist about twenty years ago we were asked by the committee running our course for suggestions about what we would like to be taught. When some of these suggestions were turned down, and some of us got rather cross, we were told by a member of the training committee that "children can't bring themselves up." As it happens I was a child then, but some of my contemporaries were in their thirties and forties, and had children themselves. So unsurprisingly, perhaps, they were rather affronted and bemused by this. (27)

It's a familiar criticism expressed unfamiliarly. Phillips was in his late forties when he described a younger version of himself, twenty years earlier, as a "child." The word elicits his feeling of infantilization when he was told he was too young to criticize his teachers. Phillips might have expressed indignation in *Equals*, perhaps citing Nietzsche's droll observation that one repays a teacher poorly by remaining a student. Instead, Phillips allows us to chuckle over the word "child," inferring the wisdom from the mouth of babes.

Going Sane

In *Going Sane* (2005), Phillips takes a subject we believe we understand and then shows we know less about it than we thought. Countless stories and textbooks have been written about "going insane," but as Phillips points out, whereas madness is a topic for daily rumination, the idea of sanity confounds us. "Like the 'good' characters in literature, the sane don't have any memorable lines" (4). Phillips begins, appropriately, with Shakespeare, reminding us that "mad" is used over two hundred times in his writings; its cognate, "madness," appears thirty-five times in *Hamlet*. Polonius advises Gertrude that her "noble son is mad," but then, struggling to define "true madness," becomes for Phillips the "first antipsychiatrist" (9).

While reading *Going Sane*, I wondered how often the word "sanity" appears in the *Standard Edition* of Freud's writings. Zero. Nor do words like psychological or mental health appear as entries. It's true that distinctions between "normal" and "neurotic" behavior appear in the index. "Now psycho-analytic research finds no fundamental, but only quantitative, distinctions between normal and neurotic life," Freud writes in *The Interpretation of Dreams* (*SE* 5: 373). He repeats this point in *Analysis of a Phobia in a Five-Year-Old Boy* (1909), the case study of Little Hans, stating that no sharp line can be drawn between normal and neurotic people. And in "Analysis Terminable and Interminable" Freud asserts that normalcy is a fiction: "Every normal person, in fact, is only normal on the average" (*SE* 23: 235). But sanity and normalcy are not identical; the former applies to a mental or psychological state, while the latter, a more general term, implies conformity to an established pattern. Phillips is right: psychoanalysts and literary critics undertheorize "sanity," which has a paradoxical quality; "it bores us, and gives us pleasure only when it is mocked" (29).

Phillips rises to the aesthetic challenge of writing a book about sanity that is neither boring nor mocking. *Going Sane* is his most philosophical book, investigating the values necessary for a good life, one in which sanity is a virtue devoutly to be wished. He proposes a blueprint for a contemporary sanity that incorporates a comment Emerson made in a diary entry: "Sanity is very rare: every man almost and every woman has a dash of madness" (178). Phillips distinguishes between the "superficially sane," who are "reassuring because they help us forget about madness," and the "deeply sane," who are "all too mindful of madness, but they have its measure" (181). He then gives us a definition that is lively and expansive enough to make anyone proud of being sane, a definition likely to become a gold standard that, paradoxically, rejects standards: "Sanity involves learning to enjoy conflict, and giving up on all myths of harmony, consistency, and redemption" (184). Deep sanity thus affirms Phillips's lifelong commitment to unknowability, uncertainty, and unpredictability. He might have added that since perfection is impossible, we should be grateful for good enough sanity.

Side Effects

If I were stranded on a proverbial desert island and had only one book to read, it would be Dickens's *Great Expectations*. It may not be considered the world's greatest novel, perhaps not even Dickens's greatest (which may be *Bleak House*), but it brings me the most intense pleasure. I've taught the novel many times and wrote a chapter on it in my 1990 book *Narcissism and the Novel*. In reading Phillips's *Side Effects* (2006), I learned something new about the novel—and about psychoanalysis—that increased my pleasure: the meaning of first impressions and second thoughts.

Of the seventeen essays in *Side Effects*, the forty-five-page "Two Lectures on Expectations" is the longest and the one that may have the greatest appeal to psychoanalytic literary critics. (The first lecture is on *Great Expectations*; the second, on *Pride and Prejudice*.) Throughout *Side Effects*, as well as his other books, Phillips rejects the practice of psycho-analysts (and literary scholars, as I did, alas, early in my career) who use literature mainly to confirm psychoanalytic theory. "The psychoanalysts never seem to say: psychoanalysis led me to believe that X was the case, but then I read, say, *Pride and Prejudice*, and realized the error of my ways. Among the psychoanalysts the literary is that which never revises a psychoanalytic insight" (47). Phillips's challenge in *Side Effects* is to show how psychoanalysis may be considered applied literature.

Great Expectations abounds in first impressions. The opening page reveals three of Pip's first impressions, all of which are enigmatic: his name, his parents, and the place in which he grew up. These first impressions, part of Pip's self-created identity, highlight the orphan's early traumatic losses. "Our first impression of Pip is of someone who needs to tell us about his first impressions, and how these are integral to his sense of himself" (222). We are often most self-revealing in our first impressions; moreover, our first impressions are often informed by great expectations, as Phillips shows is true of Pip. Psychoanalysis, Phillips adds, is about the fate of first impressions. As evidence, Phillips—who has demon-strated in his earlier books that he studies carefully the frequency of Freud's use of certain words—informs us that the word "first" appears in Strachey's *Standard Edition* translation 3,766 times, more than three times the frequency of the word "pleasure." Phillips then suggests that because of the "strange law of repetition"—screen memories, deferred action, and transference—our first impressions are substitutes for earlier, more traumatic experiences.

Repetition may be an acting out or working through of psychic trauma. Though Dickens was enthusiastic about *Great Expectations*, he feared, as he expressed to his future biographer, John Forster, that the story was an unconscious repetition of his earlier (and most autobiographical) novel *David Copperfield*, both novels dramatizing different aspects of his troubled childhood. *Great Expectations* is, of course, a masterpiece, an example of generative repetition. Unlike other psychoanalysts, particu-larly American ego psychologists, Phillips does not view the repetition compulsion principle as leading to mastering anxiety; but he does see it as a way to generate stories.

Phillips opens the second lecture with a sentence dense with paradoxical meaning. "*First Impressions*, a novel that on second thoughts was called *Pride and Prejudice*, is about, among many other things, how pride and prejudice is a better way of describing first impressions" (240). Second thoughts become the realization for first impressions. "As shorthand one could say: first impressions are radical; second thoughts are conservative" (252). Phillips's own theory of first impressions strikes me as radical, convincing us, paradoxically, that there is "nothing more anachronistic than a first impression" (227).

Phillips postulates two interrelated aesthetic principles in his discussions of *Great Expectations* and *Pride and Prejudice*. First: our initial impressions in a melodramatic story, the ability to spot immediately a villainous character, are inevitably true, suggesting lack of character development; by contrast, our first impressions in a good novel will inevitably require revision. And second: a first impression doesn't make a story good. The best stories are those where first impressions are false. After reading "Two Lectures on Expectations," I started thinking about the secret stories of first impressions, those of fictional and real characters. "Perhaps there is a book to be written about our first impressions in the nineteenth century" (226). Phillips hasn't written the book, but he may have inspired one of his readers to do so.

Intimacies

The coauthored book *Intimacies* (2008) is an anomalous work. Leo Bersani, professor emeritus of French at UC Berkeley and the author of many books on gay studies and Lacanian theory, wrote the first three chapters (along with a brief conclusion): "The It in the I," "Shame on You," and "The Power of Evil and the Power of Love." After discussing Patrice Leconte's 2003 film *Confidences trop intimes* (*Intimate Strangers*), James's *The Beast in the Jungle*, the French writer Guillaume Dustin's 1996 autobiographical novel *Dans ma chambre* (*In My Room*), and Paul Morris's pornographic 2004 film *Plantin' Seed*, Bersani examines the phenomenon of gay barebacking, having unprotected anal sex, during and following the AIDS crisis. Bersani argues for "impersonal intimacy," a jaw-dropping assertion in that the "barebacking gang-bang has none of what we usually think of as the humanizing attributes of intimacy within a couple, where the personhood of each partner is presumed to be expanded and enriched by knowledge of the other" (53). Bersani then calls for a new type of intimacy based on "impersonal narcissism," a relationality that he claims is a revolutionary reversal of the dominant relational mode that has nourished the power of evil.

Most analysts would find Bersani's vision of psychoanalysis unrecognizable. "The promises of adaptive balance and sexual maturity undoubtedly explain the appeal of psychoanalysis as therapy, but its greatness may lie in its insistence on a human destructiveness resistant to any therapeutic endeavors whatsoever" (60). He agrees with Foucault, who saw psychoanalysis, in Bersani's own words, as an "essentially sinister moment in the exercise of power in Western history" (65). Bersani's prose style is awash in rhetorical flourishes, and his intellectual critiques are even more radical than Phillips's. Writing about the "rage for death inherent in the human psyche," he concludes that "now we are in psychoanalytic territory (anathema to marry [sic] queer theorists)" (35)—a statement that may be a Freudian slip, betokening mistrust of certain types of unions of which he doesn't approve. In his 2009 book *Queer Optimism*, Michael D. Snediker offers a powerful rejoinder to Bersani's privileging of self-shattering and shame, a criticism that Phillips never makes in the fourth chapter of *Intimacies*, "On a More Impersonal Note," only thirty pages long.

As Phillips admits in the preface, his conversation with Bersani, begun nearly twenty years earlier, contains many loose ends, including questions raised by one coauthor that the other coauthor ignores. Unlike Phillips's next coauthored book, *On Kindness*, where he and his collaborator are on the same page, literally and metaphorically, sharing similar observations and conclusions, *Intimacies* proposes the need for new types of relationships, but the study itself illustrates the difficulty of achieving a balanced exchange of ideas and points of view. It is, I suspect, one of the few ironies with which the coauthors would likely agree. Bersani's tone is often acerbic, while Phillips's tone is always measured if not characteristically playful.

In one of the few moments when the coauthors speak to each other, Bersani quotes from Phillips's introduction to the recent Penguin edition of Freud's writings on psychoanalytic technique: "Psychoanalysis is about what two people can say to each other if they agree not to have sex" (*Intimacies* 1). Phillips begins his chapter by elaborating, albeit with an odd qualification, on his own words: "The preoccupation with so-called boundary-violations in contemporary psychoanalysis—the sometimes forlorn attempts to regulate psychoanalytic practice to ensure that patients are not exploited by their therapists—betrays an anxiety that the psychoanalytic setting can be rather more like ordinary life than psychoanalysts want it to be" (89). Phillips then observes that Lacan, notorious for his many boundary violations, "remarked that the well-analyzed analyst is more rather than less likely to fall in love with his patient" (89–90), a statement that does not seem to be true of Phillips himself.

Musing on the question of whether we love something because it is inside us or it is inside us because we love it, Phillips insists, in opposition to Bersani, that we must love others for their differences. If, as Bersani contends, there are no boundaries between self and other, inside and outside, the result would be, in Phillips's impish words, the "narcissism of major differences" (101), revising the "narcissism of minor differences" that Freud talks about in *Civilization and Its Discontents* (*SE* 21: 114). Using a rare double negative for which he had, years earlier, criticized Winnicott, Phillips observes that an existence without boundaries is a "picture we cannot afford not to do without" (102).

There are other differences between the coauthors. Unlike Bersani, Phillips is skeptical of the reconceptualization of narcissism as eliminating the opposition between sameness and difference. Phillips doesn't defend psychoanalysis against Bersani's withering criticisms, but he suggests that Bersani's notion of impersonal narcissism has its precursor in the early mother-child relationship, the first intimacy, based on potentiality or becoming. Phillips is no advocate of ego psychology, but Bersani's desire for the self-shattering of the ego, with its connotations of shock and fragmentation, strikes his coauthor as masochistic. In an extended review published in *Raritan*, David Kurnick noted that the "tension in *Intimacies* between the gay man's interest in sexual outlawry and the analyst's return to the family romance may represent less a miscommunication than a mild comedy of differential emphasis" (120).

On Kindness

It's not only Scrooge who would mistrust a book on kindness. Thomas Hobbes regarded Christian kindness as an absurdity in his influential *Leviathan* (1651), and though there have been many defenders of kindness, including David Hume, Adam Smith, and Jean-Jacques Rousseau, it has not fared well in a capitalist age. Christianity preaches kindness but has not always practiced it. How can one observe the Christian injunction to "love thy neighbor as thyself" if, as Lacan said, most people hate themselves?

Phillips coauthored *On Kindness* (2009) with Barbara Taylor, a Canadian-born historian who is professor of humanities at Queen Mary, University of London. The coauthors faced a daunting challenge: how to affirm kindness without sacralizing, romanticizing, idealizing, or sentimentalizing it. How can one celebrate "ordinary" kindness that is within the grasp of most people—kindness that acknowledges the centrality of ambivalence in everyday life? Kindness, the coauthors argue, has become a forbidden pleasure, and they offer psychoanalytic and historical reasons to explain the hazards of what is usually an act of generosity. A coauthored book is always a balancing act between two or more authors who rarely share similar temperaments, points of view, or aesthetic styles. Unlike *Intimacies*, *On Kindness* is a happy union of two like-minded authors. The coauthors don't specify the chapters each wrote, but it's easy to identify Taylor as responsible for "A Short History of Kindness," in part because she uses the word "paradox" only once. The chapters "How Kind?" and "The Kindness Instinct," both of which explore how psychoanalysts theorize the subject, reveal Phillips's penchant for paradoxical thinking, as when he suggests that aggression can be a form of kindness because it "contains the wish for a more intimate exchange, a profounder, more unsettling kindness between people" (48).

The coauthors acknowledge that Freud emphasized the pleasure derived from our hatreds. Phillips expresses this observation in his telltale axiomatic prose: "The pleasures of cruelty and the cruelty of pleasures are famously Freud's touchstones of modern life" (64). Phillips follows this with another paradox: "Sadomasochism is the religion of those who believe you have to be cruel to be kind" (65). In the final chapter, "Modern Kindness," Phillips conveys a psychoanalytic position that he clearly rejects: "The most long-standing suspicion about kindness is that it is just narcissism in disguise" (111).

Phillips doesn't mention that the above statement reveals Freud's thoughts about kindness. Significantly, there is no entry in the *Standard Edition* for "kindness." Only one entry appears for "compassion," with the sub-entry, "narcissistic origin of," leading readers to *From the History of an Infantile Neurosis* (1918), the story of the Wolf Man, where we learn that the patient, recalling as a young boy watching his parents have sexual intercourse, felt "compassion" for his father only because the boy thought his father's penis had disappeared. "Moreover," Freud writes, "the narcissistic origin of compassion (which is confirmed by the word itself) is here quite unmistakably revealed" (*SE* 17: 88; the German word for "compassion," *Mitleid*, means "suffering with"). Near the end of their book Phillips and Taylor offer a robust definition of kindness that doesn't require belief in God or saintly self-sacrifice. Kindness "allows for ambivalence and conflict while false, or magical, kindness distorts our perceptions of other people, often by sentimentalizing them, to avoid conflict" (91). Regardless of whether kindness is an instinct, it is as real as cruelty and not simply a reaction formation. Kindness is not a pleasure that should be forbidden, as so many cynics have complained. *On Kindness* conveys profound pleasure, a welcome corrective that we disregard at our peril.

On Balance

Psychoanalysis shows us, Phillips announces in the preface to *On Balance* (2010), "why there is often nothing more unbalancing than the demand for a balanced view" (xiv). Expanding the paradox, he suggests that our behavior is more interesting when we are off balance than when we are unbalanced. In far-ranging discussions of money, sex, parenting, religion, and education, Phillips keeps readers off balance while he challenges conventional wisdom.

The most provocative essay is the last and shortest, only four pages long, "Forsaken Favourites," which opens with a bewitching sentence: "We sometimes fall in love with people for the very things about them that will eventually drive us mad, or at least drive us away" (308). His example will surprise us, as Phillips himself was surprised when he fell out of love with his fellow Welshman, the poet Dylan Thomas. "Welshness was so alien to us as second-generation émigré Eastern European Jews, and Thomas made it seem all rather alluring in his slapdash, slapstick and apparently naively sophisticated Celtic fluency" (310). Nearly everything Phillips esteemed as an adolescent grew to annoy or bore him, including the belief in an "authentic" self, as he reveals in the only other self-disclosing comment in the book. "The culture I grew up in informed me that I had an authentic, true self; and then I discovered in my adolescence in the 1960s and early 1970s that there was no such thing. I continued to live as if I had one, but the more I looked for it, and tried to feel its presence, the more I realized it wasn't there" (107–108). Phillips presumably discovered, in D.H. Lawrence's words, that the known self will never be more than a tiny clearing in a forest. Much of what Phillips believed as a youth he came to disbelieve and reject. Dylan Thomas's poetry now strikes him as "calculated self-parody" (311). There is one author, however, whom Phillips continues to love—Freud, though it is not the Freud that modernists thought they knew.

Phillips's Freud is not "Fraud," the parapraxis made by one of his patients who exclaimed, "Don't you think Fraud is rather overrated?" (32). Nor is Phillips's Freud the scientific thinker who believed in self-mastery. Rather, Phillips's Freud described an irresolvable clash of fundamentalisms, a battle between the tyrannical id and the equally despotic superego, mediated by an insecure ego that at best can achieve only a tenuous coexistence, not unity. Noting that psychoanalysis developed at the same time that fascism and virulent nationalism arose in Western Europe, Phillips implies that Freud's creation demonstrates both Enlightenment humanism and antihumanism. Freud's key discovery, in Phillips's view, is the extent of our helplessness. "The catastrophe of being a human being is that we are irredeemably helpless creatures. And that means, helpless to do anything about our helplessness" (147–148). Phillips knows this is an overstatement, for earlier in the book he admits that the ego has a degree of agency, calling it Freud's "most radical creation, his most modern, progressivist fiction" (68). Phillips does not offer a ringing endorsement of the ego, to be sure; we have, at best, good enough self-control some of the time.

Phillips is opposed to all idealizations, but the question must be raised: Does he idealize unknowability? Two reasons suggest otherwise: First, he always avoids mystification, and second, he deepens our knowledge of the limits of knowledge. He doesn't idealize unknowability, but he makes a virtue of it. It is difficult to disagree with him when he contends that our excessive behavior reveals how obscure we are to ourselves. The atheistic Freud had religion in mind when he wrote *The Future of an Illusion* (1927), but the equally secular Phillips argues that institutionalized psychoanalysis, with its impossibly Enlightenment assumptions, is another example of an illusion that has ended in disagreement—an illusion without a future. Why not, then, consider psychoanalysis as the future of a *dis*illusion? "Any psychoanalysis that privileges knowing over being, insight over experience, narrative over incoherence, diminishes if not actually forecloses our real acknowledgement of helplessness" (157).

One can point out that this statement contains precisely the false binaries that Phillips elsewhere warns us against, but nevertheless there is truth here. Indeed, John Bayley makes a similar acknowledgment near the end of *Elegy for Iris*, when he recognizes the onslaught of his wife Iris Murdoch's Alzheimer's disease: "As in the old days, nothing needs to be done. Helplessness is all" (267). Phillips ends *On Balance* with a paradoxical statement that reaffirms our disillusionments. The sentence is likely to bring a sad smile to his readers: "Hopefully, what we learn from our mistakes is that we shall go on making them" (311).

Missing Out

Phillips is a contrarian who delights in debunking platitudes, as his next book, *Missing Out: In Praise of the Unlived Life* (2012), demonstrates. The preface opens with a startling question, one that would have rendered Socrates speechless two millennia ago. "The unexamined life is surely worth living, but is the unlived life worth examining?" (xi). We may try to live our lives in the here-and-now, Phillips suggests, but we spend much of the time lost in fantasies and daydreams, which constitute the unacknowledged stories of our lives.

Of the five chapters in *Missing Out*, "On Not Getting It" is the most fascinating and, not coincidentally, the most self-disclosing. The pleasure of reading the chapter is getting what was not gotten. Phillips's books contain few if any case studies, but *Missing Out* includes a brief clinical vignette that reveals more about the analyst than the "patient," a word he uses reluctantly. At the beginning of his career as a child psychotherapist in the late 1970s and early 1980s, Phillips worked as a consultant in what was then called a "School for Maladjusted Children." The teachers found their work both distressing and inspiring, and they were offered, on a voluntary basis, an hour a week to talk with Phillips, whom they could view as a supervisor or therapist. One of the first people to visit him was an art teacher in his forties who asked, after several minutes of uncomfortable silence during his only meeting with him, "If you look after me who will look after you?" Phillips immediately responded with his own question, one that few therapists would have raised:

> I asked, "Did you have to do a lot of looking after when you were growing up?" And he replied, as though we were in the

middle of a long conversation, "Yes, my mother was sick a lot, and my dad was away." And I said, for no apparent reason, "When you were looking after your mother, did anything really strange ever happen, anything you just didn't get?" There was a pause, and he said, "Often, very often, when I was getting up to fill the coal scuttle downstairs, my mother would shout down from her bedroom, 'Can you fill the coal scuttle' . . . so I never know whether I'm doing it because I want to or because she's telling me to." I remarked, "You said 'know' as if it's still happening now," and he replied, "It is happening now because I never really know if I'm doing what I want or whether I'm acting under instruction." I asked, "Is coming to see me an example of this?" and he smiled and said, "Yes, and I think I'll go now." He got up, walked towards the door, and as he opened it he said to me, "I am going back to my bean-field"; and I had this tremendously powerful feeling of affection for him, as if he had understood me, *Walden* having been an important book in my life, though he had no way of knowing this. (49–50)

The vignette shows how just as a good question is often better than a good answer for a patient, implicit meaning is often better than explicit meaning for a reader. The vignette is powerful because of what is left *unsaid*. The art teacher knew that he was being heard; his unverbalized insight enabled him to realize the difference between an obligation and a choice. He did not need to give Phillips a long explanation about why he was leaving. It would not have mattered to the art teacher whether Phillips grasped the allusion to *Walden*, but it mattered to the latter, who then cites the passage where Thoreau writes about loving his "small Herculean labor" of hoeing his seven-miles-long row of beans. The quoted passage from *Walden* ends with Thoreau asking—"What shall I learn of beans or beans of me?"—a question Phillips implicitly raises to his readers: What shall I learn from the art teacher or he from me?

What shall we learn from Phillips or he from us? We learn, to begin with, the importance of validation for patient and therapist alike. Psychoanalysis is an asymmetrical relationship, but patient and therapist learn from and teach the other. Phillips felt profoundly understood at that moment, able to use his literary education to apprehend the art teacher's otherwise arcane remark. The understanding between the patient and therapist parallels that between the writer and reader. "He looks after his mother. I look after him; Thoreau looks after his beans" (52)—and we look after Phillips. The art teacher's reference to *Walden* made Phillips feel they had a shared world. What Phillips leaves unsaid is that readers have a shared world with the writer: we are on the same page.

One doesn't need a literary background to appreciate Phillips's study, but we may be missing out on some of the enjoyment of the book if we don't relish his many literary allusions. Four examples will suffice. If we misconstrue the significance of frustration, we may have "had the meaning but missed the experience" (14), a reversal of T.S. Eliot's line in *Four Quartets*: "We had the experience but missed the meaning." Psychoanalysis tells us that the person we fall in love with is the person we have dreamed about before meeting him or her, "not out of nothing—nothing comes of nothing" (18), the last four words uttered by an irate King Lear to Cordelia. A person who is abandoned needs "not so much a room of one's own, but a gang of one's own" (54), reminding us of Virginia Woolf's extended essay "A Room of One's Own." And in cautioning against the supposed omniscience about the past—"Those who cannot pretend to know everything about the past are doomed to repeat it" (135–136), Phillips alters Santayana's iconic remark: "Those who do not remember the past are condemned to repeat it." Another psychoanalyst would have affirmed the art teacher's insight gleaned from the single "therapy" session. Phillips, however, warns against what Slavoj Žižek calls an "attitude of overinterpretation" (64). Throughout the brief encounter with the art teacher, Phillips raises questions rather than provides answers, suggesting unknowability; yet they are the right questions, and the one about verb tense—"know" instead of "knew"—reveals keen understanding. By leaving so much unspoken between himself and the art teacher, and between himself and the reader, Phillips shows how psychoanalysis aims to "recover the freedom not to know or be known, and so to find out what people might do together instead" (75).

Becoming Freud

Phillips opens his 2014 biography with an outrageous sentence: "The story of Freud's life is easily told" (1). Ordinarily, I would mistrust any life study that begins this way. *No one* has easily told the story of Freud's life. There are more than a dozen biographies of Freud, one of which, Ernest

Jones's authorized three-volume hagiography (1953–1957), is over fifteen hundred pages long. Peter Gay's 1988 biography, from which Phillips quotes, *Freud: A Life for Our Time*, is 810 pages; a later biography cited by Phillips, Louis Breger's *Freud: Darkness in the Midst of Vision* (2000), is 472 pages. Frederick Crews's 2017 biography, *Freud: The Making of an Illusion*, is 746 pages, not long enough to exhaust his antagonistic analysis. By contrast, *Becoming Freud: The Making of a Psychoanalyst*, based on the Clarke Lectures Phillips delivered at Trinity College, Cambridge, is a scant 178 pages long. Is the opening sentence a joke? A wisecrack? Not exactly, but it's evident that Phillips is not writing a traditional biography.

It's easy to say what Phillips's biography is *not* about. Published in Yale University Press's Jewish Lives series, *Becoming Freud* fails to explore Freud's intense ambivalence toward his own Jewishness or its impact on his work. There are only glancing references to this subject. Phillips never mentions Sander Gilman's groundbreaking books on how Freud's fraught feelings about being an Eastern European Jew unconsciously shaped the construction of psychoanalytic theory. Phillips is correct when he says that anti-Semites regarded Judaism as a "hereditary degenerative condition" (93), but his claim that Freud and other Jews of his generation identified with German culture, "taking its (gentile) history, and above all its literature, to heart" (38), omits the story of what remained for Freud a vexed and vexing question. Phillips hardly mentions Freud's lifelong struggle as an outsider to enter the privileged world of fin-de-siècle Viennese medicine and science as an insider. Nor does Phillips present new information about Freud's life. There are no startling revelations, no revisionary rereadings of Freud's writings, no biographical discoveries, in short, little that will displace earlier biographies. Phillips's footnotes indicate his limited research on the vast commentary surrounding the creator of psychoanalysis.

Phillips's major aim is to highlight Freud's writings, in particular the five books written by the young, revolutionary Freud—*The Interpretation of Dreams* (1900), *The Psychopathology of Everyday Life* (1901), and the three books published in the annus mirabilis of 1905: *Fragment of an Analysis of a Case of Hysteria*, *Three Essays on the Theory of Sexuality*, and *Jokes and Their Relation to the Unconscious*. "If Freud had died, at the age of forty-nine, having completed these five books, psychoanalysis would have been very different, but it would have been sufficiently complete"

(145). Phillips adds, in the next sentence, a typically piquing statement: "The reason so much psychoanalytic writing is so dispiriting is because it is all written by older people." Phillips himself was still a young man, only fifty, when he wrote *Becoming Freud*, but his youth was not the primary reason that his biography is anything but dispiriting.

Becoming Freud contains counterintuitive truths, expressed cryptically and elliptically, that seldom appear in other biographies. "Freud invented psychoanalysis mostly out of conversations with men but through the treatment mostly of women." Psychoanalysis is thus, Phillips writes hyperbolically, a "homosexual artifact," an allusion to Freud's overheated relationship with Wilhelm Fliess (4). After psychoanalysis, all our narratives of the past, including Freud's, are "suspect" (6). Psychoanalysis was created as an "immigrant science" (30) for a world that saw an increasing number of immigrants. Freud's wife, Martha, largely ignored by other biographers, was the "absent center of the story of Freud's life" (71). Instead of reminding us, as nearly every other biographer has done, that dreams are the royal road to the unconscious, Phillips simply says, pithily, that Freud "discovered psychoanalysis in his sleep" (126). We see throughout Phillips's book a paradoxical Freud whose most dogmatic quality is skepticism.

In the final analysis, *Becoming Freud* is Phillips's Freud, an anti-Enlightenment radical who is first and foremost a literary Freud, an author whose books were indelibly shaped by his own reading. Phillips's Freud must be seen primarily as part of the history of storytelling. Freud is the most literary of psychoanalysts, Phillips contends, and psychoanalysts must be equally literary—a near impossibility—to appreciate his writings. *Becoming Freud* is a paean to literature, to the pleasure of reading and writing, to the art of storytelling. Freud's first gift to his future wife was a copy of *David Copperfield*, a story about an ambitious young man trying to succeed, like Freud himself. As in all of Phillips's writings, there are many literary allusions that he expects us to glean, as when he tells us, echoing Matthew Arnold in "Dover Beach," that Freud came of age "between two worlds, one perhaps dying and one powerless to be born" (36). It's unlikely that many training and supervising psychoanalysts will embrace Phillips's biography. How could they when he states that Freud wrote his great books at a time when psychoanalysis was "not yet stifled and stultified by its always anxious institutionalization" (147)? "Phillips doesn't give us the whole Freud," Joshua Rothman concluded in his review in *The New Yorker*, "but, if Freud is to be believed, you can never see the whole person anyway. We see what we need to see."

Unforbidden Pleasures

Freud's favorite novel, we learn in *Unforbidden Pleasures* (2015), was *Don Quixote*. Phillips makes an intriguing connection between Cervantes's novel and Freud's often-quoted analogy, expressed in *New Introductory Lectures on Psycho-Analysis* (1933), of the ego riding on an unruly horse: "But only too often there arises between the ego and the id the not precisely ideal situation of the rider being obliged to guide the horse along the path by which it itself wants to go" (*Unforbidden Pleasures* 120; *SE* 22: 77). Unlike George Vaillant, who traces Freud's analogy to the Platonic dialogue *Phaedrus*, where Plato uses a horse-and-chariot allegory to describe the human soul, Phillips suggests that the Freudian ego is Cervantes's quixotic knight; the id is the old work-horse Rocinante; and the superego is the gullible Sancho Panza. Conceding he may be overinterpreting, Phillips raises a compelling question and then uncharacteristically answers it. "What does the Freudian superego look like if you take away its endemic cruelty, its unrelenting sadism? It looks like Sancho Panza. And like Sancho Panza, the absurd and obscene superego is a character we must not take too seriously" (121).

Phillips urges us throughout the book to recover the unforbidden pleasures that make life worthwhile. This is not a revolutionary idea, but he shows how relentless self-criticism, often the result of a punitive superego, limits our ability to experience joy. To underscore this truth, Phillips offers an example of an earlier writer who sought to recover the pleasure of literature, Oscar Wilde. Phillips quotes the best-known paradox in Wilde's 1891 novel *The Picture of Dorian Gray*: "The only way to get rid of a temptation is to yield to it" (7). It's no surprise that one paradoxicalist should be in thrall to another paradoxicalist. One might not expect a psychoanalyst to privilege Wildean aesthetics over conventional morality, but Phillips is full of surprises, including the observation that great art, in Wilde's view and his own, "enables us to forget ourselves, our rational, conforming, intelligible, law-abiding, too timid, explaining selves" (21). Phillips ends the book with a beguilingly simple sentence in the coda: "it is extraordinary how much pleasure we can get from each other's company, most of which is unforbidden" (195). Phillips succeeds in presenting us, as Mark O'Connell concludes in his *New York Times* review, with the "pleasure of conviction."

In Writing

Vintage Phillips, *In Writing* (2016) abounds in paradoxes: "The writer as so-called autobiographer must not identify with the character in his book" (40); "the only change worth having was changing by staying more or less the same" (82); "once you find your voice, lose it" (108); "The good-enough mother is always a bad-enough tantalization" (153); "all narrators are unreliable narrators" (184). The book contains his most self-disclosing interview, conducted by Paul Holdengräber, Director of New York Public Library's Public Programming. Phillips likens a psychoanalytic session to an essay, his favorite genre, one that is "very rarely a fanatical form" (251). Sounding like the psychoanalyst-novelist Allen Wheelis, to whom he never refers in his writings, Phillips admits that much of human suffering is "simply intractable" (246). Psychoanalysis has two goals: the recovery of "appetite," by which he means pleasure, and the recognition that we do not need to know ourselves, an impossible task (247).

Phillips offers two reasons for not writing about his patients. "I think what happens in analysis is entirely private, and I also wouldn't want people to be thinking they are material for my books" (257–258). When he does offer a brief clinical vignette, it's always with the patient's permission. Far from being saddened that psychoanalysis has lost the power and prestige it had half a century ago, Phillips believes this is the ideal situation: people now become analysts only if they are following their passion. If psychoanalysis disappeared, he could see himself becoming a primary-school teacher.

Attention Seeking

Phillips is a dazzlingly prolific writer, particularly for someone whose busy clinical schedule allows him to write only one day a week, on Wednesdays. His 2019 book *Attention Seeking* is an apt title for a writer who enjoys being on center stage. The twin passions in Phillips's life, psychoanalysis and literature, both make us "self-conscious about the nature and the quality of our attention" (15). Attention seeking is at its best a "comedy of errors, rather than a tragedy of failures" (31). Phillips's most recent book may not make us laugh, but it is consistently illuminating and entertaining, holding our attention throughout, performative art at its best. Phillips has mastered the art of paradox, many of them expressed as parenthetical quips. The British psychoanalyst Marion Milner (1900–1998), the author of *On Not Being Able to Paint* (1950), once told him that when she paints a tree, she looks at everything except the tree (14). Psychoanalysis "frees people to lose interest in themselves" (16). Shame makes believers of us all: "when I am ashamed I know what I am seeing, I have no doubt. Shame is a cure for scepticism" (66).

Phillips returns to unknowability in every book, including his most recent. "In our attention-seeking it could be assumed that we know neither what we want nor what we expect; and so we are in our starkest dependence on others" (31). The more attention Phillips pays to unknowability, the more darkly enlightening it becomes. Quoting a passage from Laurence Sterne's 1759 novel *The Life and Opinions of Tristram Shandy*, Phillips contrasts two types of Tristram's writings. When he is "full," he is "carefree and unfrightened," but when he is "fasting," he writes about his "scars" and "wounds." Both types of writing are necessary, Phillips points out: "It is the combination of the carefree and the terrorised that works for him" (90). The combination works for Phillips too. In calling attention to Sterne's paradoxical and provocative writing, Phillips highlights his own. Or as he jauntily asks, "When is provocation in the eye of the beholder, and when does it expose the eye of the beholder?" (77). Most psychoanalysts, I suspect, want their books to change their readers' lives, perhaps by heightening their self-understanding or by helping them learn how to overcome conflicts. Not Phillips. He simply wants his readers to enjoy his books and then forget about them (*In Writing* 258). He succeeds in the first goal and fails in the second.

JEFFREY BERMAN. You cite scores of poets and novelists throughout your books, but would you agree that Oscar Wilde, another paradoxicalist, has had a great impact on your own writing? Do you naturally think in paradoxes, or is it something you've trained yourself to do?

ADAM PHILLIPS. As far as I could tell Wilde has not been a very significant influence on my writing. But it is also true that consistently, from adolescence onwards, I have read and loved and been increasingly impressed with his work. Indeed your question makes me realize just how much he has been an informing presence for me, but behind the scenes. The importance of being earnest for psychoanalytic writing has been stifling; Wilde always makes me feel that talking and writing is the most exhilarating thing we do.

I naturally write as I do, often in paradoxes; my writing is consciously without calculation. I don't tend to train myself to do things. I can either do them or I can't; I've never tried to do anything that really mattered to me.

JB. You've said that writing comes easily to you and that you don't "fuss over your writing," as you told Joan Acocella. You stated to Jill Choder-Goldman that sometimes you leave something in your writing about which you're unsure: "unless it's patently false to me, I leave it in, and I'll find out what it's like when somebody else tells me, because I can't know." Would you describe the process of revision before you submit a manuscript for publication? Do you often soften a criticism, as you did when you removed a harsh criticism of Melanie Klein from the final version of *On Flirtation*?

AP. In so far as I revise at all it is as I go along; I never revise anything for publication because my writing is very much as it comes, with a minimum of reflection. If the sentences sound right—and if not true have some truth in them—I carry on. But it is far more to do with sound than sense, or with sound-sense. I much prefer praise to criticism, and am wary of the criticism that comes from inner superiority. We should celebrate wherever possible.

JB. The existential psychiatrist Irvin Yalom states in his 2005 novel *The Schopenhauer Cure* that "*It's not ideas, nor vision, nor tools that truly matter in therapy.* If you debrief patients at the end of therapy about the process, what do they remember? *Never* the ideas—it's *always* the relationship. They rarely remember an important insight their therapist offered but generally fondly recall their personal relationship with the therapist" (62–63). Yalom makes a similar observation in *Love's Executioner*: "It's the relationship that heals, the relationship that heals, the relationship that heals—my professional rosary" (98). To my knowledge, you've never written an essay about the patient-analyst relationship. Would you agree with Yalom's observation? Can you foresee writing about the patient-analyst relationship?

AP. I do agree with Yalom's observation but I could never write about the patient-analyst relationship because each one is different, and analysts should neither write nor speak in public about their patients; it is unethical.

JB. Near the end of *Promises, Promises*, you write that an "analysis, like a work of literature, is potentially a transformational object" (372), a term that comes from Christopher Bollas, who was one of your analysts. Which contemporary psychoanalytic theorists and literary writers have most influenced you?

AP. There would be too many to list, and too many that I have been affected by without entirely noticing. The psychoanalytic writers I am most moved by are Pontalis, Bollas, Loewald, John Gray, Harold Boris, Milner, Winnicott, John Forrester, Matte-Blanco, Enid Balint, Coltart, Khan, Eigen, Tustin, Searles, Leclaire, Hirsch, Dimen, Ghent, Lear, Stoller, Bersani, Laplanche, Joseph Smith and others I can't bring to mind at this moment. But what used to be called Literature has been infinitely more important to me than most of the psychoanalytic literature. I think I felt that Literature had already taught me a lot about so-called psychoanalysis, and then when I read Freud and Ferenczi it was all formulated.

JB. In the conclusion to your coauthored *Intimacies*, Leo Bersani observes that what he finds appealing about your work is your use of "anti-psychoanalytic arguments *for* psychoanalysis" (119). Would you agree with that characterization? What was it like coauthoring *Intimacies* with Bersani?

AP. Yes I would agree with Leo's remark. He is a very close friend of mine, and has been tremendously important to me as both a friend and a writer, so I don't want to go into the writing of *Intimacies*. Suffice it to say it was one of the most thrilling writing experiences of my life; and that it couldn't have been easier. I still feel slightly amazed that I wrote a book with him; and *Intimacies* is one of the books I am proudest of (although proud doesn't sound like the right word here). It is, I still think, one of the most interesting books I've written.

JB. When you were writing *Houdini's Box*, did you realize that a psychoanalyst is, in many ways, an escape artist, helping to free patients from their manacles? Do patients help release you from your own manacles?

AP. I had no idea at the time why I was writing *Houdini's Box*. I was not interested in magic, nor, ostensibly, in escapology; nor was I remotely interested then in Houdini. I was in a bookstore in New York and found a recently published biography of Houdini; and I realized at that moment that I was going to write a book about him. It was completely unintelligible to me at the time why I was doing it, and the book virtually wrote itself. I don't think of psychoanalysis, as far as I am aware, as much to do with escape (I was much impressed from an early age by Balint's remark that if someone is running away from something they are running towards something else). I think of it as being more about acknowledgment; and, in the pragmatic way, about what we can do to get the life we want, though in the full knowledge that we can never know what we want beforehand. Wants are discoveries not weapons or tools. Psychoanalysis shows us what we are using the rather complex idea of escape to do.

Of course analysts use their patients to cure themselves. If analysis is not in some sense mutual it is indoctrination.

JB. In reading your books chronologically, I'm struck by the consistency of your psychoanalytic vision. Have many of your views of psychoanalysis changed over the years?

AP. I think they have mostly changed, as they say, by remaining the same. It feels to me that my sense of psychoanalysis was clear to me very early on, but it took time to articulate it. I have been greatly helped by not being much involved in psychoanalytic institutions, and their conversations.

JB. Your biography of Freud, unlike other biographies, is remarkably nonjudgmental. ("The real problem with pathography," you observe, "is that it makes everybody sound the same; the distinctiveness of the individual dissolves into his symptomatology" [*In Writing* 57].) How do you manage to be so nonjudgmental when you write about other people?

AP. Wherever there is judgment there is an uncompleted experiment. Psychoanalysis is very good at showing us what can happen when judgment is suspended. I am probably no less judgmental than most people but writing and talking in psychoanalysis enable you to think about what's going on in our judging, why we want our judgments to be our second nature.

JB. "Cover-up" (or "cover story"), one of your favorite expressions, implies something that is concealed which you then reveal. Your writings dramatize the dialectical tension between concealing and revealing, a process best embodied in the paradox. This seems to be part of your sensibility and aesthetic. Does this observation ring true for you?

AP. Yes it does. I'm very struck by development as hide-and-seek, about the fear and the desire for both, and how you can't have one without the other. The privacy of being able to hide is essential, as is hiding as a love-test to the world.

Conclusion

Psychoanalysis—A Work in Progress

Striking differences exist among the six psychoanalytic clinicians and theorists in this book. Perhaps the major difference concerns the question of the scientific validity of psychoanalytic theory. Sander Gilman is less concerned with the scientific underpinnings of psychoanalysis than with Freud's hidden ideological assumptions that shaped the construction of psychoanalytic theory. Allen Wheelis was skeptical of psychoanalysts for claiming a scientific status for non-verifiable theory, but Joan Wheelis, a medically trained psychoanalyst, is committed to evidence-based analysis. She has sought to integrate psychoanalysis with behavioral treatments, embracing dialectical behavior therapy, an approach that interested her father after she began studying it. Nancy Chodorow's academic training in the social sciences instilled in her the value of empirical research, of which British and European analysts remain wary. Though most of the early psychoanalysts were, like Freud, physicians, psychoanalysis developed in England and Europe largely independent of psychiatry, allowing non-physicians to become analysts. By contrast, American psychoanalysts were, until the end of the twentieth century, physicians. Neither Christopher Bollas nor Adam Phillips is medically trained; consequently, neither one is preoccupied with the scientific validity of the talking cure.

Was Freud mainly a medical scientist, as he claimed repeatedly, or a humanist discovering (or rediscovering) literary, psychological, and philosophical truths? One of Freud's favorite sayings was from his mentor, the French neurologist Jean-Martin Charcot (after whom Freud named one of his sons): "Theory is good, but it doesn't prevent the facts from existing." The facts, however, never prevented Freud from formulating theory that went counter to empirical evidence. As usual, Freud tried to have it both ways, claiming psychoanalysis was based on universal truths when theory could not be confirmed empirically. Freud was the recipient of the Goethe prize for literature in 1930, but he was annoyed when his name was mentioned for the Nobel Prize in literature, not medicine.

Psychoanalysts continue to debate the question of the scientific validity of their profession. Joseph Schwartz speaks for many of his colleagues when he observes in *Cassandra's Daughter* (1999) that the question of whether psychoanalysis is scientific is a distraction that is sometimes maliciously intended. "What we need from an account of psychoanalysis," argues Schwartz, who earned a PhD in physics before becoming a psychoanalyst, "is not a sterile debate about whether psychoanalysis conforms to the criteria of past scientific successes but an analysis of the problems of human subjectivity that psychoanalysis has set itself to solve and an evaluation of its successes and failure" (8). There are other questions. If psychoanalysis is not a science, what is it? An art? A hermeneutic? A cult, as cynics maintain? Should psychoanalysts modify their treatment to make it more in line with other psychotherapy treatments?

There is no question, however, of the interdisciplinarity of psychoanalysis. Indeed, it would be more accurate to speak of *psychoanalyses*. The six psychoanalytic thinkers whom I discuss in this book represent a cross-section of the liberal arts: cultural history, German and English studies, creative writing (including memoir and fiction), sociology, and literary criticism. Contemporary psychoanalysts embrace branches of knowledge far remote from medicine, as Freud wrote in *The Question of Lay Analysis*—including academic disciplines that Freud did not mention, such as modern languages, social work, law, linguistics, philosophy, and the social sciences.

The Dodo Bird Effect

Do all forms of psychotherapy produce equally good results? This was Saul Rosenzweig's conclusion when he published in 1936 an article with the colorful subtitle, "At Last the Dodo Bird Said, 'Everybody Has Won and All Must Have Prizes.'" The subtitle comes from Lewis Carroll's 1865 novel *Alice's Adventures in Wonderland* in which all the contestants who run around a lake are judged to be winners. Rosenzweig's counterintuitive conclusion was that all forms of psychotherapy lead to beneficial outcomes. As Bruce E. Wampold and Zac E. Imel note in *The Great Psychotherapy Debate* (2015), common factors—"hope, expectation, relationship with the therapist, belief, and corrective experience" (33)—are far more important in therapy than a particular theoretical approach. The Dodo bird effect, also called the common factors theory, remains highly controversial, but as Wampold and Imel remark, dozens of meta-analyses used to compare multiple evidence supported treatments confirm Rosenzweig's thesis. The differences among treatments, Wampold and Imel maintain, are small or non-existent. "The Dodo bird conjecture has survived many tests and must be considered 'true' until such time as sufficient evidence for its rejection is produced" (156).

The Dodo bird effect anticipates the classic 1979 study by Hans Strupp and Suzanne Hadley that concluded that any form of psychotherapy is effective provided that both the therapist and patient acted in good faith, that the patient respected the therapist, and that the therapist knew how to create a positive therapeutic relationship. In his magisterial study *The Noonday Demon: An Atlas of Depression* (2002), Andrew Solomon cites the 1979 study, pointing out, in Solomon's words, that Strupp and Hadley "chose English professors with this quality of human understanding and found that, on average, the English professors were able to help their patients as much as the professional therapists" (111). Christopher Bollas and Adam Phillips would not have been surprised by this conclusion.

Marital Inequality

Freud lived in a colonial age that coincided with psychoanalysts' efforts to colonize and dominate academic disciplines. "I am glad you share my belief that we must conquer the whole field of mythology," Freud wrote to Jung on October 17, 1909. "Thus far we have only two pioneers: Alexander and Rank. We need men for more far-reaching campaigns" (Freud and Jung 255). I recall with chagrin that my early publications, written in the 1970s, were efforts to show how literature "proved" psychoanalysis. It took me longer to abandon this imperial approach than I care to admit. It was not until the 1990s, when I became the general editor of New York University Press's Literature and Psychoanalysis series (1991–1997), that I rectified the error (without acknowledging guilt) in the foreword:

The literary critic's insights into psychoanalysis are no less valuable than the psychoanalyst's insights into literature. Gone are the days when psychoanalytic critics assumed that Freud had a master key to unlock the secrets of literature. Instead of reading literature to confirm psychoanalytic theory, many critics are now reading Freud to discover how his understanding of literature shaped the evolution of his theory. In short, the master-slave relationship traditionally implicit in the marriage between the literary critic and psychoanalyst has given way to a healthier dialogic relationship, in which each learns from and contributes to the other's discipline. ("Foreword")

Had I taken a graduate course with Sander Gilman, who began teaching at Cornell when I was a doctoral student, I might have avoided this error. But Cornell's English department was conservative in 1967 when I began graduate studies, still dominated by New Criticism, and not yet sympathetic to interdisciplinary approaches to literature. I remember feeling uneasy using clinical (considered "extra-literary" at the time) research on suicide for my 1971 doctoral dissertation, later published as *Joseph Conrad: Writing as Rescue* (1977).

The desired marital equality between literature and psychoanalysis was long honored in the breach. The psychoanalytic authoritarianism of the 1950s and 1960s carried over into psychoanalytic literary criticism. Norman N. Holland (1927–2017), whom I call in a recent book the "dean of American psychoanalytic literary critics," was one of the first English professors to receive a training analysis. His seven-year analysis with Elizabeth Zetzel, while he was studying at the Boston Psychoanalytic Institute, was the turning point in his intellectual life. In one of the most astonishing claims made by a literary theorist, Holland opined that readers who had not, like himself, been analyzed were unqualified to criticize the psychology of a literary text:

It is a little surprising that there should be any literary critiques of this kind, that is, attacking the Freud-Jones analysis of *Hamlet* [a reference to Jones's *Hamlet and Oedipus*, inspired by Freud's comments on the play], not from a literary but a psychological point of view. With all due respect to my literary colleagues, it seems to me that they are somewhat out of their depth, psychologically. Surely criticisms of a psychoanalytic diagnosis as such are the province of the expert—in psychoanalysis. For literary critics not trained in psychoanalysis there are plenty of cogent criticisms of the Freud-Jones view of *Hamlet* that can be made from the point of view of an expert in literary criticism: misreadings, misunderstandings of tone, treating a play as a puzzle, reading back to Shakespeare, treating the characters as real people, and so on. It seems to me the purely literary critic would do well to confine himself to those, if he wishes to object. (*Psychoanalysis and Shakespeare* 185)

If Holland's Freud was entirely scientific, casting an illusory objective shadow over literary interpretation, Harold Bloom's Freud was purely subjective and literary. Arguably the most influential American literary critic of the second half of the twentieth century, Bloom (1930–2019) regarded Freud as one of the century's greatest creative writers, believing, as he asserts in *The Western Canon* (1994), that Freud was far greater than his creation, psychoanalysis. "Freudian literary criticism of Shakespeare is a celestial joke; Shakespearean criticism of Freud will have a hard birth, but it will come, since Freud as a writer will survive the death of psychoanalysis" (350). One week before his death, Bloom was scheduled to give a talk on Freud to the American Psychoanalytic Association in New York City. No doubt it would have both pleased and dismayed his audience. He believed that Shakespeare anticipated everything valuable in Freudian theory. Freud is "essentially prosified Shakespeare," Bloom claimed (*Shakespeare* 377). Bloom asserts near the end of the book that, "as ever, Shakespeare is the original psychologist, and Freud the belated rhetorician" (714).

The asymmetrical marriage between literature and psychoanalysis has slowly become more equal. In the introduction to *The Cambridge Companion to Literature and Psychoanalysis* (2022), Vera J. Camden, a Professor of English at Kent State University and a training and supervising analyst at the Cleveland Psychoanalytic Center, refers to the new "companionate" marriage (xiv), a term the early Puritans used to describe a union of "two mentalities, two languages of meaning" (3). Literature and psychoanalysis "draw from the heart of each other," Camden remarks, "and in doing so foster new creations" (3). In the same volume, Jeremy Tambling calls literature and psychoanalysis an "inseparable if odd couple," each bringing out in the other insights that would not have been apparent without their pairing (239).

A New Translation

The "golden age" of psychoanalysis occurred in the 1950s and early 1960s, when, as Douglas Kirsner points out in *Unfree Associations* (2009), half the people chairing university departments of psychiatry were analysts. The golden age has long passed. Nevertheless, psychoanalysis remains alive if not entirely flourishing. One cannot imagine more antithetical approaches to a new translation of Freud's writings than those offered by Gilman and Phillips.

Our understanding of psychoanalysis is based largely on our reading of Freud's work translated into English. The authorized translation, the *Standard Edition*, was published between 1955 and 1974. In *Freud and Man's Soul* (1982), Bruno Bettelheim was one of the first psychoanalysts to point out the limitations of James Strachey's translation, which, despite its magisterial prose, depicts a more scientific Freud than in the original German edition. Strachey invents awkward neologisms such as "cathexis" and "parapraxis" and translates Freud's "das Ich" and "das Es" as "ego" and "id" instead of "I" and "it," respectively. Gilman offers in *Inscribing the Other* a practical, far-reaching proposal for a new translation based on Freud's original German text and reflecting the subtleties of his language and culture. "Thus the new reader will be able to have access in English to psychoanalysis as the representation of multiple strands of Freud's fictive personality—simultaneously scientist, writer, anthropologist, cultural critic, and, perhaps, most important, middle-class Jewish male of turn-of-the-century Vienna" (210).

Gilman's characteristic inclusiveness frames his concrete suggestions for a new edition. He has no doubt about the intellectual and commercial value of a new translation, given the renewed interest in psychoanalysis among humanists from a variety of disciplines. Translators of the new edition must have, he recommends, a fluent command of fin-de-siècle Austrian German, a cultural historian's insights into late-nineteenth- and early-twentieth-century intellectual and psychiatric history, and a profound respect for Freud's work. Gilman's recommendations, made two decades ago, call for a highly scholarly edition that appeals to cultural and intellectual historians. In other words, though he would never say this, translators must be scholars like Gilman himself. Regrettably, his recommendations for a new translation of Freud have not yet been implemented.

By contrast, Adam Phillips, the general editor of the seventeen-volume *Penguin Modern Classics Freud* translation, created a distinctly non-scholarly translation. In the Appendix to *In Writing*, "On Translating Freud," Phillips claims, oddly, that he is not a "scholar by nature or inclination" and that he has never done anything that people call "research" (267). Despite not knowing German, he agreed to be the general editor of the Penguin translation of Freud, selecting non-psychoanalysts to introduce each volume, which would not contain a scholarly apparatus. Phillips chose ten different translators for the seventeen volumes. The goal of the new edition, for the new century, would be to allow readers to see Freud as another modernist writer—an appeal to what Phillips calls, echoing Virginia Woolf, the "common reader": those who are as passionate about literature as she was. The great twentieth-century novelist and essayist, no Freudian herself, was married to Leonard Woolf, the owner of The Hogarth Press, which continues to publish the *Standard Edition*.

In an interview with Robert S. Boynton in *The New York Times* in 2000, Phillips expressed his goal in creating the new edition. "I think a literary translation will capture some of what has been lost in Freud: an unconscious and a conscious ambiguity in the writing, and an interest in sentences, in the fact that language is evocative as well as informative." Boynton presents the advantages and disadvantages of the Penguin edition, but in summarizing Phillips's intentions, he uses a reductive word. "Psychoanalytic theory, writes Mr. Phillips, is simply 'a new set of stories about how we can nourish ourselves to keep faith with our belief in nourishment, our desire for desire.'" But "simply" scarcely does justice to the complexity of Phillips's thinking. Nor does Boynton's description of Phillips, whose "sad eyes and shaggy rock-star mane resemble a poet more . . . than a revolutionary," convey the radical nature of Phillips's approach to a new Freud translation.

One can only hope that Phillips's edition for the common reader will flourish—and hope that one day there will be a new scholarly translation of Freud based on Gilman's recommendations. I can imagine buying my grandchildren copies of Phillips's edition of Freud and hoping that, years later, I'll be around to buy them copies of Gilman's edition.

Translating Freud's works into English raises a larger question: How do we express psychoanalytic ideas into words? Is psychoanalytic writing different from non-psychoanalytic writing? John Forrester (1949–2015) raises this question in his posthumously published book *Thinking in Cases* (2017). A professor of history and the philosophy of science at the University of Cambridge and the author of several books on psychoanalysis, Forrester suggests that writing about case studies inevitably (re)mobilizes the writer's transference and countertransference that are inherent in the patient-analyst relationship:

> Psychoanalytic writing is not just writing *about* psychoanalysis; it is writing subject to the same laws and processes as the psychoanalytic situation itself. In this way psychoanalysis can never free itself of the forces it attempts to describe. As a result, from one point of view, all psychoanalytic writing is exemplary of a failure. Psychoanalytic writing fails to transmit psychoanalytic knowledge because it is always simultaneously a symptom. . . . On the other hand, the fact that psychoanalysis enacts the very forces it attempts to "capture" could be taken as a demonstration of the very facts it is "communicating." (65–66)

Acknowledging Dostoevsky's observation in *The Brothers Karamazov* that psychology is a knife that cuts both ways, Forrester admits there is no interpretation-free zone in human communication. Adam Phillips underscores this insight in his introduction to *Thinking in Cases*. "Psychoanalytic writing is a failure—as is all writing, from a psychoanalytic point of view—in the sense that it is always saying something other than it intends to. Its intentions are only a small part of its intention" (xv).

Psychoanalytic writing also involves what Thomas Ogden calls the "intersubjective analytic third," which he defines as a "set of unconscious experiences jointly, but asymmetrically, constructed by the analytic pair." This idea is "disconcerting," he concedes, because it implies that the analyst's and patient's dreaming and reverie are no longer conceived as their own. "Conversations at the frontier of dreaming are not always private" (11–12). Ogden's analytic third describes the intersubjectivity co-created by the analyst and patient, but it also enables us to track the dialectical movement of intersubjective relationships. To convey the enigmatic meaning of the analytic third, Ogden cites a poem by A.R. Ammons in which the poet looks for a shape that may mysteriously summon itself through him—an example of the interdisciplinary marriage between literature and psychoanalysis.

Unfinished Business: Two Tragedies

While writing this book, I have thought about one of the paradoxes of my life. Although I have been deeply fulfilled in love and work, Freud's definition of a psychologically healthy life, many of my books are about the two tragedies in my life. The first occurred on Labor Day, 1968, when my mentor, Len Port, took his own life. His suicide compelled me to study psychoanalysis in an effort to understand why he ended his life—and to understand its devastating impact on me. Much of my teaching and writing has been an effort to come to terms with his death.

I had an aha! moment when reading the following sentence from *Attention Seeking*, where Phillips observes, after noting that Freud uses the word "shame" thirteen times in his *Three Essays on the Theory of Sexuality*, "in shorthand we can say that for Freud, where there is repetition there is unfinished or unfinishable business" (60). Many of my books have the words "death," "dying," "grief," "suicide," or "widowhood" in their titles, an example, I have long thought, of Freud's repetition-compulsion principle, ongoing efforts to work through and live with traumatic experiences. I still believe this, but I recognize the truth of Phillips's words—I continue to grapple with unfinished or unfinishable business. As Peter Brooks remarks in *Reading for the Plot* (1984), narrative "always makes the implicit claim to be in a state of repetition, as a going over again of a ground already covered" (97). Repetition implies a return to an event, a doubling back, but we are never sure, Brooks adds, whether this return is a "return *to* or a return *of*: for instance, a return to origins or a return of the repressed" (100).

My unfinished business, I suspect, is related to my body's convulsions while watching films, as I suggested in the introduction. In Adam Phillips's terms, I must be playing hide-and-seek, both hiding from and seeking the weeper in myself. This is only a partial insight, admittedly, but it reveals something important to pursue further. My convulsions are trying to tell me something, and if Bessel van der Kolk is correct in his bestselling 2015 book *The Body Keeps the Score*, the meaning has something to do with ongoing trauma encoded in my body. Like psychoanalysis, I am a work in progress, trying to accept my good enough sanity or, as Slavoj Žižek might say, enjoy my symptoms. By exposing publicly my bouts of unpredictable self-weeping, I am, in Phillips's terms, engaged in attention seeking, which is at its best a comedy of errors rather than a tragedy of failures.

Some of the authors in this study hint at the therapeutic implications of their own writing. Interestingly, these hints appear not in their books or articles but in their responses to my questions. Sander Gilman doesn't use words like "therapy" or "healing" to describe the motivation behind his scholarly work, but in "Why and How I Study the German" he describes "burn[ing] with those fires that define you as the outsider." Changing metaphors, he refers, in his response to one of my questions, to the "emotional excavation" behind his writing. Nietzsche's observation in *Thus Spake Zarathustra* illuminates the obsessional quality of Gilman's scholarship: "Of all that is written, I love only what a person hath written with his blood. Write with blood, and thou wilt find that blood is spirit" (*The Philosophy of Nietzsche*, 39). It's true that elsewhere Nietzsche warns of the danger of following one's obsessions, as when he observes that "he who fights with monsters should be careful lest he thereby become a monster. And if thou gaze long into an abyss, the abyss will gaze into thee" (466). Nevertheless, to recite one more Nietzschean insight, "What does not kill me makes me stronger." Joan Wheelis acknowledges that "Last Cut," the first vignette she wrote in *The Known, the Secret, the Forgotten*, was "therapeutic" in helping her come to terms with her father's death. "It also initiated a process of self-analysis as I revisited some of the vicissitudes of my relationships with my parents and my son in each vignette I wrote." Adam Phillips never mentions in any of his books why he writes, but he doesn't hesitate to answer my question whether helping release patients from their manacles allows him to free himself from his own. "Of course analysts use their patients to cure themselves. If analysis is not in some sense mutual it is indoctrination." It is not an exaggeration to say that for many analysts, including psychoanalytic literary critics such as myself, psychoanalysis is the talking and writing self-cure.

The second tragedy in my life occurred when my first wife, Barbara, died on April 5, 2004, at age fifty-seven, of pancreatic cancer. We had been married for thirty-five years. Immediately after her death I began writing a book about her, *Dying to Teach: A Memoir of Love, Loss, and Learning*, published in 2007. In reading everything I could about bereavement, I came across a new theory, formulated by Dennis Klass, Phyllis R. Silverman, and Steven L. Nickman in their 1996 book *Continuing Bonds: New Understanding of Grief*, which suggests that contrary to what Freud conjectured in "Mourning and Melancholia," the bereaved can maintain a relational bond with the deceased while forming new bonds with the living. As Madelon Sprengnether has shown in her 2018 book *Mourning Freud*, the founder of psychoanalysis never acknowledged his painful early childhood losses, including the death of his younger brother Julius in early infancy; the departure of his first nanny, who was dismissed when she was caught stealing; and the disruption caused by the family's move twice in two years as a result of his father's business failures. Freud's insistence in

"Mourning and Melancholia" that "mourning impels the ego to give up the object by declaring the object to be dead and offering the ego the inducement for continuing to live" (*SE* 14: 257) represents, Sprengnether contends, a failure to theorize the importance of grief and bereavement. Regrettably, psychoanalysis remains unaware of the theory of continuing bonds, a theory that immediately resonated with me when I first read about it. To my knowledge, Sander Gilman, Nancy Chodorow, Christopher Bollas, and Adam Phillips have never experienced widowhood, nor have they called attention to Freud's questionable injunction that the living must "decathect" from a lost loved one. Sometimes one must experience a tragedy to reorient one's theoretical thinking. I don't believe I'm "stuck" on grief: in 2011 I remarried, and Julie has returned joy to my life.

Life Lessons: My Impressions of Our Conversations

I learned much from my conversations with the authors in this book, not only about psychoanalysis but also about life. The best stories are those that gift us, undogmatically, with memorable life lessons. Some of these life lessons include stumbles in my discussions of the authors in this study or in the questions I asked them.

"A teacher affects eternity," Henry Adams famously said; "he can never tell where his influence stops." Nowhere is this more evident than with Sander Gilman. He has not only created courses on literature, psychoanalysis, and cultural history wherever he has taught but he has also established new intellectual disciplines. To be a master teacher is an accomplishment; to be the world's most prolific psychoanalytic scholar is extraordinary. An intellectual lightning rod, Gilman is rarely dogmatic or defensive in his writings. His acknowledgment that psychoanalysis requires constant revision and refinement, like other disciplines, bodes well for the future. I chuckled when he referred to his "procrastination" in beginning new projects. I wish I suffered from that kind of procrastination. I remember feeling awe when I first met him in the 1970s. I feel the same awe today. I must ask myself, however, whether that awe prevents me from seeing whatever limitations may appear in Gilman's scholarship. Would I feel the same way toward him if we were in the same department, working together, day after day, seeing him, in other words, as human, all too human? Is this what it feels like to be in psychoanalysis, idealizing one's shrink? All I can say is that the more closely

I examine Gilman's scholarship, the more I admire his work. Or to cite Phillips's observation to me, "We should celebrate wherever possible."

I can only imagine what it must be like having parents who were psychoanalysts, one of whom was a world-famous novelist who repeatedly evoked grim portraits of married life and depicted male analysts who were clinicians of despair. Joan Wheelis writes with great delicacy about her parents, and I suspect that the word she uses to describe the experience of reading her father's books, "complicated," is understated. (In her 2019 memoir *In Another Place*, the psychoanalyst Susan Mailer uses the same word to describe her relationship with her father, Norman Mailer.) Had I been in Joan Wheelis's situation, I might have struggled more than she apparently did in accepting her father's "literary license." Yet given the nuanced portrait of her father in *The Known, the Secret, the Forgotten*, "complicated" seems the right word. I guess one must embrace Keats's idea of Negative Capability—"When man is capable of being in uncertainties, Mysteries, doubts, without any irritable reaching after fact and reason" (Keats 261)—and give up trying to separate fact from fiction in Wheelis's novelistic world. *Kirkus Reviews* characterized the vignettes in *The Known, the Secret, the Forgotten* as "allusive and elusive"; that's the way Joan Wheelis responded to my questions. I wonder why she wrote much more about her father than her mother. She politely but firmly corrected me when I suggested that it was easier for her to love her mother than her father. I felt it would be intrusive to ask her anything about her divorce after a 20-year marriage or her son.

I'm struck by Joan Wheelis's observation that "Mortality felt less tethered to existential angst" as a result of writing *The Known, the Secret, the Forgotten*. She was, after all, leaving behind a written record for those who come after all, creating a posterity self that would outlive her, as her father had done. Surprisingly, she makes no mention in her memoir of her father's loss of the beloved pen she had given him: "She knows my fetishistic addiction to elegant writing instruments," Allen Wheelis observes in his last book, *The Way We Are*. I regret I didn't ask her whether she was tempted to use that pen to write her memoir.

I had the most fun during my conversation with Nancy Chodorow—it felt, indeed, like a genuine conversation, with the greatest flow and spontaneity. I enjoyed her humor, which might be called, in the words of my late colleague Sarah Blacher Cohen, Jewish wry. Chodorow commented the most fully on my questions, and I could feel her affection for her teachers, colleagues, and students. I'm also the most familiar with Chodorow's writings, having quoted from many of them in my own books. I know many of the same feminist scholars that she mentions, Claire Kahane, Marilyn Yalom, Brenda Webster, and Madelon Sprengnether. The latter two are not only excellent psychoanalytic scholars but also superb creative writers; in *Psychoanalytic Memoirs* I discuss Webster's *The Last Good Freudian* (2000) and Sprengnether's *Great River Road: Memoir and Memory* (2015).

I suspect that of all the writers in this book, Chodorow has the largest network of colleagues and friends. I was surprised by her response to my question whether she was aware of the distinction English teachers often make between showing and telling: "Actually, I wasn't. It's always really nice to learn something new." I was even more surprised that she doesn't like first-person novels, regarding them as "often a false, or cheap, way to bring you into the story." Some of my favorite novels are narrated in the first person: Mark Twain's *Huckleberry Finn*, Fitzgerald's *The Great Gatsby*, J.D. Salinger's *The Catcher in the Rye*, Vladimir Nabokov's *Lolita*, Philip Roth's *Portnoy's Complaint*, and Toni Morrison's *Beloved*. First-person novels convey an intimacy, immediacy, and spontaneity usually lacking in third-person novels; the former gives us the illusion of being inside a character, seeing the world as the character sees it. Part of the challenge of reading a first-person novel is locating narrative distance, the relationship between the author and the narrator. If I were interviewing Chodorow again, I would remind her that *Wuthering Heights*—she refers to Cathy and Heathcliff as two of literature's great lovers—contains several first-person narrators.

Some of my comments on Christopher Bollas's work proved wrong or misleading. I assumed that his decision to "throw away" his PhD dissertation and start again must have been an act of "desperation—and courage," neither of which was true. I also assumed, again incorrectly, that his training in English literature was more important than his formal psychoanalytic training. I made still another error when I assumed that Bollas must have deliberately used Freud's essays "Delusions and Dreams in Jensen's *Gradiva*" and "The Uncanny" in the creation of *Theraplay*. It's possible, of course, that Bollas was *unconsciously* influenced by Freud's essays, but I didn't want to pursue this question lest I come across as pigheaded. My biggest error, which I deleted from the final version of the chapter, occurred when I observed that Bollas had misattributed Keats's "Negative Capability" to Freud rather than to Keats. I reached this conclusion from the following statement in *The Shadow of the Object*: "Just as Freud asked his patients to achieve a 'negative capability,' to suspend assumption and prejudice and to report the thoughts that come across the mind . . ." (67). I asked myself, how could an English professor *not* know this? Bollas later told me that he *knew* Negative Capability was a Keatsian idea and assumed his readers knew this too. Fortunately, Bollas was not put off by my mistaken criticisms, my efforts to be "smarter" than the person I was discussing. Bollas alerted me to his obituary on Masud Khan, "Portrait of an Extraordinary Psychoanalytic Personality," which conveys Bollas's own extraordinary insight and empathy.

Adam Phillips's wit sparkles in his responses to my questions—as when, responding to his love for Oscar Wilde, he observes, slyly alluding to one of Wilde's best-loved plays, that "The importance of being earnest for psychoanalytic thinking has been stifling." Wildean wit! Phillips told me that he finds it unethical to write about patients, but he does this in several books. Is he aware of the contradiction? If so, is he troubled by it? I'm perplexed by his statement, "I've never tried to do anything that really mattered to me." Is he implying that his work is inconsequential? Or that what he does is natural, effortless? Here, and elsewhere, Phillips invests the greatest meaning into the fewest words. Like a poet. One must suspend judgment in psychoanalysis, Phillips suggests, even if one cannot be entirely nonjudgmental in life. The same is true about teaching, which requires us to be as open-minded and empathic as possible. I'd like to know more about Phillips's writing process. Are his manuscripts free of additions, deletions, revisions, like Mozart's compositional method, where everything was composed in his head but not yet written? I can't imagine writing without endless revision, "without calculation," with a "minimum of reflection."

One of the anonymous reviewers who evaluated this book before publication raised an intriguing question I wish I had asked all of the interviewees: might there be a "shadow analyst" in their lives, as there was in Phillips's life—Winnicott? The question can be expanded to include whether there is a "shadow teacher" in most professors' lives. The shadow teacher in my own life was my mentor, Len Port, who first awakened my passion for reading Freud.

"Every psychologist," Freud observes in *The Interpretation of Dreams*, citing an insight by the Belgian experimental psychologist Joseph Delboeuf, "is under an obligation to confess even his own weaknesses, if he thinks that it may throw light upon some obscure problem" (*SE* 4: 105 n.1). Psychoanalytic literary critics are not required to confess their own weaknesses, but I learned much from the anonymous reviewers of my book. "There is so much transference operating in the work (the author's attraction to these analysts and various works of fiction) that could have been engaged more but these could be for the next books." The reviewers, likely psychoanalysts, called attention to something of which I was not entirely aware: how my admiration or idealization of the psychoanalytic thinkers in this book resembles an analysand's idealization of his or her analyst. I tried to respond to this criticism in my revision of the manuscript by omitting certain statements that proved problematic to the external readers. For example, after discussing how Gilman felt like a "fraud," I initially wrote: "A fraud?! How can one of the country's most productive scholars, one who has written, coauthored, or edited over ninety academic books, many published by the world's most esteemed university presses, feel like a fraud? (I just mistyped 'Freud,' signifying my association of Gilman with the person I regard as one of the world's great geniuses.)" I still feel this way; it's hard to know the line between healthy admiration and idealization. Recall Nancy Chodorow's reference to her unresolved positive transference to her research subjects in *Feminism and Psychoanalytic Theory*. It is a question I continue to think about, as does probably every psychoanalytic scholar.

Elisabeth Young-Bruehl, the biographer of Anna Freud and Hannah Arendt, raises this question in *Subject to Biography* (1998). She disagrees with the traditional definition of empathy as "putting yourself in another's place" and instead offers a more intriguing definition. "Empathizing involves, rather, putting another *in yourself*, becoming another person's habitat, as it were, but without dissolving the person, without digesting the person" (22). In this way, the biographical subject lives within the biographer, and the latter is able to maintain the difference between self and other. Young-Bruehl makes another valuable observation: recognizing when a biographer's idealization of a subject, or a literary critic's idealization of a writer, becomes narcissistic. "The mechanism is narcissistic: the subject is constructed as how you wish to be in the eyes of some one or ones; you are looking, in the medium of the subject, for the you who would be most lovable to someone else or to you yourself (which may come to the same thing)" (46). Again, recognizing the distinction between admiration and idealization remains a challenge for every writer—and for every person. Regardless of whether one has been in psychoanalysis, self-analysis remains a lifelong goal, especially for the psychoanalytic scholar. In his 1994 edited volume *Self-Analysis in Literary Study: Exploring Hidden Agendas*, Daniel

Rancour-Laferriere argues persuasively that "self-analysis can be a boon to other-analysis, including psychoanalysis of literature. Literary analysis informed by self-analysis is in principle superior to literary analysis not so informed" (29).

The Future of Psychoanalysis

It's unlikely that many psychoanalytic institutes will include Adam Phillips's own books on their syllabi, if only because of his dismissive statements about psychoanalytic institutes, as Boynton reported in *The New York Times*: "Psychoanalysis has become a very dreary profession indeed. It is terribly puritanical, moralistic and coercive. The institutionalization of analysis has killed its wilder spirit. The craving for academic respectability has made analysts want to be recognized either as real scientists or real artists. They aren't comfortable sustaining the ambiguity that comes with being neither." Douglas Kirsner, professor of psychoanalytic studies and philosophy at Deakin University, Melbourne, agrees with the conclusion offered by Christopher Bollas and David Sundelson in their 1995 book *The New Informants* that psychoanalysis fosters the "trappings of expertise, not the substance" (137). "Most psychoanalytic institutes," Kirsner writes in his updated book *Unfree Associations: Inside Psychoanalytic Institutes* (2009), based on over 150 interviews with leading analysts,

> are unfree associations of psychoanalysts where the spirit of free inquiry has been replaced by the inculcation of received truth and the anointment of those who are supposed to possess knowledge. Through their institutions, psychoanalysts can easily become blind to the spirit of sceptical inquiry on which psychoanalysis was based. This method is rarely applied to their institutions, which are mostly unfree oligarchies, and which rewarded conformity and punished difference. The story of psychoanalytic institutions is central to psychoanalytic history, and to what has gone so wrong with psychoanalysis. (10)

Institutional psychoanalysis confronts vexing questions about its continued existence. These questions include the distinctions, if any, between psychoanalysis and dynamic psychotherapy; the length of time and frequency of a training analysis, and whether a training analysis should continue to be mandatory for an analyst-in-training. Some analysts believe that the role of a training analysis blurs the boundaries between education and therapy. Liberal analysts interested in reform wish to eliminate the present training analysis system, which they regard as elitist and authoritarian; other analysts, more conservative, worry that the elimination of national standards for training analysis will result in a profession whose members cannot agree on anything. Many have lamented the lack of multicultural diversity in the American Psychoanalytic Association, whose membership continues to dwindle.

The spirit of inquiry will be fostered by psychoanalyst-novelists like Allen Wheelis and Christopher Bollas who offer us inside accounts of the failures and triumphs of the talking cure. Books about clinicians of despair written by psychoanalysts who have not given up on their profession will prepare readers for the inevitable challenges that accompany verbal therapy, including the hazards of being an analyst. Reading Wheelis's fiction reminds me of Thomas Hardy's sobering insight: "If a way to the Better there be, it exacts a full look at the Worst." Reading Joan Wheelis's *The Known, the Secret, the Forgotten* affirms the value of storytelling, offering us through evocative, lyrical prose the mystery of love, loss, and resilience. Gilman's scholarship on Freud encourages us to see how the creation is inseparably connected to the creator himself. In shining a light on what Freud thought was the dark continent of female psychology, Nancy Chodorow charts a new direction based on sociology and feminism. Bollas helps us verbalize the unthought known, reminds us of the importance of free association, and in his fiction conjures up a viral spirit that destroys the human soul—much like life in the coronavirus pandemic. And appreciating Phillips's Wildean wit highlights a post-Enlightenment Freud who was, unexpectedly, a disillusioner.

For psychoanalysis to succeed, we will need more people like the ones I discuss in this book: bold, original, interdisciplinary scholars, clinicians, and creative writers who are not afraid to chart new directions. It is possible, decades from now, that Sander Gilman, Allen Wheelis, Joan Wheelis, Nancy Chodorow, Christopher Bollas, and Adam Phillips will fall out of favor and be forgotten, the fate of even extraordinary thinkers. And yet I can imagine that, in a still more distant future, their writings will be rediscovered and considered "classics" that will provide insight, guidance, and pleasure to those who study them. As Adam Phillips remarks in his conversation with David James Fisher, "I think people falling out of favor is the best thing that can happen to them in psychoanalysis" (937).

Their writings, all taught in a university's interdisciplinary individuology department, inspired by Nancy Chodorow's idea, will then be studied only by people who are interested in them.

Works Cited

Abraham, Nicholas, and Maria Torok. *The Shell and the Kernel*, vol. 1, edited and translated by Nicholas T. Rand. U of Chicago P, 1994.

Acocella, Joan. "This is Your Life: Adam Phillips." *New Yorker*, February 18, 2013.

Adams, Tim. "*In Writing* by Adam Phillips Review—The Psychoanalyst as Unreliable Narrator." *Guardian*, June 5, 2017.

Adler, Alfred. *Understanding Human Nature*, translated by Walter Beran Wolfe. 1928. G. Allen & Unwin, 1968.

Alexander, Franz, and Thomas M. French. *Psychoanalytic Therapy: Principles and Application*. Ronald Press, 1946.

Alford, C. Fred. "Allen Wheelis: Philosopher of Despair, Poet of Desire." *Explorations*, vol. 9, 1999, pp. 199–227.

Almond, Richard. "Thoughts on the Future of Psychoanalysis." *American Psychoanalyst*, vol. 54, 2020, pp. 10–13.

Anonymous. *The Incest Diary*. Farrar, Straus and Giroux, 2017.

Bakan, David. *Sigmund Freud and the Jewish Mystical Tradition*. D. van Nostrand, 1958.

Bart, Pauline. Review of Chodorow's *The Reproduction of Mothering*. *Mothering: Essays in Feminist Theory*, edited by Joyce Trebilcot, Rowman & Allanheld, 1984, pp. 147–152.

Bayley, John. *Elegy for Iris*. Picador, 1999.

Benvenuto, Sergio, and Anthony Molino, editors. *In Freud's Tracks: Conversations from the Journal of European Psychoanalysis*. Jason Aronson, 2009.

Berman, Jeffrey. *Diaries to an English Professor: Pain and Growth in the Classroom*. U of Massachusetts P, 1994.

———. *Dying in Character: Memoirs on the End of Life*. U of Massachusetts P, 2012.

———. "Foreword to New York University Press's Series on Literature and Psychoanalysis." New York UP, 1991–1997.

———. *Joseph Conrad: Writing as Rescue*. Astra Books, 1977.

———. *Mad Muse: The Mental Illness Memoir in a Writer's Life and Work*. Emerald, 2019.

———. *Narcissism and the Novel*. New York UP, 1990.

———. *Norman N. Holland: The Dean of American Psychoanalytic Literary Critics.* Bloomsbury Academic, 2021.

———. *Psychoanalytic Memoirs.* Bloomsbury Academic, 2022.

———. Review of *Houdini: A Mind in Chains. Journal of Psychohistory*, vol. 5, 1977, pp. 307–309.

———. Review of Sander Gilman, *The Case of Sigmund Freud* and *Freud, Race, and Gender. Psychoanalytic Review*, vol. 82, 1995, pp. 778–783.

———. *Risky Writing: Self-Disclosure and Self-Transformation in the Classroom.* U of Massachusetts P, 2001.

———. *Surviving Literary Suicide.* U of Massachusetts P, 1999.

———. *The Talking Cure: Literary Representations of Psychoanalysis.* New York UP, 1985.

———. *Writing the Talking Cure: Irvin D. Yalom and the Literature of Psychotherapy.* State U of New York P, 2019.

Berman, Jeffrey, and Paul W. Mosher. *Off the Tracks: Cautionary Tales About the Derailing of Mental Health Care*, 2 vols. International Psychoanalytic Books, 2019.

Bersani, Leo, and Adam Phillips. *Intimacies.* U of Chicago P, 2008.

Bettelheim, Bruno. *Freud and Man's Soul.* Knopf, 1982.

Bloom, Harold. *Shakespeare: The Invention of the Human.* Riverhead Books, 1998.

———. *The Western Canon: The Books and Schools of the Ages.* Harcourt, 1994.

———. *Yeats.* Oxford UP, 1970.

Bollas, Christopher. *Being a Character: Psychoanalysis & Self Experience.* Hill and Wang, 1992.

———. *Catch Them Before They Fall: The Psychoanalysis of Breakdown*, with Sacha Bollas. Routledge, 2013.

———. *The Christopher Bollas Reader*, introduction by Arne Jemstedt, foreword by Adam Phillips. Routledge, 2011.

———. *Cracking Up: The Work of Unconscious Experience.* Hill and Wang, 1995.

———. *Dark at the End of the Tunnel.* Free Association Books, 2004.

———. *The Evocative Object World.* Routledge, 2009.

———. *Forces of Destiny: Psychoanalysis and Human Idiom.* Free Association, 1989.

———. *Hysteria.* Routledge, 2000.

———. *I Have Heard the Mermaids Singing.* Free Association, 2005.

———. *The Infinite Question.* Karnac, 2009.

———. *Mayhem.* Free Association Books, 2006.

———. *Meaning and Melancholia: Life in the Age of Bewilderment.* Routledge, 2018.

———. "Melville's Lost Self: Bartleby." *American Imago*, vol. 31, 1974, pp. 401–411.

———. *The Mystery of Things.* Routledge, 1999.

———. "Obituary: Masud Khan—Portrait of an Extraordinary Psychoanalytic Personality." *Guardian*, June 26, 1987.

———. *The Shadow of the Object: Psychoanalysis of the Unthought Known*. Columbia UP, 1987.

———. *Theraplay & Other Plays*, introduction by Anthony Molino. Free Association Books, 2006.

———. *When the Sun Bursts: The Enigma of Schizophrenia*. Yale UP, 2015.

Bollas, Christopher, and David Sundelson. *The New Informants: The Betrayal of Confidentiality in Psychoanalysis and Psychotherapy*. Jason Aronson, 1995.

Boynton, Robert S. "The Other Freud (the Wild One); New Translation Aims to Free the Master from His Disciples' Obsession." *New York Times*, June 10, 2000.

———. "The Return of the Repressed: Psychoanalysis' Fallen Angel." *Boston Review*, January 2003.

———. "Till Press Do Us Part: The Trial of Janet Malcolm and Jeffrey Masson." *Village Voice*, November 28, 1994.

Breger, Louis. *Freud: Darkness in the Midst of Vision*. Wiley, 2000.

Breuer, Josef, and Sigmund Freud. *Studies on Hysteria*. 1895. *The Standard Edition of the Complete Psychological Works of Sigmund Freud*, translated by James Strachey, vol. 2. The Hogarth Press, 1975.

Brooks, Peter. *Reading for the Plot: Design and Intention in Narrative*. Knopf, 1984.

Broyard, Anatole. *Intoxicated by My Illness and Other Writings on Life and Death*, compiled and edited by Alexandra Broyard, foreword by Oliver Sacks. Ballantine, 1992.

Camden, Vera J., editor. *The Cambridge Companion to Literature and Psychoanalysis*. Cambridge UP, 2022.

Canby, Vincent. "*The Crazy Quilt* Begins Run: Unusual Film Opens at Cinema Rendezvous." *New York Times*, October 4, 1966.

Carey, Benedict. "Expert on Mental Illness Reveals Her Own Fight." *New York Times*, June 23, 2011.

Choder-Goldman, Jill. "An Interview with Adam Phillips." *Therapy Route*, August 16, 2019. www.therapyroute.com/article/an-interview-with-adam-phillips-by-j-choder-goldman.

Chodorow, Nancy J. "Being and Doing: A Cross-Cultural Examination of the Socialization of Males and Females." *Woman in Sexist Society: Studies in Power and Powerlessness*, edited by Vivian Gornick and Barbara K. Moran, Basic Books, 1971.

———. *Femininities, Masculinities, Sexualities: Freud and Beyond*. U of Kentucky P, 1994.

———. *Feminism and Psychoanalytic Theory*. Yale UP, 1989.

———. *Individualizing Gender and Sexuality: Theory and Practice*. Routledge, 2012.

———. *The Power of Feelings: Personal Meaning in Psychoanalysis, Gender, and Culture*. Yale UP, 1999.

———. *The Psychoanalytic Ear and the Sociological Eye: Toward an American Independent Tradition*. Routledge, 2020.

———. *The Reproduction of Mothering: Psychoanalysis and the Sociology of Gender*. U of California P, 1978; 2nd ed., 1999.

Clark, Judith, and Adam Phillips. *The Concise Dictionary of Dress*, photography by Norbert Schoerner. Violette, 2010.

Crews, Frederick. *Freud: The Making of an Illusion*. Metropolitan, 2017.

———. *The Sins of the Fathers: Hawthorne's Psychological Themes*. 1966. Oxford UP, 1970.

Didion, Joan. *We Tell Ourselves Stories in Order to Live: Collected Nonfiction*. Knopf, 2006.

Eilberg-Schwartz, Howard. "Freud as a Jew." *New York Times*, January 9, 1994.

Eliot, T.S. *The Complete Poems and Plays, 1909–1950*. Harcourt, Brace & World, 1952.

Elovitz, Paul H., and Bob Lentz. "Nancy J. Chodorow: Psychoanalyst and Gender Theorist." *Clio's Psyche*, vol. 11, 2005, pp. 113, 134–143.

Faimberg, Haydée. "Listening to Listening." *International Journal of Psychoanalysis*, vol. 77, 1996, pp. 667–677.

Fisher, David James. "A Conversation with Adam Phillips." *Journal of the American Psychoanalytic Association*, vol. 66, 2018, pp. 913–940.

Fitzgerald, F. Scott. *The Crack-Up*, edited by Edmund Wilson. New Directions, 1945.

Forrester, John. *Thinking in Cases*. Polity, 2017.

Forster, John. *The Life of Charles Dickens*, 2 vols. 1872. Chapman and Hall, 1899.

Freud, Anna. *The Ego and the Mechanisms of Defense*, rev. ed. International Universities P, 1976.

Freud, Sigmund. *Analysis of a Phobia in a Five-Year-Old Boy*. 1909. *The Standard Edition of the Complete Psychological Works of Sigmund Freud*, translated and edited by James Strachey (*SE*), vol. 10. The Hogarth Press, 1955.

———. "Analysis Terminable and Interminable." 1937. *SE*, vol. 23. The Hogarth Press, 1964.

———. *An Autobiographical Study*. 1925. *SE*, vol. 20. The Hogarth Press, 1959.

———. *Beyond the Pleasure Principle*. 1920. *SE*, vol. 18. The Hogarth Press, 1955.

———. *Civilization and Its Discontents*. 1930. *SE*, vol. 21. The Hogarth Press, 1961.

———. "'Civilized' Sexual Morality and Modern Nervous Illness." 1908. *SE*, vol. 9. The Hogarth Press, 1959.

———. *The Complete Letters of Sigmund Freud to Wilhelm Fliess, 1887–1904*, translated and edited by Jeffrey Moussaieff Masson. Harvard UP, 1985.

———. "Constructions in Analysis." 1937. *SE*, vol. 23. The Hogarth Press, 1964.

———. "Delusions and Dreams in Jensen's *Gradiva*." 1907. *SE*, vol. 9. The Hogarth Press, 1959.

———. *Fragment of an Analysis of a Case of Hysteria*. 1905. *SE*, vol. 7. The Hogarth Press, 1953.

------. *From the History of an Infantile Neurosis.* 1918. *SE*, vol. 17. The Hogarth Press, 1955.

------. *The Future of an Illusion.* 1927. *SE*, vol. 21. The Hogarth Press, 1961.

------. *The Interpretation of Dreams.* 1900. *SE*, vols. 4–5. The Hogarth Press, 1953.

------. *Introductory Lectures on Psycho-Analysis.* 1916–1917. *SE*, vols. 15–16. The Hogarth Press, 1961, 1963.

------. *Jokes and Their Relation to the Unconscious.* 1905. *SE*, vol. 8. The Hogarth Press, 1960.

------. *Letters of Sigmund Freud,* selected and edited by Ernst L. Freud, translated by Tania Stern and James Stern. Basic Books, 1960.

------. *Moses and Monotheism.* 1939. *SE*, vol. 23. The Hogarth Press, 1964.

------. "Mourning and Melancholia." 1917. *SE*, vol. 14. The Hogarth Press, 1957.

------. "On Narcissism." 1914. *SE*, vol. 14. The Hogarth Press, 1957.

------. *An Outline of Psycho-Analysis.* 1940. *SE*, vol. 23. The Hogarth Press, 1964.

------. *Psycho-Analytic Notes on an Autobiographical Account of a Case of Paranoia (Dementia Paranoides).* 1911. *SE*, vol. 12. The Hogarth Press, 1958.

------. *The Psychopathology of Everyday Life.* 1901. *SE*, vol. 6. The Hogarth Press, 1960.

------. *The Question of Lay Analysis.* 1926. *SE*, vol. 20. The Hogarth Press, 1959.

------. "Recommendations to Physicians Practicing Psycho-Analysis." 1912. *SE*, vol. 12. The Hogarth Press, 1955.

------. *Three Essays on the Theory of Sexuality.* 1905. *SE*, vol. 7. The Hogarth Press, 1953.

------. *Totem and Taboo.* 1913. *SE*, vol. 13. The Hogarth Press, 1953.

------. "The Uncanny." 1919. *SE*, vol. 17. The Hogarth Press, 1955.

Freud, Sigmund, and Carl Jung. *The Freud/Jung Letters: The Correspondence Between Sigmund Freud and C.G. Jung.* Edited by William McGuire, translated by Ralph Manheim and R.F.C. Hull, Princeton UP, 1974.

Freud, Sigmund, and Oskar Pfister. *Psychoanalysis and Faith: The Letters of Sigmund Freud and Oskar Pfister.* Edited by Heinrich Meng and Ernst L. Freud, translated by Eric Mosbacher, Basic Books, 1963.

Gabbard, Glen O. "Review of *Hysteria.*" *Journal of the American Psychoanalytic Association,* vol. 49, 2001, pp. 688–690.

Gardiner, Muriel. *Code Name "Mary": Memoirs of an American Woman in the Austrian Underground.* Yale UP, 1983.

Gay, Peter. *Freud: A Life for Our Time.* Norton, 1988.

------. *A Godless Jew: Freud, Atheism, and the Making of Psychoanalysis.* Yale UP, 1987.

Geller, Jay. "*Atheist* Jew or Atheist *Jew*: Freud's Jewish Question and Ours." *Modern Judaism,* vol. 26, 2006, pp. 1–14.

Gilbert, Sandra M. *Wrongful Death: A Memoir.* Norton, 1995.

Gilman, Sander L. *The Case of Sigmund Freud: Medicine and Identity at the Fin de Siècle.* Johns Hopkins UP, 1993.

———. *Difference and Pathology: Stereotypes of Sexuality, Race, and Madness.* Cornell UP, 1985.

———. *Disease and Representation: Images of Illness from Madness to AIDS.* Cornell UP, 1988.

———. *Diseases and Diagnoses: The Second Age of Biology.* Transaction, 2010.

———. *The Fortunes of the Humanities: Thoughts for After the Year 2000.* Stanford UP, 2000.

———. *Franz Kafka.* Reaktion Books, 2005.

———. *Franz Kafka: The Jewish Patient.* Routledge, 1995.

———. *Freud, Race, and Gender.* Princeton UP, 1993.

———. *Inscribing the Other.* U of Nebraska P, 1991.

———. *Jewish Self-Hatred: Anti-Semitism and the Hidden Language of the Jews.* Johns Hopkins UP, 1986.

———. *The Jew's Body.* Routledge, 1991.

———. *Jews in Today's Culture.* Indiana UP, 1995.

———. *Love + Marriage = Death: And Other Essays on Representing Difference.* Stanford UP, 1998.

———. "Psychoanalyzing Psychoanalysis: *Freud and the Hidden Fault of the Father.*" *Contemporary Psychoanalysis*, vol. 2, 1983, pp. 213–215.

———. "Psychotherapy." *Companion Encyclopedia of the History of Medicine*, edited by W.F. Bynum and Roy Porter, vol. 2, Routledge, 1993, pp. 1029–1049.

———. "Review of Gay's *A Godless Jew* and *Freud: A Life.*" *Jewish Quarterly Review*, New Series vol. 79, 1988, pp. 251–253.

———. "Review of Yosef Hayim Yerushalmi, *Freud's Moses: Judaism Terminable and Interminable.*" *American Historical Review*, vol. 97, 1992, pp. 1178–1179.

———. *Smart Jews: The Construction of the Image of Jewish Superior Intelligence.* U of Nebraska P, 1996.

———. "Why and How I Study the German." *German Quarterly*, vol. 62, 1989, pp. 192–204.

———, editor. *Introducing Psychoanalytic Theory.* Brunner/Mazel, 1982.

Gilman, Sander L., Jutta Birmele, Jay Geller, and Valerie D. Greenberg, editors. *Reading Freud's Reading.* New York UP, 1994.

Gilman, Sander L., and James M. Thomas. *Are Racists Crazy?: How Prejudice, Racism, and Antisemitism Became Markers of Insanity.* New York UP, 2016.

Glass, James M. "A Conversation with Allen Wheelis, San Francisco, 1993." *Explorations*, vol. 9, 1999, pp. 85–123.

Godley, Wynne. "Saving Masud Khan." *London Review of Books*, vol. 23, 2001.

Gopnik, Adam. "Man Goes to See a Doctor." *Tales from the Couch: Writers on Therapy*, edited by Jason Shinder, William Morrow, 2000, pp. 18–37.

Griffin, Fred. "Memoir: Finding Order in Meaning, Being, and Becoming: Interview of Joan Wheelis about *The Known, the Secret, the Forgotten.*" American Psychoanalytic Association Conference, February 12, 2020.

Hamilton, Victoria. Review of *Dark at the End of the Tunnel* and *I Heard the Mermaids Singing*. *Psychoanalytic Review*, vol. 95, 2008, pp. 528–534.

Heti, Sheila. "Second Selves." *New York Times*, January 18, 2013.

Hoffman, Roy. "Family Memoirs: The Ties That Bind and Those That Fray." *New York Times*, May 16, 2019.

Holland, Norman N. *Psychoanalysis and Shakespeare*. 1966. Octagon Books, 1976.

Hopkins, Linda. *False Self: The Life of Masud Khan*. Other Press, 2006.

Hughes, Judith M. Review of Sander L. Gilman's *The Case of Sigmund Freud* and *Freud, Race, and Gender*. *American Historical Review*, vol. 99, 1994, pp. 1285–1286.

Jacobs, Daniel. *The Distance from Home*. International Psychoanalytic Books, 2019.

Jaffe, Lee. "APsaA Apology to Non-Medical Psychoanalysts." *American Psychoanalyst*, vol. 54, 2020, pp. 1, 4.

Jamison, Kay Redfield. *Robert Lowell: Setting the River on Fire*. Knopf, 2017.

Jones, Ernest. *The Life and Work of Sigmund Freud*, 3 vols. Basic Books, 1953–1957.

Jung, C.G. *Memories, Dreams, Reflections*, recorded and edited by Aniela Jaffé, translated by Richard and Clara Winston. 1963. Vintage, 1989.

Jutras, Lisan. "Review: In *Unforbidden Pleasures*, Adam Phillips Is at His Most Exciting and Fatiguing." *Globe and Mail*, May 27, 2016.

Kahn, Coppélia. "The Hand That Rocks the Cradle: Recent Gender Theories and Their Implications." *The (M)other Tongue: Essays in Feminist Psychoanalytic Interpretation*, Cornell UP, 1985, pp. 72–88.

Keats, John. *Selected Poems and Letters*. Riverside Press, 1959.

Kierkegaard, Søren. *Philosophical Fragments, Johannes Climacus*, edited and translated by Howard V. Hong and Edna V. Hong, with introduction and notes. Princeton UP, 1985.

Kirkus Reviews. "Review of *The Known, the Secret, the Forgotten*." *Kirkus Reviews*, April 23, 2019.

Kirsner, Douglas. *Unfree Associations: Inside Psychoanalytic Institutes*, updated ed. Jason Aronson, 2009.

Klass, Dennis, Phyllis R. Silverman, and Steven L. Nickman, editors. *Continuing Bonds: New Understanding of Grief*. Taylor and Francis, 1996.

Kleinschmidt, Hans J. "The Angry Act: The Role of Aggression in Creativity." *American Imago*, vol. 24, 1967, pp. 98–128.

Kolk, Bessel van der. *The Body Keeps the Score: Brain, Mind, and Body in the Healing of Trauma*. Penguin, 2015.

Kurnick, David. Review of *Intimacies*. *Raritan*, vol. 29, 2010, pp. 109–123.

Laslett, Barbara. "The Gendering of Social Theory: Sociology and Its Discontents." *Contemporary Sociology*, vol. 25, 1996, pp. 305–309.

Lehrman, Philip R. "Freud's Contributions to Science." *Harofe Haivri* [*Hebrew Physician*], vol. 1, 1940, pp. 161–176.

Levy, Lisa. "Fantasies of Understanding: Adam Phillips's *Missing Out.*" *Los Angeles Review of Books*, January 22, 2013.

Lichtenstein, Heinz. *The Dilemma of Human Identity*. Jason Aronson, 1977.

———. "Identity and Sexuality." *Journal of the American Psychoanalytic Association*, vol. 9, 1961, pp. 179–260.

Lindner, Robert. *The Fifty-Minute Hour: A Collection of True Psychoanalytic Tales*. Rinehart, 1955.

Linehan, Marsha M. *Cognitive Behavioral Treatment of Borderline Personality Disorder*. Guilford, 1993.

Loewald, H.W. "On the Therapeutic Action of Psychoanalysis." *Papers on Psychoanalysis*. Yale UP, 1960.

Maeder, Thomas. *Children of Psychiatrists and Other Psychotherapists*. HarperCollins, 1989.

Mailer, Susan. *In Another Place: With and Without My Father Norman Mailer*. Northampton House P, 2019.

Makari, George. *Soul Machine: The Invention of the Modern Mind*. Norton, 2015.

Malchow, H.L. "Review of *Freud, Race, and Gender.*" *Journal of Modern History*, vol. 67, 1995, pp. 898–899.

Malcolm, Janet. *In the Freud Archives*. Knopf, 1984.

———. *The Journalist and the Murderer*. Vintage, 1990.

———. *Psychoanalysis: The Impossible Profession*. 1981. Vintage, 1982.

McLaughlin, J.T. *The Healer's Bent: Solitude and Dialogue in the Clinical Experience*. Analytic Press, 2005.

Merkin, Daphne. "A Neurotic's Neurotic." *New York Times*, December 20, 2007.

Meyer, Bernard C. *Houdini: A Mind in Chains*. Dutton, 1976.

Miller, Elise. "Writing Under the Influence: The Scholarly Writer at Work." *American Imago*, vol. 76, 2019, pp. 623–647.

Molino, Anthony. "A Conversation with Christopher Bollas." *The Vitality of Objects: Exploring the Work of Christopher Bollas*, edited by Joseph Scalia, preface by Malcolm Bowie, Wesleyan UP, 2002, pp. 179–222.

———. "Into Fiction, Through Catastrophe: A Conversation with Christopher Bollas." *In Freud's Tracks: Conversations from the Journal of European Psychoanalysis*, edited by Sergio Benvenuto and Anthony Molino. Jason Aronson, 2009.

Mosher, Paul W. "Frequency of Word Use as an Indicator of Evolution of Psychoanalytic Thought." *Journal of the American Psychoanalytic Association*, vol. 46, 1998, pp. 577–581.

Mosher, Paul W., and Jeffrey Berman. *Confidentiality and Its Discontents: Dilemmas of Privacy in Psychotherapy*. Fordham UP, 2015.

Mosse, George. "Anatomy of a Stereotype: Review of *Difference and Pathology* and *Jewish Self-Hatred.*" *New German Critique*, vol. 42, 1987, pp. 163–168.

Nabokov, Vladimir. *Lolita*. Weidenfeld, 1959.

Nathan, Debbie. *Sybil Exposed: The Extraordinary Story Behind the Famous Multiple Personality Case*. Free Press, 2011.

Nettleton, Sarah. *The Metapsychology of Christopher Bollas: An Introduction*. Routledge, 2017.

Neusner, Jacob. "Review of *Jewish Self-Hatred*." *Journal of the American Academy of Religion*, vol. 55, 1987, pp. 149–151.

Nietzsche, Friedrich. *Beyond Good and Evil*, trans. R. J. Hollingdale, with an introduction by Michael Tanner. Penguin, 1973.

———. *Human, All Too Human: A Book for Free Spirits*, translated by Marion Faber with Stephen Lehmann, introduction and notes by Marion Faber, new introduction by Arthur C. Danto. U of Nebraska P, 1996.

———. *The Philosophy of Nietzsche*. Modern Library, 1954.

O'Connell, Mark. "Review of *Unforbidden Pleasures*." *New York Times*, May 20, 2016.

Ogden, Thomas. *Conversations at the Frontier of Dreaming*. Jason Aronson, 2001.

Parish, Margaret. Review of *Catch Them Before They Fall*. *American Journal of Psychoanalysis*, vol. 75, 2015, pp. 232–234.

Phillips, Adam. *Attention Seeking*. Penguin, 2019.

———. *The Beast in the Nursery: On Curiosity and Other Appetites*. Pantheon, 1998.

———. *Becoming Freud: The Making of a Psychoanalyst*. Yale UP, 2014.

———. *Darwin's Worms: On Life Stories and Death Stories*. Basic Books, 1999.

———. *Equals*. Basic Books, 2002.

———. *Going Sane*. 2005. Harper Perennial, 2007.

———. *Houdini's Box: The Art of Escape*. Pantheon Books, 2001.

———. *In Writing*. 2016. Penguin, 2019.

———. *Missing Out: In Praise of the Unlived Life*. Farrar, Straus and Giroux, 2012.

———. *Monogamy*. Random House, 1996.

———. *On Balance*. Farrar, Straus and Giroux, 2010.

———. *On Flirtation*. Harvard UP, 1994.

———. *On Kissing, Tickling and Being Bored: Psychoanalytic Essays on the Unexamined Life*. Harvard UP, 1993.

———. *One Way and Another: New and Selected Essays*, introduction by John Banville. 2013. Penguin, 2018.

———. *Promises, Promises: Essays on Psychoanalysis and Literature*. Basic Books, 2001.

———. "'Rebecca, Take Off Your Gown': Review of *Jewish Self-Hatred*." *London Review of Books*, vol. 8, 1986.

———. *Side Effects*. Harper Perennial, 2006.

———. *Terrors and Experts*. Harvard UP, 1996.

———. *Unforbidden Pleasures*. Farrar, Straus and Giroux, 2015.

———. *Winnicott*. Harvard UP, 1988.

Phillips, Adam, and Barbara Taylor. *On Kindness*. Farrar, Straus and Giroux, 2009.

Poland, W.S. *Melting the Darkness: The Dyad and Principles of Clinical Practice.* Jason Aronson, 1996.

Rancour-Laferriere, Daniel. *Self-Analysis in Literary Study: Exploring Hidden Agendas.* New York UP, 1994.

Reed, John R. Review of Sander L. Gilman, *Difference and Pathology*, and Elaine Showalter, *The Female Malady. Victorian Studies*, vol. 30, 1987, pp. 410–411.

Roazen, Paul. *Freud and His Followers*. New American Library, 1976.

———. *The Historiography of Psychoanalysis*. Transaction, 2001.

Rodman, Robert F. *Not Dying: A Psychoanalyst's Memoir of His Wife's Death.* Random House, 1977.

———. *Winnicott: Life and Work*. Da Capo Press, 2003.

Rosenzweig, Saul. "Some Implicit Common Factors in Diverse Methods of Psychotherapy: 'At Last the Dodo Bird Said, Everybody Has Won and All Must Have Prizes.'" *American Journal of Orthopsychiatry*, vol. 6, 1936, pp. 412–415.

Ross, Lillian. *Reporting Always: Stories from The New Yorker*. Scribner, 2015.

Roth, Philip. *My Life as a Man*. Holt, Rinehart and Winston, 1974.

———. *Portnoy's Complaint*. Random House, 1969.

———. *The Professor of Desire*. Farrar, Straus and Giroux, 1977.

Rothman, Joshua. "The Freud We Wish For." *New Yorker*, June 19, 2014.

Ruddick, Lisa. "Beyond the Fragmented Self." *The Cambridge Companion to Literature and Psychoanalysis*, edited by Vera J. Camden, Cambridge UP, 2022, pp. 256–274.

Rudnytsky, Peter L. *Psychoanalytic Conversations: Interviews with Clinicians, Commentators, and Critics*. The Analytic Press, 2000.

Rustin, Susanna. "Adam Phillips: A Life in Writing." *Guardian*, June 1, 2012.

Schafer, Roy. *Aspects of Internalization*. International Universities P, 1968.

Schneiderman, Stuart. "Everybody's Mother is a Mother." *New York Times*, January 21, 1990.

Schreiber, Flora Rheta. *Sybil*. Warner, 1974.

Schwartz, Joseph. *Cassandra's Daughter: A History of Psychoanalysis*. 1999. Routledge, 2018.

Schwartz, Murray M. "Psychoanalysis in My Life: An Intellectual Memoir." *American Imago*, vol. 75, 2018, pp. 125–152.

Schwartz, Murray M., and Christopher Bollas. "The Absence at the Center: Sylvia Plath and Suicide." *Criticism*, vol. 18, 1976, pp. 146–172. Reprinted in *Sylvia Plath: New Views on the Poetry*, edited by Gary Lane. Johns Hopkins UP, 1979.

Seelye, Katharine Q. "Janet Malcolm, Provocative Journalist with a Piercing Eye, Dies at 86." *New York Times*, June 17, 2021.

Seidman, Naomi. "Carnal Knowledge: Sex and the Body in Jewish Studies." *Jewish Social Studies*, New Series vol. 1, 1994, pp. 115–146.

Shorter, Edward. "Women and Jews in a Private Nervous Clinic in Late Nineteenth-Century Vienna." *Medical History*, vol. 33, 1989, pp. 149–183.

Silverman, Kenneth. *HOUDINI!!!: The Career of Ehrich Weiss*. HarperCollins, 1996.

Smith, Dinitia. "How Even 'Good' Stereotypes Can Be Bad; Myriad Subjects with a Common Thread: The Images We Build to Define Ourselves." *New York Times*, November 21, 1998.

Snediker, Michael D. *Queer Optimism: Lyric Personhood and Other Felicitations*. U of Minnesota P, 2009.

Solomon, Andrew. *The Noonday Demon: An Atlas of Depression*. Touchstone, 2002.

Spence, Donald. *Narrative Truth and Historical Truth: Meaning and Interpretation in Psychoanalysis*. Norton, 1982.

Sprengnether, Madelon. *Crying at the Movies: A Film Memoir*. Graywolf Press, 2002.

———. *Great River Road: Memoir and Memory*. New Rivers Press, 2015.

———. *Mourning Freud*. Bloomsbury Academic, 2018.

Stein, Jean. "Interview with William Faulkner." *Paris Review*, vol. 12, 1956. www.theparisreview.org/interviews/4954/william-faulkner-the-art-of-fiction.

Stekel, Wilhelm. *The Autobiography of Wilhelm Stekel: The Life Story of a Pioneer Psychoanalyst*, edited by Emil A. Gutheil, introduction by Hilda Stekel. Liveright, 1950.

Strupp, Hans, and Suzanne Hadley. "Specific vs. Nonspecific Factors in Psychotherapy: A Controlled Study of Outcome." *Archives of General Psychiatry*, vol. 36, 1979, pp. 1125–1136.

Tambling, Jeremy. "Why Literature? Why Psychoanalysis?" *The Cambridge Companion to Literature and Psychoanalysis*, edited by Vera J. Camden, Cambridge UP, 2022, pp. 239–255.

Tanner, Stephen L. "Allen Wheelis: Philosopher-Novelist Behind the Couch." *Explorations*, vol. 9, 1999, pp. 1–27.

Thomas, D. M. *The White Hotel*. Viking, 1981.

Twain, Mark. *The Mark Twain-Howells Lectures*, edited by Henry Nash Smith and William M. Gilson, 2 vols. Harvard UP, 1960.

Vaillant, George. *The Wisdom of the Ego*. Harvard UP, 1995.

Wampold, Bruce E., and Zac E. Imel. *The Great Psychotherapy Debate: The Evidence for What Makes Psychotherapy Work*, 2nd ed. Routledge, 2015.

Webster, Brenda. *The Last Good Freudian*. Holmes & Meier, 2000.

Weinstein, Harvey. *A Father, a Son and the CIA*. James Lorimer & Company, 1988. American edition: *Psychiatry and the CIA: Victims of Mind Control*. American Psychiatric Press, 1990.

Wheelis, Allen. *The Desert*. Basic Books, 1970.

———. *The Doctor of Desire*. Norton, 1987.

———. *The End of the Modern Age*. Basic Books, 1971.

———. "Goodbye, Mama." *New Yorker*, October 13, 1951.

———. *How People Change*. Harper & Row, 1973.

———. *The Illusionless Man: Some Fantasies and Meditations on Disillusionment*. 1966. Harper & Row, 1971.

———. *The Life and Death of My Mother*. Norton, 1992.

———. *The Listener: A Psychoanalyst Examines His Life*. Norton, 1999.

———. *The Moralist*. Basic Books, 1973.

———. *On Not Knowing How to Live*. Harper & Row, 1975.

———. *The Path Not Taken*. Norton, 1990.

———. "The Place of Action in Personality Change." *Psychiatry*, vol. 13, 1950, pp. 135–148.

———. *The Quest for Identity*. Norton, 1958.

———. *The Scheme of Things*. Harcourt Brace Jovanovich, 1980.

———. *The Seeker*. Random House, 1960.

———. *The Way Things Are*. Baskerville, 1994.

———. *The Way We Are*. Norton, 2006.

Wheelis, Joan. *The Known, the Secret, the Forgotten*. Norton, 2019.

———. "Mending the Mind." *Psychoanalytic Dialogues*, vol. 20, 2010, pp. 325–336.

———. "Theory and Practice of Dialectical Behavioral Therapy." *Textbook of Psychotherapeutic Treatments*, edited by Glen O. Gabbard, American Psychiatric Association Publishing, 2009, pp. 727–756.

Whitebook, Joel. *Freud: An Intellectual Biography*. Cambridge UP, 2017.

Wilde, Oscar. *The Picture of Dorian Gray*. Oxford UP, 1982.

Yalom, Irvin D. *Love's Executioner and Other Tales of Psychotherapy*. Perennial Classics, 2000.

———. *Lying on the Couch*. Harper Perennial, 1997.

———. *The Schopenhauer Cure*. Harper Perennial, 2006.

Yeats, William Butler. *The Collected Poems of W.B. Yeats*, edited by Richard J. Finneran. Collier Books, 1989.

Young, Iris Marion. "Is Male Gender Identity the Cause of Male Domination?" *Mothering: Essays in Feminist Theory*, edited by Joyce Trebilcot, Rowman & Allanheld, 1984, pp. 129–146.

Young-Bruehl, Elisabeth. *Anna Freud: A Biography*. Summit Books, 1988.

———. *Subject to Biography: Psychoanalysis, Feminism, and Writing Women's Lives*. Harvard UP, 1998.

Index

9 781438 495699